YOU GET *PAID* FOR THIS?

From industry to adventure

Peter Dyer

DISCLAIMER

This is a memoir of my life change.
Names and the chronology of events may have been changed.

Front cover from top left, clockwise: Students sailing in the Holy Loch / Winter
climbing in Glencoe / A slalom competition / Peter in the Alps

Back page: Winter at Benmore Adventure Centre.

Contents

CHAPTER 1: A CHANGE OF LIFE

It's not what you know but who you know. Perhaps we're lucky if we meet people who teach us new and exciting things - people who can show us an exciting way to change our lives. I must have been very lucky.

The sleek yacht, with its deep keel, surged through the green sea and heeled well over so that water sloshed over the gunwales on the port side. The clients and I, all in full yellow waterproofs suits, sat in a line high up on the windward side of the cockpit. It was the last afternoon of a sailing course and we were sailing back to our mooring in the Holy Loch on the beautiful west coast of Scotland.

Sally, one of the clients, shouted above the rushing water, "Well Pete, it's been a great week."

I smiled. "Yes, the weather's been perfect for us."

A man sitting next to me said. "So, Peter, it's the end of the course for you, too. What are you doing next week?"

I bent forward and eased the mainsheet out a little to take some pressure from the huge sails, and then said, "Rock climbing, I think. I'll be instructing a climbing course. It'll make a change from the sea."

He looked vaguely interested. "Rock climbing, eh? Yes, but what do you do for a living? What do you get paid to do?"

I had been instructing this group of adults all week and was rather surprised with his question.

"What do I do for a living?" I smiled. "Well, this. Instructing these activities is my job."

There was silence while they looked out to the green water, sparkling as it rushed by, and to the sunny fields along the shore and the glorious mountains in the distance. Then Sally said with a smile and an amazed expression, "You do this for a living? Do you mean to say you actually get *paid* for this?"

I grinned and nodded. "Mm, lucky eh?"

Yes, I certainly had been lucky to find this way of earning a living. But I had never grown up in this wonderful environment or with such an interesting job. Growing up as a child in the terraced streets of London I had never sailed a boat in wide oceans. I had never canoed a wild river or been down into a deep limestone cave. Before the age of eighteen, I'd never even seen a mountain, so how these adventures became a major part of my life might seem a mystery.

*

The Boy Scouts was probably the start. When I was little my mum and dad thought I would like to be a boy scout, so one evening mum took me to join a Cub Scout group. I wasn't very bright at school but the Cubs and later the Scouts suited me perfectly. We met in a disused building on the edge of the canal in a rundown industrial area of west London. Life for me began to revolve around the Scouts with games, camping at weekends, lighting fires, 'wide' games in the forest, leadership and friendship.

Years later, when I was eighteen, I was still active as the leader of the Venture Scouts. Scouting was one of the things that helped to change my life.

CHAPTER 2: FROM SCHOOL TO WORK

I was fifteen when I left school with no qualifications and no idea what work I wanted to do. My dad worked in the print industry in London, and for most of his working life in Fleet Street, he was in a photographic dark room. For no particular reason, I was not keen on anything like that. I used to help my dad in his shed making things in wood, and that was my real interest.

So, I got on my bicycle and went round my part of London to see if I could get an apprenticeship as a joiner. None of the firms were interested until I cycled into the yard of a small building firm. I went across to a scruffy door and quietly opened it to see an old man sitting at a desk covered with large drawings. Around the floor were pieces of building supplies.

He looked up at me and said sharply. "What do you want lad?"

"I want to be an apprentice joiner, sir."

He looked at me for a minute and then waved a finger to a scruffy chair at the front of his dusty desk. "Sit down son."

I sat down and he continued.

"Now, you don't want to work in a little firm like this. I'm only a small building firm and couldn't afford to send you off to college. You need to work in a big firm where they will send you to a technical college one day each week. You will have to do two evenings at night school as well.

He smiled and said. "Get an apprenticeship in a big firm, lad."

I had never met the man before or since but he was someone who set me on the right road.

*

A friend of our family called Harry, who lived along our road, worked as a joiner in a large joinery factory. Mum had a word with Harry who spoke to the boss of the timber firm where he worked. An interview was arranged, and after a few days Harry took me in his car for a meeting with the boss of the firm.

It was a big factory on a large industrial area in north-west London. On one side of a driveway was a very large timber yard and on the other side was the large machine shop and joiner's workshop with offices above.

I was told to wait in the foyer and shyly watched the office workers coming in to start the day of work.

Sharp at eight o'clock, deafening machines started up and I could see through the window down to the machine shop where men in boiler suits were beginning the day of work. After half an hour, I was shown into a panelled office where an old man in a suit was sitting behind a dark polished desk.

I had brought a large folder of my technical drawings I'd done at school. I remember little of the interview except when he was looking at my drawings of different types of timber doors. He pointed a finger at the picture of a door and looked up at me. "Which side of that door would you put the hinges?"

I pointed. "Er…. That side."

He smiled and shook his head. "No, the other side, so the brace stops any drop."

I was a bit depressed as I went home on the train. However, two weeks after the interview I received a letter telling me to start on the first day of August. So, with no great excitement and not at all sure how I would manage, I started my five years of apprenticeship.

*

It was a very good firm but a savage world for a kid straight from school. At one end of the vast dusty factory was the machine shop full of screaming and dangerous machines operated by skilled men dressed in boiler suits. At the other end was the joiners' shop, which got a bit quieter towards the far end where all the craftsmen wore a white apron.

The first day I was set to work with a pleasant old man called Sam. His constant work, and mine, was smoothing long timber moulds that we did by rubbing with glass paper by hand using various shaped blocks. Half way though the morning I must have been working hard with my head down, when I suddenly noticed a man the other side of the workbench. It was the foreman who looked down at me.

"What was your name, son?"

"Er, Peter, sir."

He smiled. "Well, Peter, take it easy. You'll not last till lunch time."

In the afternoon my fingers were very painful and old Sam at the next bench came over to see my problem. I showed him my fingers that had been worn so badly by the glasspaper that blood was seeping through the skin.

Sam was a kind old chap. "Good lord, lad, why didn't you say something?" He got a large roll of masking tape and bound up my fingers so that I could carry on until the end of the day.

*

So, my days became routine. After a good fried breakfast with my dad coughing at his first cigarette, I would leave early each morning on my bicycle for the five-mile ride to the factory where we had to 'clock in' each day.

I soon got to know the many other apprentices, and at lunchtime we all played cricket in the huge timber yard opposite the factory. The wicket was an old door, and the first time I was given the bat I was bowled out the first ball. I went to give the bat over but 'Big John' shouted, "No, okay lad. Stay there."

When I was out the very next ball everyone laughed. However, over the years I did eventually get so good they couldn't bowl me out and I would give up the bat for the next lad.

I had been working with other joiners for two months when the foreman told me to go out the next day on a site job up town. I walked to the station very early each morning and went on the underground train to the building site. It was a new construction that was a six-storey extension to a big hospital. I was working with our foreman on the site who was called Frank. We were working one day on the fourth floor when he told me to go down the scaffold to fetch some special hinges from the site office.

I went down the ladders, picked up the small box of hinges and started up the ladders again. I was just going up the ladder to reach the fourth floor when a chap started coming down above me. I stepped down to get out of his way but had not realized how far up the ladder I was. I lost balance and went head first through the ladder opening below. I was not aware of what happened but after a painful jolt, found myself hanging with a scaffold pole under my arm and hanging three floors above the ground. I sat down on a nearby platform and only then noticed that my left wrist was very painful.

Other workers had seen my very lucky escape and took me down to the site office. It was soon obvious that my left wrist was broken and it was easy to go next door to the hospital. After an X-ray a nurse was putting my arm in plaster when she said with a smile. "How did you break this?"

I grinned weakly and said, "I fell off the scaffold."

She frowned. "You naughty boy. Why were you playing on the scaffold?"

I gave her a serious look. "I wasn't playing, I was working."

When I got home, mum was a bit shocked but soon got over it and of course I could not go into work. After two weeks the old boss, who had interviewed me, telephoned me at home to ask if I could go and help out in the office. So, I went in each day on the train and worked in the general office with about ten other workers. The men in the factory thought that the office workers were rather 'above' the tradesmen but I soon realized that the clever workers were the craftsmen.

Eventually, my wrist mended and I started back in the joiners' shop. I was pleased to be put to work with a joiner called George in the quieter end of the factory. He was a very short squat man with a little round head and muscular arms and looked rather like a chimpanzee. He had a low stool to sit on during the morning tea break, and as he sat there his head was not much higher than his bench. His tools were of an ancient type but were all looked after carefully, showing years of use. In those days, joiners had no power tools, so each craftsman had a big variety of hand tools. George had four different types of planes, each one with a razor-sharp cutting 'iron' with the metal and timber polished by hands over many years.

Holes were drilled by hand with different types of brace, and screws were twisted in by hand with a screwdriver. I used to watch George putting a screw in and saw the muscles on his short powerful forearm ripple. In time I developed that hand strength too, and soon built up a big selection of hand tools that I still treat with loving care today.

George was not very cheerful but was known to be the most skilled joiner in the big firm and was always given the most technical jobs to do. With my bench next to his he taught me a huge amount and we were always working with timbers like oak, teak, mahogany, iroko, walnut, sycamore and ash. The foreman never gave George a job that was to be made in any cheap softwood, but only work in the finest timber that would eventually be given a beautiful finish in the polishing workshop next door.

Life became routine, and although I would get very tired it was okay. However, I was never able to see the sky or sunlight outside. During the winter months it was still dark in the morning when I would ride the long way to work in the factory district. By the time I joined the line of quiet and weary men to clock off at the end of each day, it would be dark again.

Saturday morning was a normal working day and I cycled the five miles home in the rain one winter afternoon. The day was grey. The factories were grey and the rows of terrace houses, each with smoke from a blackened chimney, were grey. The smell of the gas works that I passed was almost overwhelming, with the stagnant air and thick with the stench of sulphur.

After turning by the rough pub and passing the iron foundry at the end of our terraced road, I was home. With nothing exciting to do, I was in our kitchen, leaning on the washing mangle that stood in front of the window. We called this room the kitchen, but there were no facilities for cooking, as that was all done in the tiny scullery that had a door out to the yard.

*

Perhaps it was my mum who first showed me there might be a different life. I was looking out to the row of terrace houses opposite, which blocked any view from the end of our narrow garden, when mum, wearing her usual wraparound floral apron, came from the scullery with a tray of tea and sat down at the scrubbed wood table. She poured herself a cup of tea and, without looking up, said, "Tea Peter?"

"Er, no thanks."

She pushed her sleeves up and I could sense she was trying to pick the right moment and the right words to say something to me, her spotty teenage son. "Peter," she said. "There's a talk on up town, a talk with pictures that I thought we might go to."

I frowned. "A talk with pictures? A talk about what?"

She put her cup down and folded her ample arms. "Well it's a talk about climbing the highest mountain in the world, Mount Everest. The men that first climbed it are going to give the talk."

I looked at her with amazement. She had never shown any interest in mountains or anything like it. She and my dad had both spent their youth in the slums of London. At her age, and certainly a little plump, she was hardly likely to start climbing mountains now.

I looked out to the grey afternoon where lights in houses were already on and tried to imagine what a mountain might look like. "A talk with slides eh?" I was getting quite enthusiastic, but as a teenager I felt it was not the cool thing to show this enthusiasm, especially to one's parents. "Yeh, alright. I'll come if you want to go."

So, after an early dinner we walked to the underground station and got a train 'up town'.

Mum bought tickets and we went into the big, bright lecture hall. The lights eventually dimmed and the mountaineers came onto the stage led by John Hunt, the leader of the whole expedition. I didn't realize it at the time but just a few years later I was to meet him when he had become 'Sir' John Hunt.

13

The men seemed a casual group of friends, all bright and upright. Various members of the team spoke while brilliant pictures of mountains, valleys and climbers were projected. I remember that I was impressed by their genuine team spirit, their arduous struggle over many weeks and their shared dangers. I was particularly impressed with the hard work and sacrifice of glory by some team members so that just two climbers would receive the fame of the summit. These things had bound them into a friendship that really impressed me.

This 'talk with slides' might have sparked an interest in mountains, an interest in all the adventurous activities that grew to fill my time away from work in the factory where I could never see grass, trees, sky and certainly not mountains.

CHAPTER 3: ABROAD AND FIRST MOUNTAIN

During my apprenticeship I was still an active scout, leading older lads called Venture Scouts. In our district of London, we also formed a Rover/Ranger group, which involved older teenagers, both lads and girls. Mixing lads and girls like that was rather frowned upon by the National Scout Association, so I made a large mascot for our Rover/Ranger group. The mascot was a giant teaspoon. It was four feet long with the bowl and handle all carved and polished from mahogany. Along the handle I carved out the words: 'Always ready to stir'. I met a scout leader many years later who told me they are still using the spoon mascot in that part of London.

That summer there was an international Scout jamboree near Birmingham, and our Rover Ranger group went north to join the meeting. There were scouts from all over the world, camping in close contact covering a great area of mown grass. It was here that I first met Roger, who was a bright venture scout from Sweden who spoke perfect English.

Roger was about my own age and a person who changed my life more than he would ever know. He was camping next to me and at the door of his small, yellow tent was a pair of brown leather boots.

"What are the boots for?" I asked.

He picked up one of the boots and grinned enthusiastically. "Mountaineering".

I picked up the other boot. "Mountaineering?"

"Yes, I have just come from Switzerland."

"Switzerland?"

"Yes, I went on a mountaineering course in the Alps. Glaciers, snow peaks, it was fantastic." His eyes shone with the memory of it.

"Oh." I sat down on the grass. "The Alps. It sounds good. A course on climbing mountains, eh?"

"Yes, it was brilliant." He looked into the distance and smiled, showing a great sense of past memories.

"Had you done any mountaineering before?"

"No." He smiled. "Most of the people were beginners, just like me. Of course, we had a guide and climbed some great mountains. Any scout our age can go."

I put the boot down. "Mm, the course was just for Scouts eh…. How did you get on the course?"

"Oh, you just have to write to them." He passed me a mug of black tea. "It's run from the scout chalet at Kandersteg. You have to write off and send your money to book a place." It sounded simple so I wrote down all the details.

Back in London, I sat at our kitchen table and carefully sent off my application. I was accepted on the mountaineering course and now had to buy some equipment. I bought an ex-army rucksack with a heavy metal frame and a pair of work boots that, I know now, were completely unsuitable. My mum cut down a pair of dads old check trousers to make breeches, for we thought mountaineers wore that sort of thing. I only had two weeks of annual holiday from the factory and booked this holiday to go on the mountaineering course.

*

So, in July I set off by myself on my first journey abroad. It was very early and still dark when I set off with my heavy rucksack to the underground station, then took a train to the centre of London to catch a very early train south to the port of Dover. Once I was on the ferry, I became quite relaxed and went on deck to watch the famous white chalk cliffs recede into the distance. I was so ignorant that I had not even considered that I spoke not a word of French, but I still managed to find my train to Paris and the Gare du Nord. Then, after stumbling about and asking, I found my way underground to the Metro and the main line station going to Switzerland.

I was careful to ask and find the signs on the train. Yes, it was going the right way. What I had not realized was that the back half of the train was going to Switzerland but the front half was going on to Belgrade and I got into the wrong half.

I think it was at Basle that there was a bit of noise and some shunting but with my boots off and coat in the rack I was having a lovely sleep so didn't notice much. We jerked off again and I turned over and shut my eyes.

I was woken a little later by the train guard speaking to me in a language I didn't understand. Eventually I realized he was asking for my ticket. With a confident smile I found it and passed it over. He took a double look at it and then pointing at the ticket, started to tell me something in his perfect French. I must have made a grin like an idiot for he scratched his head and pointed back to the direction that we had come from. With his broken English I eventually understood that I should have changed at the last station and the only thing to do was get off at the next station and get a train back to Basle. So, it seemed that all was not lost and I began to pack loose things into my sack.

However, before I had finished packing, we stopped at a station. I was rushing to try and put my boots on but before I was ready the train was

16

moving off again. It was only a few minutes before the conscientious guard came back and when he saw me still sitting there, he threw one hand to the top of his head and with exasperation started pointing and telling me what I already knew, that I should have got off the train at that station. I pointed to my heavy boots and tried to explain but he got the message and left the carriage muttering to himself and shaking his head.

It wasn't long before we stopped at another quiet little station and I got off, crossed over to the other side and eventually found out when the next train was due. I was lucky for it wasn't long before I was on the next train back to Basle. There was a wait of about an hour and this time I made sure that the train was the one I wanted. I settled into a comfortable carriage, quite relieved, and as the train thundered south, I slept again.

When I woke, we were in the mountains and I was thrilled at the beautiful countryside. Green little fields around trim farms and clean little villages in deep but open valleys. Then higher above the fields were the forested lower slopes of the hills. I had never seen such beautiful countryside. As the valleys closed in on both sides the hillsides became steeper and the train began to work hard, climbing and winding higher and higher until we had left the farms and fields and were now going through the real mountains. I can still remember how I was overwhelmed by the mountains that I saw from the train as it cut through gorges and trundled from tunnels into the bright mountain light. I don't know what I had really expected of the Alps but these snow-capped mountains were magnificent and I moved about the windows so that I shouldn't miss anything.

It was still light when the train pulled into the station at Kandersteg. The village was everything one would imagine a clean alpine village would be: the timber buildings with steep roofs and verandas covered with flowers around the first floor. Everyone seemed to understand my cockney English and a pleasant old lady directed me along the road to the outskirts of the village where there was a large timber framed building. This was the scout chalet.

I was shown my room that had three bunk beds and met the other twelve scouts who were doing the mountaineering course. They were about my age, some wearing scout uniforms from many European countries. We all sat together on a long wooden table for the evening meal, and I was delighted to meet Roger again, the Swedish scout who had told me about the course a year before. They seemed a bright and intelligent group, and as I spoke no foreign language, I was pleased to realize that most understood my broad London English.

I slept well and after a good breakfast we were given ice axes, briefed about what to wear, and met Fritz, who was our guide for the course. He seemed old and quietly confident, and spoke German or good English that most could understand. We had lunch all together on a long wooden table outside on the terrace.

Then, with rucksacks packed, we walked out of the village where glorious flowers hung from every balcony. We turned off the road onto a good track and followed Fritz past sloping fields where two men were skilfully cutting golden hay with scythes. Gaining height, we followed on through pine forests, alongside rushing streams, until the trees started to thin out and there was little left but alpine flowers, rocks, stony scree and the mountains sweeping up to snow summits. We had a rest by a blue lake that mirrored the mountains around and Fritz pointed up to a hut in the distance where we were to sleep the night.

Two hours later and we arrived at my first alpine hut. It was a building of solid stone, nestled in a vast snowy bowl which was surrounded by wonderful snowy peaks with a glacier filling the valley below us. Outside the entrance of the hut was a wide stone terrace and I stood looking at the magnificent scenery; I had never seen anything like it in my life. Other groups of mountaineers were talking and although I couldn't understand their various languages, I could gather they were talking about the mountains as they pointed up to routes and faces that they had just climbed, or perhaps were intending to climb.

Boots were not allowed in the hut so we changed into felt slippers that were neatly stored on a rack in the foyer. We then followed Fritz up a pine stair to a long dormitory. There were no separate beds but on each side was a row of continuous bunk beds called matrazen lager. All the walls were bare timber panels including the dining room where a good meal was provided on two long polished wooden tables. Our dormitory was for people who had to rise early at two in the morning, so I prepared my kit for an early start.

It was getting dark so I went outside to find the toilet. It was a simple timber shed, twenty metres from the hut without any water. When looking down the wooden box toilet seat I was amazed to see right down to a glacier a hundred metres below. A simple hut and a simple system.

Fritz came into the dormitory, switched the light on and woke us. It was about one thirty and, sleepy eyed, we got dressed and went down to the dining room. There were already plenty of other mountaineers busily getting breakfast and sorting their kit out.

After a good simple breakfast Fritz checked that we had everything and then led us out into the cold night air. There was little talking as we followed Fritz in a single file on a rough track that ran along the top of a rocky lateral moraine. After a couple of hours, the sky lightened and by the time we had gained a rocky ridge, the sun was shining and I was looking in all directions to take in the magnificent scenery. We gained more height, and the ridge, now covered with hard snow, became more serious.

Fritz stopped and arranged for us to be tied onto ropes and told us to use our ice axes to stop any possible slip on the steepening, firm snow. Wearing dark glasses and a peaked cap as protection from the sun, I was pleased to be tied onto the rope just behind Fritz. It was still not noon when we eventually gained the summit, which was fairly flat, and we stood looking around and into the far distance.

It was perfect weather and Fritz pointed out various mountains that we could clearly see. "That sharp one," Fritz pointed in the distance, "is the Matterhorn."

Roger touched my arm. "I am going to climb that one day," he said with a grin.

To me it seemed completely out of the question but just four years later I had climbed many mountains in the Alps, including the Matterhorn. We remained tied on the rope as it seemed a lot more serious going down than going up. In just two hours we were back at the mountain hut and had a break with a big mug of tea and a good snack. Some of the lads had been in the mountains before and after leaving the hut and on a good track I followed them down with youthful enthusiasm, going faster and faster until they decided to wait at the blue lake for the others.

So, we arrived back in the village, a bit sunburnt, but ready for another peak the following day. The weather was perfect for the whole of the course and Fritz was keen to give us a very full programme. We climbed four mountains, each peak taking two days, and I found that I was fit and strong on the hills, probably from the physical work in the factory and riding my bike both to work and then night school every day. However, the walk up to each mountain hut and the gallop down two days later in my hard, new work boots was a real punishment for my feet. Over the ten days I gained the worst blisters that I have ever had, either before or since, but the seeds of mountaineering had been sown. The beautiful scenery, the wilderness freedom, the spectacular views, the challenge, the excitement of shear faces dropping down from snowy summits.... I was hooked.

> *I leave the busy road*
> *and step to the mountain track*
> *I'll never look back.*

CHAPTER 4: ADVENTURES IN BRITAIN

To gain my woodwork qualifications I attended night school on two evenings each week, and it was there that I met Bernard. He was the same age as me and also an active Scout. It was Bernard who introduced me to climbing on rock out–crops just a few miles south of London. They are not very high but the sandstone rock proved hard climbing.

The long bicycle ride to work and then to night school was now a thing of the past, as I had bought a motorbike. Bernard had a climbing rope and slings and we travelled on my motorbike to the cliffs on Sundays – Sunday being our only day off work.

I continued to improve and gained strength, sometimes leaving my hands so strained after climbing all day that I had difficulty pulling the clutch in to change gear on the ride back home.

*

However, working conditions were changing and our hours of work were reduced to just forty, which meant that we no longer worked on Saturday mornings. This made a huge difference to me for now I was free to go further afield at weekends – and where I went was not to the mountains but underground.

*

While at night school my twin sister Joyce had met some lads who were cavers. She joined them on a few trips and it sounded exciting. So, on a cold snowy night in February I was given a lift in their car to the caving club cottage. It was there, in the limestone area of Somerset, where I was introduced to potholing.

My introduction to those hardy speleologists was rather strange for I had taken my sister's kit bag by mistake. When I unpacked, the first clothing that came out was a fine selection of women's underwear. There was an embarrassed silence as I tried to explain to my new friends. However, they had a good sense of humour and I joined their club, The Mendip Caving Group.

So, after work on Friday, I would get a lift with one of the older men to the caving club cottage that was in the Mendip Hills of Somerset. I began to spend most weekends underground. On Thursday evenings we would all meet in a local pub and plan the trips for the coming weekend. We explored all the bigger cave systems, splashing along stream passages, abseiling down into vast black caverns, squeezing through crawls and climbing ladders through freezing waterfalls.

Without modern wetsuits and only wearing a boilersuit with woollen underwear and sweaters, it was a cold business. Even more uncomfortable was free diving through passages completely filled with water. These 'sumps' were only short but were always a serious challenge. As soon as we plunged down into the water the acetylene lamps on our helmets went out, so we were in complete blackness, crawling on hands and knees through the water, with the helmet scraping along the rock ceiling. It was dangerous, free diving these sumps, but we had to keep calm for all the time we knew that the only air was at the far end of the waterlogged passage. We even went on to discover new cave systems in Somerset.

There was a big depression of grass that we knew of and thought it was probably a 'sink hole'. We started digging out at the bottom of the depression and after a couple of days broke through to a 'pot'.

We lowered a flexible ladder and went down to the bottom of the pot hole that was only about forty feet. With out lights shining round we were surprised to see two human skeletons.

After coming out and before returning to London we phoned the police about the skeletons. They went down the pot with an expert and after studies told us that the skeletons were from the times of the 'Black death' and probably thrown down when the shaft was open.

There were two caves that were known called 'Longwoods' and 'August hole'. After doing a rough survey of them we decided that two of the passages were very close and were probably all the same cave system. We went down with picks and shovels and dug away some rocks and mud and eventually broke through.

Now it's possible to go in one entrance and go through both caves to come out at the other entrance.

We also went up to Yorkshire one Easter weekend to meet up with the local club who organised a dramatic winch to descend down the massive Pot hole called Gaping Gill. We explored other big pots in the same area that were quite different to those in Somerset.

During a few weekends we went to explore the caves of south Wales. With rivers and fine passages, we found these caves excellent.

I had two weeks of holiday each year and decided to use one of my weeks on a dinghy sailing course on the south east coast. This was my first taste of sailing and with an instructor in every boat, I learned a lot in the week.

The other week of my annual leave I went on a rock-climbing course that I had heard about. Courses were run at a new National Mountain Centre in North Wales that is called Plas Y Brenin, the 'Kings Palace' in English.

I loaded my motorbike with everything I might need and, with no motorways yet, took the rather long journey up to North Wales. I had never been to Wales before and was very impressed with the wonderful scenery as I got closer to the mountains.

The National Mountain Centre is well situated at the meeting of two valleys and at the end of a lovely lake, Llynnau Mymbyr. There were ten clients on our course and we had a very good week of instruction in rock climbing. Each day we followed an instructor on various rock climbs up cliffs on the sides of the valleys. The valleys had steep barren sides where rocky cliffs had been created by the ancient glaciers that had carved out the valleys during the last ice age. I had a good chance to see for the first time this mountain area, and to my pleasant surprise I found it really was great mountain scenery with rocky mountain faces, vertical cliffs and mountain lakes in the bowl-shaped 'cwms'.

Each evening we had illustrated lectures and I was very keen to soak up as much knowledge as possible. I thought Plas Y Brenin was a great place, and didn't realise that, just two years later, I would get to know it and North Wales very well indeed.

I now thought of climbing clubs and found details of the London Mountaineering Club. One late autumn evening I got a train into the centre of London and went to their meeting. I knew nobody, but decided to join a weekend meet at their club hut in North Wales. It was a Friday in January and the long freezing ride on my motorbike after a week of work was a real test. Travelling through dark winding roads I eventually passed Plas Y Brenin and went down the rugged Llanberis pass. The club hut was a stone cottage in a small hamlet and as it was late evening, most club members were in the local pub. After a full day of work and then the very long ride I was tired and after a simple meal from tins, I found an empty bed and was soon deep in my sleeping bag and fast asleep.

In the morning, club members were making breakfast and planning their day. Being a new member, I knew nobody, but a pleasant couple of chaps, a bit older than me, asked if I wanted to join them. I knew little of the area, so I was very pleased to join Brian and Karl for any trip they were planning. By now I had bought proper mountaineering kit, and with a packed lunch we set out to climb a ridge on the far side of the valley.

I followed them up through patches of snow and rocks gaining height. Higher up we came to the snow line and eventually stopped at the foot of our intended rocky buttress. They began to get out a rope and other kit when Brian turned to me and said, "Well Peter, do you want to lead?"

I was a bit surprised but thought it didn't look too steep even though it was well-plastered with snow. "Okay," I said. "I'll have a look." So, with the rope tied round my waist and with a couple of slings fitted with karabiners I set off upwards.

The icy conditions were tricky, and as I had never led a multi-pitch route before, or one with snow and ice, I didn't know quite how far I should go. Eventually, I found a suitable stance and belay fixing and tied on. However, I had to stop for five minutes as I was doubled up with pain in my fingers. As the blood came back to one finger the pain was severe.

I brought Brian up first and when he reached the ledge and tied on, he said, "A good lead, Peter."

So, I continued to lead, and by the time we arrived back at the club hut just before dark I was feeling confident with new friends and felt part of the team. In the evening a large white blister appeared on two fingers and when I returned home, I went to see the doctor.

 He looked at the fingers and then said. "Frost bite. Not seen this very often. How did you do it?" I told him about my weekend and he gave a knowing smile but said it didn't need treatment. So, my life was changing and revolved more and more around the weekends when I would go caving or climbing.

However, there were also changes for me at work. I had been working in the big workshop with George, the top craftsman, for more than two years and could see that if I wanted to progress it had to be while still an apprentice. Once I had finished my 'time' I thought it would be difficult to move up the ladder. However, this was a good firm and they might risk me taking on more responsibility. I approached the manager, who was a miserable chap about 'setting-out' and he grunted and walked away.

Setting-out is a key skill in the joinery trade, for it's the setter-out who produces the technical drawings, called 'rods', orders the timber and then finally marks the joints etc., so any mistake on his part is serious.

A couple of weeks went by and I was surprised when the manager stopped at my bench. "Try this job," he said, and handed me some architect's drawings. "Work in the office with Eric."

So, I went along to Eric's office that was alongside the big noisy machine workshop and worried over the drawings. Before I had finished, I was given another job, and so it went on until I took my woodworking tools home. I stopped wearing my white apron like all the joiners and bought a brown 'smock' coat like the other three setters-out, and this gave the other apprentices a chance to joke and call out as I would walk through the factory.

So, I eventually finished my five years' apprenticeship as a setter-out. On my very last day at the factory I was busy leaving things straight when an apprentice came into the office and told me that Jean, who ran the work kitchen, wanted to see me urgently. What an earth would she want with me? I went upstairs to the kitchen and when I opened the door I was amazed to see all the apprentices and young workers in there. They all had a mug of tea and gave me a cup while 'big John' said a few words wishing me all the best of luck for the future.

The surprise made me almost speechless for I didn't realize they knew that I was even leaving that day. I should have shown more feeling but surely this number of people missing in the factory would soon be noticed, so we drank up and all went back to work. So, I left the factory without looking back or saying 'thanks' to anyone. The boss and workers had been good to me and, to this day, I still regret that I had not shown my gratitude.

So, I had finished five long years as an apprentice and now I could state I was not only a joiner but could apply for work as a setter-out, which was a very big step up the ladder. My apprenticeship was done and now I was free. However, my mind was already on other things for I had plans of a much longer holiday for the coming summer.

CHAPTER 5: SWITZERLAND AND FRANCE

I had booked in for another alpine climbing course at the Scout chalet in Switzerland, and from there I was going straight to France. I had been invited to join a French caving expedition on the big limestone plateau just a few miles north of the Mediterranean Sea, and as it was all free, I had accepted the invitation eagerly. The climbing course, again in perfect weather, was a great success, and I was better equipped with proper climbing kit. We followed Fritz up to huts and beyond, to the summits of four glorious peaks. After the wonderful ten-day course, I said farewell to my new scout friends.

*

With my heavy rucksack that was full of climbing and caving kit, and also carrying a large suitcase, I took a train for France and eventually arrived just north of the Mediterranean at the little town of Draguignan. Here, I met the leader of the speleological expedition, and he took me in his little car to a camp where I met French and Belgian cavers.

Few of them spoke much English and my French was limited to things I had learned at a night school class I attended with my elder sister. Learning some French phrases, I soon picked up plenty of new words until an older chap said to me one day, "Pierre, that word you use, it's not a very nice word."

So, I realized one had to be careful of some words that the French lads were using. However, we got by and during the month we discovered some new caves and descended deep potholes, some as deep as 80 metres, by flexible ladders.

Towards the end of the month-long expedition, I had been looking for unknown caves on the high limestone plateau all day in the blazing heat. The next morning, I woke with the most terrible headache and was a bit delirious. A doctor was called and diagnosed sunstroke.

I was given medication, and as the expedition finished a couple of days afterwards an older French chap invited me to join him in his holiday home. He took me in his car to a small fortified village a couple of hours north and we had a pleasant few days playing 'jou de Boule' with other people around the dusty streets.

*

This had been a convenient stop for me as I only had to take the local bus north to the town of Grenoble where I was meeting my twin sister and a team from our caving club. From a local map we had agreed to meet at a particular time at the junction of two roads. Sure enough, there was a café on that corner and I bought a coffee and sat outside in the sunshine.

Right on time my six club members arrived in their Land Rover and pulled up beside the café as arranged. We had planned to be shown some of the caves in that amazing limestone area by one of the locals. We were very impressed with the spectacular caves with lakes and wonderful stalactites and stalagmites. This was the limestone area that had the Goufre de Berger that was the deepest cave in the world at that time.

After two weeks exploring these wonderful deep caves we had to start driving north and I had suggested that we go a bit east and visit my aunt who lived in an alpine village. She had come to work in France in the 1930's and met a French lad who she married, and lived there for the rest of her life in the wonderful alpine village of Les Contamine. I had never been there before but we all squashed into the Land Rover and after a long drive, eventually found the village of Les Contamine and my aunt's house.

We arrived about midnight, when she was in bed, and I had failed to tell her there would be seven of us arriving! However, she didn't complain, and by waking her friend who lived in the mountain chalet next door she found a place on the floor for all of us to sleep.

I am embarrassed when I think how thoughtless I was in just turning up with seven strangers when she didn't even know what day we were going to arrive.

May's husband had died a few years before and her house was really only a simple extension at the end of the big timber chalet that was the home of her very good friend, Rose. My aunt's house had only one bedroom and May kindly moved up to the 'grange' in the roof to sleep. There were no taps in the house and water was collected from the 'basin' just outside. The toilet was also outside and was simply a terrible pit toilet that had not been emptied for many months. But, despite a crowd of young people descending on them, May and old Rose next door made us very welcome.

We did a few walks in the area – and what a glorious area it was. It is a beautiful valley on the western end of the Mont Blanc mountain chain where huge glaciated mountains rise above forests on the eastern side. Above the few alpine houses on the western side were steep fields developed for the cattle.

So, after a few days, our holiday was over and we drove north to the English Channel and home. But I was to see a lot more of the beautiful village of Les Contamine and those alpine mountains.

When I returned to London, I went to see my doctor about the heatstroke that I had developed on the caving expedition. He looked at my file on his desk for a while and then said, "In the winter, did you not see me about frost bite?"

I grinned and nodded my head. "Yes."

He shook his head wearily. "Frost bite and heat stroke in the same year."

CHAPTER 6: THE END OF SUMMER

It had been a great summer for me but now, back in London, I had to get work. A shopfitting firm not far from my home needed a setter-out, and I started just a week after arriving home. It was a small firm and the first job I had to do was a fancy metal staircase for an office block. Not quite the work I was used to, but it went well and the boss of the small firm probably thought I would be there for some time.

However, at the weekly meeting of the London Mountaineering Club I met Brian again and he invited me to join three others for a two-week winter climbing trip in Scotland. I immediately accepted. So, I was only working at the shopfitters for five months before I gave in my notice and we left in Brian's car for the long drive north.

*

I had never been to Scotland before and was very impressed with the rugged snow-capped mountains around the steep glaciated valley of Glencoe. We stayed in a climbing club hut and were active every day. Now with an ice axe and crampons on my boots I led a few easy snow gullies. I was getting good experience and was now more confident on snow and ice climbs.

However, after many days of kicking steps in hard snow my knees had swelled up very badly and on arriving back home I went to the doctor, who was getting to know me. He grinned and told me to try and rest for a while, which I did, and I have never had trouble since. So, after two good weeks with pleasant friends I was looking for work again.

*

Within a couple of days, I was appointed as the setter-out for a busy joinery firm just ten minutes ride from my home. This type of joinery work was easy for me, and being the only setter out in the firm I was also the assistant foreman and was in charge of the machine shop and joiner's workshop on Saturday mornings.

On my first morning of this new job, the foreman was showing me round and the first person I met working at a bench was Harry, the man who lived along our road. This was the friend of our family who had introduced me to the company where I had started as an apprentice just five years ago. I had been a naive, ignorant schoolboy, and was now his boss. It might have been depressing for him but he just smiled and shook my hand.

28

However, once again I soon developed plans for the coming summer and gave my notice in and left at the end of June.

*

I joined members of my club to go caving in France again, and after that I went by myself to visit my aunt May in her little home in the French Alps at Les Contamine. I had a pleasant week exploring the beautiful alpine valley with its fields and orchards and lower slopes of the mountains, where I could look across to the magnificent rugged snow and ice peaks of the Mont Blanc range.

By the end of August, I was back in London and knew that I could get a job in the joinery business as a setter-out very easily. However, I did not look for joinery work for I had other ideas that eventually led me away from joinery and city life altogether.

CHAPTER 7: NEW HORIZONS

I had not forgotten Plas Y Brenin, the National Mountain Centre in North Wales, where I had done the rock-climbing course two summers before. It would be a great place to stay if there was a job I could do. So, I wrote to the principal offering to be a volunteer who could do all types of building and maintenance work. In just a few days he wrote back saying I would have free board and lodging if I could help out on the maintenance of the house and kayaks. I was delighted, and arranged to go to Wales the very next week.

*

So, this started a new direction for my life, a permanent direction away from busy city life and the industry of the timber trade. With my motorbike stacked high I made the long journey north again and arrived in the mountains of Wales on a glorious evening. The autumn colours were beautiful, with a range of green and yellow in the random fields that were surrounded by dense oak woodlands, and beyond the trees the steep slopes of the mountains were covered with bracken.

I went to the reception desk where a secretary smiled up at me. "Hello. I'm Peter Dyer. I've come to do some voluntary work."

"Ah, yes," she said, and stood up. "I'll go and find the assistant housekeeper."

I put my heavy rucksack down and waited. The building seemed empty and I looked around the foyer at the black and white mountain photographs that I remembered from the course I had attended two summers ago. It all seemed very exciting and professional. It wasn't long before I heard footsteps and a young lady, a few years older than me, came along.

She gave me a wide smile and held out her hand. "Hello, I'm Morag. And you're Peter Dyer?"

"Yes." We shook hands. "I'm doing some voluntary work."

"Aye, I ken all abooot it. John told me to expect you." Morag didn't seem to be Welsh for she spoke with a lovely Scots accent. "I'll show you to your room, Peter."

At that first meeting I was not to know that Morag and I would work together in later years. So, the principal of the centre, Mr. Jackson, was called John. It seemed that first names were used for everyone. Already it was not quite like the world of industry that I'd left.

The main building of the National Mountain Centre closely edges the country road but Morag led me to a row of cottages away from the road at the back of a courtyard and above a sloping grass bank that dropped down to a beautiful mountain river.

As I followed her down a short corridor she said. "Some of the domestic staff live in this cottage. You have to share the toilet and bathroom at the end." She opened the door of one of the rooms. "Here you are."

I put my rucksack down. "Oh, thanks."

"I'll leave you to settle in." And as she left, she turned and said, "dinner is at seven."

My small bedroom was very basic with just a wardrobe and single chest of drawers, but it seemed perfect for my needs. It had only one window, but what a wonderful view from that small window. Grass ran down the bank to the river, and on the far side a forest of mixed conifers and oaks covered the lower slopes of our nearest mountain. Higher up, the trees cleared to show patches of purple heather and yellow gorse. Then, if I bent my head a little, I could see the summit of yellowed grass with plenty of solid rock wearing through.

After leaving my kit I walked down to the river where a few people were kayaking in the fast-flowing water. A narrow shoot of water ran down from a long lake that stretched away into the distance, where shadows of vertical cliffs highlighted the steep mountains not too far away.

A wooden footbridge crossed the narrow river and led across to the forested mountain. I stood on the bridge and looked around at the evening colours and it all seemed wonderful. Here there were no smells of sulphur or the noise of industry; just the fine smell of pine trees and the gurgle of the river under the bridge. I knew that I was going to enjoy it here.

I started work the next day. Life was good; I worked around the house or in my workshop, taking instructions from the domestic bursar or John, the principal. Food was good and I ate with everyone else in the lovely big dining room with windows overlooking the lake. I went into the staff room for tea and a cake at five and listened to the instructors talking about their day on the mountains, climbing on crags or kayaking on the lake, sea or river.

Then after dinner in the evenings there was always a lecture for the clients, usually with slides given by one of the instructors. I would sit at the back and learned all sorts of things about the activities, the history, glaciation, and the nature and geology of the area.

Apart from maintenance around the big mansion I was responsible for the kayaks. On one occasion John came to see me. "Peter, we have a big problem. There is a kayak course starting tomorrow and we need ten kayaks and we are short of one as we only have nine."

"Oh. I see. Okay John. You need another kayak. I'll see what I can do." In those days, kayaks were made from timber with a canvas 'skin' stretched tightly round the frame. I started work to make a kayak, and by working right through the night it was all finished by breakfast time, so now we had enough kayaks for the course that would arrive in a few hours.

I had been living at the mountain centre for a couple of months, and must have been some use, for one afternoon the principal called to me. "Peter, come in will you."

I went into his office, which was charming, with white panelled alcoves round the windows that looked out to the lake, and the Snowdon massive in the near distance. "Yes John?"

"Peter. You're a great help around the place – around the house, and mending the kayaks and things."

I smiled with embarrassment. "Oh, thanks."

"Are you thinking of staying on over the winter?"

"Well … er. Yes, if you want me to. I'd like to stay."

"Good." He leaned forward with his elbows on the desk. "We need a full-time maintenance man. If you want the job, Peter ... it's yours."

"Maintenance?"

"Yes. Maintenance of the boats and the house. The wages are not too bad." I was delighted. "Yes…. Yes. Thanks John. I'd love the job."

"Good." He stood up and shook my hand. "That's settled then. I can backdate your pay for a month.

So, although I was not, at that stage, a great help at instructing, I was to get paid to live in the most beautiful countryside, had all my meals provided, and worked with the most interesting of colleagues.

Saturday was the only day off for me each week and I would wander for long days over the mountains that were covered with snow and ice during the winter. My mountain skills improved and so did my navigation as I went out no matter how bad the weather. I was gaining all sorts of experiences that I would never have had back in the city – but not all of these were happy experiences.

*

It was late November and I had started some repairs in the workshop when John came in. "Peter, we have a rescue callout. Stop this and get kitted out for the hills."

I put my saw down. "Oh, okay John."

He turned to leave and said, "Meet Don by the Land Rover as soon as you can."

The instructors were not part of any mountain rescue team as they were involved every day with the clients who had paid for a one-week programme. However, Don Roscoe, the senior instructor and well-known rock climber, who had written a rock-climbing guide to the area, had gathered seven people like me and we drove the few miles to the Climber's Club hut in the valley of Llanberis. It seemed that a person had been seen below a crag called Main Wall, so in a line behind Don we set off up the hill with a stretcher and first aid kit.

When we got to the person, who was on a rock ledge, we immediately knew we didn't need a first aid kit. The young man had been dead for some hours. Apparently, he had been trying to get down from the grassy ridge high above. He must have slipped and fallen the full length of the huge cliff called Main Wall. We lifted the cold body onto the stretcher, tied the head on firmly as it was wobbling grotesquely, and with everything covered we carried the stretcher down to the road. The body was lifted off and put straight into a waiting ambulance.

Back at Plas Y Brenin I went back to work, and it wasn't until the evening that sadness came over me when I thought of the terrible tragedy that had hit the young man's family.

*

But not all rescues ended in tragedy. It was a very cold, wet and windy morning in January and we were all at breakfast when, out of the window, I saw a man run across the river footbridge. A few minutes later John came to the staff table and told six of us who were not instructing that day, to eat up quickly and kit out for a rescue.

It seemed that the bedraggled man I had seen was a teacher who had a group of students on a mountain course from another outdoor centre. They had been camping high up on Moel Siabod when the weather became so bad that the instructor from the outdoor centre had decided to break camp and bring the whole group down in the dark. The teacher was at the back with the last four lads when one of them needed to tie a boot lace. The delay in the dark had got them separated from the leading group. The four students were still on the hill and could go no further and were apparently in a bad way. The teacher told me later it was a very long night and at the first sign of dawn he forced himself to stand up and was ready to get the five boys down. However, he was stunned to find that the lads could not

33

stand and were not even capable of talking coherently let alone walking down.

"I knew of this centre," he said. "So, I came down through the forest as soon as I could."

With the teacher leading we set off up the hill with a first aid kit, hot sweet drinks, emergency food and clothing. The teacher seemed a good man and we followed him up the overgrown hillside of tall trees. We followed on, pushing through the sharp little branches but as we got higher the teacher became more and more hesitant until he stopped.

We all gathered round him and Don said, "Where are they?"

The teacher looked left, right and ahead. "I thought it was about here." He looked around again and then said. "Perhaps it was a bit further."

We followed on but only went another hundred metres when he stopped again and looked in all directions through the dense forest. The poor chap looked worried and frustrated at the same time. "They were here … somewhere." He looked suddenly very tired.

"Spread out in a line," said Don. "We will do a sweep search." We spread out in a line across the forested slope and continued up hill.

We had only walked for a few minutes when the teacher shouted. "Over here."

I was shocked when I saw the teenage students. They had rucksacks with tents, sleeping bags and good clothing but none of this kit was being used. Two had bare torsos, one had his trousers round his ankles and the other had lost his boots. It was my first experience of hypothermia and how one's brain starts to fail when blood temperature drops.

We wriggled each one of the boys into a sleeping bag and fed them hot sweet drinks and treacle flapjack. By the time we had packed up the kit that was lying around three of the lads had rapidly improved. With a firm shoulder for support they were able to slowly walk down, but one lad had to be carried.

Don made a 'split rope carry' and we lifted the lad onto his back. With the boy's legs through the rope loops Don made his way carefully down.

John met us outside the centre and as we unloaded from the mini-bus he said, "It's really warm in the boiler room. Put them all in there. Chairs are set out and Morag is bringing hot tea and food."

There was nothing else I could do, so I changed and went back to work. When I went for lunch the teacher and the four teenage lads were at a table eating a hot meal. If still on the mountain they might have been dead by now, so I was amazed how quickly they had recovered with the right treatment. I was learning all the time.

*

34

The last night of every course at the centre could be rather quiet, and I felt there should be some sort of social gathering for the clients on the last evening. As a teenager in downtown London I had learned nothing about outdoor adventures - but one thing I had learned to do, was to dance. My sisters and I went to dance classes every Wednesday evening and, in those days, it was ballroom dancing with the jive just coming in.

So, on the last evening of every course at the mountain centre I collected a stack of dance music records and a record player and I took over the dining room and became a 'disc jockey'. With chairs moved round to the walls and the tables stacked at one end it made the perfect dance hall. These last night 'socials' became so popular with all the clients that even the instructors and their wives would come in specially.

When spring came, I made the very most of all the daylight hours. After work in the evenings I would carry a kayak down to the water and taught myself the basics of kayaking and canoeing and then progressed to the 'white water' of the flowing river.

During any time off, visiting instructors often wanted a partner for rock climbing, and I was the one who was always keen and available. I followed good climbers up harder and harder routes and started to improve my climbing and rope management. As the months went by, I was asked more often to assist instructors.

John, the principal, would come bursting into my workshop. "Ah Peter. We're short of an instructor." He would quickly look over the kayak that I might be repairing. "Drop what you're doing, will you, and help Don with his rock-climbing course?"

"Sure, John." I was delighted and helped out on kayaking as well, and I even led a few mountain walking parties by myself. On one occasion I was to lead a two-day mountain camp for a group of twenty-year-old women who were training to be physical education teachers.

John met me in the staff room, and with a cup of tea he said, "So, Peter, where are you going to take the group for this camp?"

"Well, the weather is brilliant and hot, so I thought of taking them up to the high cwm with the lake."

"Yes, could be fine." Then he took a sip of tea and after a pause said. "Yes, should be a good camp up there. The group are all young ladies, aren't they?" He took another sip of tea and stopped to think for a minute. Then said. "I did that with a group just like yours from the same college. It was also a lovely hot day and the girls all stripped off to their underwear and went for a swim." He raised a warning finger and smiled.

By the time spring came I had raised my own standard of rock climbing. My years of working in the factory were paying off. Using hand tools for eight hours every day must have made my hands quite strong. I could rest on small handholds with confidence and I began to realise that I had some talent on the rock. I led the easier climbs and gradually worked up the grades until I was leading harder routes.

After a spell of dry weather, I approached a volunteer instructor who was also a qualified British Mountain Guide, and a little older than me. "Hugh, are you free to climb tonight?"

His face lit up with enthusiasm. "Sure, Pete, what did you have in mind?"

"I'd like to try the Corner."

"The Corner? What, Cenotaph Corner?"

I grinned. "Yes, I want to have a go, if it's dry."

"Well, I'm keen if you're the one leading."

Cenotaph Corner is now a regular route for most good climbers, but in those days, with less sophisticated protection and no specialist rock boots, it was still a test piece for the better leaders. We went out on my motorbike, over the head of the mountain pass and down the empty valley of Llanberis. A steep walk up rough scree and a scramble to a wide ledge put us at the bottom of the vertical corner that is like an open book with great rock walls on either side.

I looked up the clean line of thirty-five metres to the blue evening sky, way above. "It looks dry, Hugh"

"Well, yes, except that black streak half way up."

We sat on a rock to put on our black 'gym shoes'. I sorted out the few rope slings of various sizes, all tied with a double fisherman's knot, and to each one I clipped a heavy steel karabiner. These slings I hung round my neck. Hugh had sorted out the climbing rope and I tied onto one end with a bowline knot.

I looked up at the perfect corner and said, "Okay Hugh?" He checked his belay.

"Yes, ready when you are."

I started up. I'd heard that a hard move was only about seven metres up, but it was difficult to get a 'runner' on for protection. I climbed to that point fairly easily and took off the thin sling I had brought specially to thread through a hole. I was there for ten minutes but I couldn't thread the line through.

My strength was beginning to go and I called down to Hugh. "No good, can't thread it. I'll push on."

He grunted. On the rope slings I had threaded different sized nuts that I'd collected from engineering workshops. I slotted the nuts into any suitable cracks in the rock so that they might jamb if a weight was put on the sling. With these 'runners' in place it meant that if I fell off, I would be unlikely to hit the ground. I managed to fix a few of these slings for protection so that the rope ran through and this gave me the confidence to enjoy the spectacular position. As I gained height, the vertical, smooth rock walls on either side gave a wonderful sense of exposure. The left wall in particular seemed to hang over the steep valley below.

I eventually pulled over the top, tied onto a sound little oak tree, and called down to Hugh. "Right Hugh, climb when you're ready."

I sat and looked across the deep valley to the rugged mountains around Snowdon. I could see tiny puffs of smoke from the last tourist train of the day going up to the summit of Snowdon. Little red trains, like toys, pulling their single carriage of tourists up the rack railway. The sun was getting low and the rocky glaciated bowls of each hanging valley were in deep shadow. This darkness in the 'cwms' contrasted dramatically with the bright sunlight, that lit the sides of the mountain ridges. The milky blue sky and the hazy greens of the hills were beautiful. I sat there, taking in the climbing rope as Hugh climbed. There was a great drop below me but I was at peace with the world.

*

By coincidence, on the very next day, the management committee of the National Centre was meeting. The chairman of the committee was Sir John Hunt, the leader of the expedition to first climb Mount Everest; the very same man, with his team, that had presented the 'talk with pictures' that my mum had taken me to see when I was an apprentice just a few years before. During five o'clock tea in the staff room this famous man was brought in by the principal and introduced to everyone. I was sitting in the corner, a little to one side, and after shaking the hand of all the instructors the principal came to me.

"And this, Sir John, is Peter Dyer." And as I stood up and shook the great man's hand the principal added, "Peter climbed Cenotaph Corner yesterday."

"Oh, well done," said Sir John. He smiled at my boss. "I didn't know you had instructors of that quality."

But of course, I wasn't an instructor, and the principal quickly corrected him. "Oh, no. Peter is not an instructor. He's the maintenance man."

As none of the instructors had climbed Cenotaph Corner, they found this comment of John's very amusing, and it was some time before the laughter died down.

John Jackson must have thought that he had embarrassed me, for when we were alone, he mentioned the comment again. "Hope I didn't offend you, Peter."

I laughed. "Not in the slightest, John."

He tapped me on the shoulder. "Oh, good."

*

Each week we had a new batch of clients for a variety of outdoor activity courses. Many were adults, some were teachers in training and some were youth groups. I had been working at the National Mountain Centre for about seven months when one of these youth groups came with a smart chap in charge. I had done quite a bit of instructing with this group and while in the staff room one evening I said to the leader of the teenage group. "So, is this work for you?"

He smiled. "Oh, yes."

"Are you a teacher, then?"

He shook his head. "Oh no. I'm a youth leader."

"A youth leader? And this is your full-time job?"

He chuckled. "Yes. I run a big youth club in Stafford. We open six nights each week and have a staff of ten."

I was intrigued and asked him all about it. Until leaving London just a year ago, I had run the venture scout troop, and never realized that one could get paid for doing this type of youth work. I asked him all sorts of questions including how to get a youth leader's job.

"Well," he poured another cup of tea. "You have to be qualified."

"Qualified?"

"Yes. You would need to do a two-year college course."

I had never thought of going to college for anything as the only qualifications I had were in building work.

He continued. "If you're interested, I can give you the contacts." He tore off a piece of the newspaper on the coffee table and wrote down the name and address of a college near Birmingham. "There. Write to this college and tell them that I recommend you."

I don't remember the man's name and have never seen him since but he was another person who changed my life in more ways than he would ever know.

*

I wrote to the college in Birmingham and, to my delight and surprise, they accepted me for a course in youth leadership. The two-year course would

38

start in early September, so there was still a summer of activity ahead of me, and I made plans for a good season in the Alps.

CHAPTER 8: AN ALPINE SEASON

Hugh, the guide and voluntary instructor who had climbed Cenotaph Corner with me, was keen to climb in the Alps that summer, and I agreed to join him. So, I left the National Mountain Centre with a good alpine season ahead, and a very different future sorted out for the next couple of years.

Hugh and I hitchhiked down through France to my aunt May's house at Les Contamines. It was late spring, and the alpine valley looked beautiful with spring blossom on the fruit trees and everything green and fresh. Her house, with water only available outside in the basin, and a pit toilet, was primitive but it suited us fine.

After a day of sorting kit and buying food in the village we said goodbye to my aunt and set off on our first trip. We went south to the end of the valley and over the col de Seine that was on the border with Italy. We made our way through the high valley and down through the forests to camp near the Italian mountain village of Courmayeur. This was before the Mont Blanc rail tunnel had been built, and Courmayeur was a sleepy little alpine village.

The next day we went into a mountain equipment shop and bought a number of pitons and karabiners and I bought a good pair of climbing boots as these things in Italy were much cheaper than back in Britain. While in the shop we mentioned that we were going to climb the Grandes Jorasses mountain the next day. The shopkeeper was concerned, as he thought it was too early in the season, and he went across the road to ask advice from a guide. He came back and told us that we must not leave the high mountain hut later than midnight on the day of our ascent. We thanked him but quietly thought this a little overcautious.

We left our camp for the mountain hut the next day. It is a long and steep hike to the hut and when we arrived late in the afternoon, we were rather surprised that there was nobody there and the hut had not been used since last summer.

The mountains on this Italian side looked magnificent but sinister, with sharp rock ridges and steep snow and ice faces above serious glaciers. But we settled in with a meal and plans to wake at 2 am. However, when we woke at two the cloud was right down to the hut and light snow was falling. We went back to bed ready to start at 7am. However, when we woke again the weather was worse, so this climb was out in such bad weather. We retreated to our sleeping bags, and after breakfast made our way back down to the valley. Perhaps we had been lucky, for it's a serious mountain even in good weather.

The only map I had was one that covered the whole of Switzerland, so details were rather lacking. However, we thought there was a possible route marked on the map that went up a glacier and over a pass, called a Col in French, and down another glacier that led directly to my aunt's village of Les Contamines.

We decided to try this route and left camp the next morning with very heavy loads that included the kit I had bought in Courmayeur, such as new climbing equipment, a new pair of boots and all our camp kit. By late afternoon we were lucky to find a deserted stone hut on the edge of our glacier and settled in for an early night.

After a quick breakfast we left at four the next morning and started up the glacier in darkness in good weather with stars shining brightly in a clear sky. As the hours went by it got steeper and steeper. We stopped to fit crampons to our boots, and still the col looked a long way upwards. It was four in the afternoon when we eventually reached the ridge, which to my amazement was knife sharp.

Roped together, we made our way carefully along to a place where we could see a descent to the glacier we wanted to reach far below. The weather was still perfect and these high glaciated mountains looked magnificent but very serious.

Hugh belayed and I set off, down and across, very steep, firm snow. Halfway across I put in one of the new screw ice pitons that I had bought in Courmayeur, and clipped the rope through it. I then continued down and across before running the rest of the rope out, and made a secure belay. "Right, Hugh," I shouted up.

He started off but had not gone far when he slipped. I watched him slide faster and faster down the steep face and braced myself for a shock on the rope. However, the piton between us held and he swung to a stop and eventually came across to join me.

So, we carried on down this steep open face, only getting off the snow and ice when any daylight had already gone. Down and down through the dark forest to eventually reach the village and my aunt's house just after midnight.

It had been a very long and tough day so we took a day off to rest and shop in the village. The next day, after saying Thanks to May for her generous stay, we took a bus down the valley alongside the turbulent river, passing small orchards in pink blossom, and a patchwork of small green fields. At the village of St Gervais, we changed buses and went east, gaining height through the mountain village of Chamonix to Argentierre, where we set up camp.

After a snack lunch with a large mug of tea we closed the tent and left the valley for the Argentierre mountain hut. We reached it in good time, and after booking in and sorting out our bedding and kit we took a big mug of tea and sat out on the wide stone terrace. The high mountains around looked great in this perfect weather, and with map and guide book we planned our route for the next day. We made a big but simple meal from tins and, leaving a crowd of other mountaineers in the dining room, we settled in for an early night.

We crept out of the dormitory in the dark the next morning and after a good quick breakfast we left the hut to a cold but sparkling dark sky. Feeling fit, we did a pleasant route across glaciers and then up to the summit of Chardonnet. We were back at the hut quite early in the afternoon and sat on the stone wall surrounding the terrace drinking tea and talking to other climbers.

We stayed in the alpine hut another night and the next day did an easy ascent of a rocky peak at the end of the valley. We were off the mountain early and after packing our kit we ambled down to the main valley to the camp site and our tent for the night.

The next day we packed up our camp and took a bus east across the border to Switzerland and the little mountain village of Arolla. We camped there for a few days. We went up to the vignettes hut and climbed Mont Collon and later did the Pigne d'Arolla.

It was here that I had a fall. We were roped up with Hugh going first down a long rocky ridge. We were moving together, with me belaying where I could. I was hurrying to safeguard Hugh and took hold of a spike of rock that broke away. I fell backwards down the opposite side of the ridge and only stopped when the rope came tight over the ridge. I was lucky, for I only had a few bruises and soon climbed up and over the ridge to join Hugh, who had hardly noticed my fall.

The weather was still holding well and after a week of doing a few good peaks we packed up our camp again and made our way up the glacier and over the col on the east. Then it was down to eventually pass the north face of the Matterhorn and to reach the mountain village of Zermatt.

We settled into a camp field just outside the busy little village, and the next day set off for the Tasch hut and stayed for a few days. The weather was perfect and we climbed the Allalinhorn and the Alphubel.

Down at our camp in the valley we took a day to sort kit and buy food. The weather was still perfect and we were getting quite used to the beautiful alpine scenery and were fit and well equipped for any of the peaks. We decided to go across to the western side of the valley, and made our way up to the Rothorn hut. The next morning after an early start we went up the Zinalrothorn. Still the weather held, and the next day we climbed the Gabelhorn before eventually descending to Zermatt and our little camp.

We had been climbing in the area for a couple of weeks when Hugh's mountaineering club from Birmingham arrived at our campsite in the valley. This was their club's alpine meet for the year and there were about fifteen of them. One of the club members was Gill, who was Hugh's girlfriend. Gill seemed a bright, confident person who was a fit and keen climber.

She was to climb with Hugh, so I was invited to join another couple of pleasant chaps from the club. After a day to sort out kit and buy food in Zermatt we all set off to the Breithorn hut ready for an ascent of the Stralhorn. At three the next morning, there was little wind and the stars were bright in a dark silken sky when we left the hut. Our rope of three made good time up the easy glacier onto the ridge, and we were at the summit before noon. There was little technical climbing for this peak and we eventually took the rope off when we left the wide glacier early in the afternoon.

We strolled back to the hut and made ourselves some lunch, and with a mug of tea we sat out on the sunny terrace looking at the magnificent alpine peaks that could be seen in all directions. With more tea we got talking about climbing, particularly in North Wales where these club members had a hut. It wasn't long before the other teams from the Birmingham club came along the track, dumping their rucksacks, and joined us to talk about their day.

Eventually everyone was back, all except Hugh and Gill. A few jokes were made about the 'courting couple' but as the hours went by, we began to wonder where they were. It was now getting quite late and I suggested that we walk up to see if we could see them. The club members were also having concerns, as it would be dark in an hour, so some of the fitter members agreed to join me. We put our boots and gaiters on again and collected ropes and other kit.

We set off at a good pace up the path, but had only been going for half an hour when Hugh came down the track. There was dried blood on his face. "Hugh – you okay?" Before he could answer I said, "Where's Gill?"

"Crevasse," he said. "Down a crevasse. We both went down but I couldn't get her out."

He looked tired but he was a fit chap and he turned around to lead us up to the crevasse. By the time we reached the glacier it was dark but Hugh thought he knew where to go. However, conditions had changed during the heat of the afternoon and crevasses on the lower part of the wide glacier had opened up all over the place. We followed Hugh from one great fissure to another, and after half an hour began to get quite worried. Apparently,

43

Gill was not injured, but the crevasses were very deep and if she were to be stuck deep down all night it would be very serious indeed.

Then, with a torch, Hugh saw one of our Italian pitons down the wall of a crevasse. "This is it. That's the peg I used to get out." He laid flat and shouted down into the darkness. "Gill!"

From deep down we were relieved to hear a faint "Here!" In a few minutes, with two ice axes, we had rigged up a good solid belay and I went over the lip and started to descend. It was about twenty metres down and got quite narrow to where Gill was crouched. She was a bit bruised but I tied her onto the rope and with me helping and the others pulling the rope we came out to the surface.

She was so cold that we helped her while descending the dangerous glacier, but she was a strong lass and had recovered by the time we had gone off the moraine, and we walked easily down the track to the hut. The members who had stayed behind had made a simple but ample meal and over big mugs of tea we talked about the rescue. All agreed that it could have ended far worse.

After two weeks of climbing, the club members left for home and Hugh and I left our little tent and walked up to the Breithorn hut to do the Breithorn. We were talking to a guide in the dining room and he told us that for the next couple of days all the local guides were going to be down in the valley as they were attending a funeral of an old guide.

This was interesting news for us. It would mean there would be no guided parties, particularly on the Hornli ridge of the Matterhorn. This famous ridge gets busy on all the good days during the season and with so many parties it can get very slow and dangerous.

We wanted to do the Matterhorn, so we made plans to be on the ridge on the day when the guides would be down in Zermat. We left in the dark very early the next morning and made excellent time to the summit of the Breithorn in perfect weather. It was still early in the day when we were off the mountain and made our way down towards the west to eventually reach the Furggletshcher glacier that was ankle deep in an icy slush.

With wet feet we eventually reached the Hornli ridge and climbed up to the hut, perched way above the glaciers far below. We suspected that the hut would not be too busy, but to our delight the hut was completely empty. We had no food left so we raided the 'left over' bins near the kitchen and found enough to make a meal. We spread out in a dormitory and after getting everything ready for the morning we had an early night.

Breakfast was easy as nobody had arrived during the night and after checking our kit we left the hut at 2am to a very cold but beautifully clear night. Sometimes moving together, we made good time up the sharpening rock ridge to eventually make the summit in the bright early morning light.

It certainly is a sharp peak, and we looked down the sinister north face that was not catching any of the glorious sunshine. We took more care going down the ridge but made the hut in good time and stayed for a few cups of tea and a talk with the ever-growing parties who were arriving with their guides. Then it was an easy descent to the valley, Zermat, and our cosy tent.

We had done many of the standard routes from this valley and the next morning we packed up our camp and, with heavy packs again, made our way up and over a high col on the eastern side to drop down to the charming village of Saas Fee. We spent another good week climbing the peaks from alpine huts. As we came down to the valley from out last peak, I knew that time was up for me. Hugh and I had managed to have a great alpine season with perfect weather every day, and being fit we had achieved a lot.

But now my mind was once again on the future. We sorted kit, packed up our tent and the next day turned our backs on the glorious Alps. By bus and train, I made my way north to Paris, the channel and London. I had two weeks to prepare for my new life as a college student and the prospect of new friends. These friends were to change my life.

CHAPTER 9: COLLEGE LIFE

Back at my parents' home in London, I packed my kit. But this time it wasn't mountaineering equipment but a tennis racquet, soccer boots and casual clothes for college life. With my motorbike stacked high with a suit case and a couple of other bags I rode north to Birmingham.

The college campus was lovely with lecture rooms, the dining room and the students' halls of residence, all built around lawns, woodlands and tennis courts. All the students lived on site. About five hundred of these were training to be teachers in primary schools, most being girls who had come straight from highschool.

On my course there were about thirty students who were mostly men in their early twenties. We were all doing the course in youth leadership that would qualify us to run a full-time youth club. The youth leadership students were a good group, coming from industries of various sorts, and all had some experience of helping in their local youth groups.

Alan, who I was to share a room with, had a similar background to me, and from the start we got on famously. He was a local Birmingham chap, twenty-two years old like me, who had come from industry and already had good experience of voluntary youth leadership. He was a fit chap and keen on all sports playing: soccer, rugby and basketball. He was also the life and soul of any party scene and could get on with everyone.

I was considered to be a 'mature student' so my tuition, accommodation and even food was all free. I soon realized that college life was great. The room that Alan and I shared was on the ground floor of a three-story hostel block. This nice hostel had a strict lock up time of 10 o'clock. This was probably because all the residents were girls training to be teachers – Alan and I were the only men in that hostel. Perhaps they thought that as Alan was married, we would be the steady ones to be in the girls' hall of residence.

However, almost every night we were continually being woken by girls who had been locked out. They would tap on the casement window at the head of my bed so that I could open it and they would climb through, cross our room and creep up the stairs to their own rooms.

Perhaps it was inevitable that I was moved at the end of the first year to a room in another halls of residence. Although Alan was married and lived locally the college wanted him to live on campus for his first year. Now in his second year he was allowed to live back at his home. This meant that he used my hostel room as his daytime room. Often, I might be studying in my room and find that he had invited a crowd of our mates in for coffee! However, he was a good mate and, although moving into different careers, we have been friends ever since.

During the days we had lectures and were given written assignments. As most of us had not had any academic training since leaving school at the age of fifteen, we found these written projects quite taxing. Alan and I were part of a group that required special tuition in English.

The practical aspect of the youth leadership course was working in the evenings at local youth clubs that were situated around Birmingham. These clubs for teenagers were run on one night each week at places like community centres or church halls.

*

Although my recent life had been involved in the outdoor activities such as mountaineering, caving and kayaking, I had already decided to return to conventional sports while at college. Alan and I were enthusiastic members of the soccer and rugby teams and played every week. We also played basketball and I played tennis almost every day when free. The tennis courts were overlooked by a few lecture rooms and I played so much in the summer that one of the tutors questioned me as he thought I must be missing a lecture. I joined all the various college clubs and even taught a bit of ballroom dancing.

Our youth leadership course involved other projects. We put on a drama production each winter and I was an enthusiastic actor on each show. In our second year we had to come up with a big project for all the youth clubs in Birmingham. We decided to run an orienteering course for about one hundred teams, each team having six club members. We arranged to run the course in the great park at Sutton Coldfield that has woodland and a few lakes. We even got the sea cadets involved to ferry the teams across the lakes. We had to close the park to run our competition and as the council would not close the park during the day, the whole orienteering course took place at night, finishing around breakfast time.

On our course we also had a 'camp' for two weeks, so we could be taught outdoor skills. This was perfect for me and I got involved in helping the tutors to teach climbing and canoeing, and I led some mountain trips. I also had the chance to join a university camp on the shore of lake Coniston in the lake district. I did plenty of dinghy sailing that proved to be good experience for the future.

*

47

During the college summer break of two months, I gained a position as a voluntary instructor at a new outward-bound school on the Welsh coast. These outward-bound courses would each last for one month, but the school was so new that the first course hadn't even started. It was the first O.B. school solely for girls, so that when the first students arrived the queen and Prince Philip came to meet the staff and make a grand opening. When the royal couple came, we instructors lined up and shook hands with both of them. I was a young, fit chap and when I smiled and shook hands with the queen, I gripped her little hand confidently. Perhaps too confidently, for I felt her poor little bones grind together.

Each group of ten students had a female instructor, and us four men were involved in teaching climbing, canoeing and camping. During each course I also ran a workshop programme where each group of girls built a slalom kayak that was made in timber and canvas. It was good experience for me.

*

Back at college for my second year I went abroad twice. The youth leaders all went to Germany for two weeks to look at the work being done in large, professional youth centres. We saw impressive work in Berlin and Koln. I also had a chance to go through the 'Berlin wall' to see parts of east Berlin that were completely different from the thriving west side.

*

The other trip abroad was not work but skiing. We had a students' outdoor club, and one of the girls found a very cheap skiing holiday in Italy. Six girls and five chaps paid up and we had a great time on the slopes. A student who was training to be a primary school teacher, called Catherine, organized it, and her teenage brother joined us. Like me, he had skied before, so we seemed to team up on most days. However, as my college course was coming to an end, I had other distractions.

Catherine, with her blue eyes and blond hair, had attracted me. We were in the same hostel block and played tennis together, and her skiing and outdoor interests were the same as mine. I would constantly see her passing my window and it distracted me from the studying I should have been doing. I wasn't really ready for a steady girlfriend for my future was still uncertain. However, I realized that after leaving college I would be unlikely to meet anyone so perfect as Cath. I tried to meet her alone, but she was always with a group of friends. I eventually met her in the dining room one evening and with her friends all nearby it took all my courage to invite her out. Her friends looked at me and then at her and then pretended to be interested in something across the room. She accepted, and we began to do more together.

I was no great 'catch' so my college mates were amazed and joked with me when she invited me to go home one weekend to meet her parents. Cath's dad had bought her a minivan and she drove us north to Yorkshire to the village of Penistone where her dad had an optician practice. Her mum and dad were interesting and charming to me, but not at all certain that I was a good catch.

*

But it seemed that Cath and I were both thinking of the future. However, there were problems. I had already decided that I would not go straight into youth work and had been accepted as a volunteer with the 'International Voluntary Society'. After leaving college I was sent on a training course in France and was due to be sent out to the Cameroon in west Africa. Then, at the last moment, there were problems in West Cameroon and my trip was postponed for a year. Cath had moved to Leicester to start her teaching career in a primary school and was sharing a flat with a couple of other girls from our college. Cath might wait a year for me but in two years I might lose her, so with some regrets I pulled out of the IVS and now had to look for work.

*

Even when I could find a vacancy in youth leadership it would be a month or two before I could be appointed, so I had to look for something else. Back with mum and dad in London I immediately got a cabinet-making job nearby. It was interesting work but I knew that I could get joinery work anywhere. So, after only a week, I left the job in London and, with all my tools, went up to Leicester where Cath had begun her teaching career.

I got a room not far from her flat and it took me only two days to get work as a joiner. Cath was doing well in her first teaching job and I started to apply for work as a youth leader. A month later I applied for a leadership job just west of my home in London. It was a completely new establishment and they appointed me as the full-time youth leader. So, after two months working as a joiner in Leicester, I packed my motorbike again and went home to London to start up this new youth centre in Southall.

*

The youth centre was a new building and the facilities were excellent. I appointed a part-time and voluntary staff of about ten, and we soon had more than one hundred teenagers coming every night of the week. We established all sorts of activity groups that took place in the big hall or other rooms every evening but most members would also come to the wonderful big coffee bar to chat and meet friends. Each afternoon I worked in the office to organize things. Most of my evening work was talking in the coffee bar, for these relationships, I felt, were the most important thing. With the right relationship one can change the lives of teenagers.

On one occasion, all the ash trays in the lovely committee room were stolen. I felt sure they had been taken by one of a gang. The next evening, I had a quiet word with Ralph, the leader of this gang. He was a bit shocked. "I didn't take them Pete."

I smiled. "No, I know you wouldn't, Ralph. Just ask around and bring them back to me."

He looked thoughtful. "Mm. Leave it to me Pete." The next evening, he came in early when I was still in the office. He put a carrier bag on my desk. "There you are, Pete. It won't happen again."

All the ashtrays were there and I smiled. "Thanks Ralph." He left the office walking tall. On another occasion, a big lad and I were chatting near the coffee bar and he was swearing on every other word.

Eventually, I quietly said. "Ken, I would rather you didn't swear. It makes me embarrassed." He grinned and certainly never swore again in my presence. One evening two men came into the crowded club. Although they were dressed in casual clothes everyone knew they were policemen. They had a coffee with me while leaning on the bar and after looking round said. "You have some hard cases in here, you know."

I grinned. "Perhaps, but we never have any trouble."

Every morning I wrote a letter to Cath and every morning the postman delivered one to me. We managed to have a few camping holidays in Wales, and had a week in her aunt's holiday house on the coast in Northumberland. I also joined Cath when she visited her parents in Yorkshire, and I seemed to get on well with her mum and dad.

Cath had been teaching in Leicestershire for a year but then left that school to live at home and took a teaching post in a small Yorkshire village.

The youth centre was going very well, but this was not the future I wanted for Cath and myself. We didn't speak about our future but I knew that we wanted a life away from the busy city. After a year as a youth leader, I started to apply for work as an instructor at various outdoor activity centres.

CHAPTER 10: INTERVIEWS AND DREAMS

I wrote applications for work all over the country. All the letters of rejection came in thin envelopes as they only contained a single sheet of paper, and I had received a number of similar letters during the last few months. Usually, I only received a polite letter on the lines of, 'thank you for your application, but on this occasion, you have been unsuccessful'.

However, sometimes the envelopes were thicker, and this usually meant that I was asked to attend an interview. One interview was in Devon at the outward-bound school. Another had been in the Lake District on a day when I could hardly see the hills because of the cloud and rain. I had a nervous interview on a bleak winter day at the outdoor centre in Derbyshire. The chairman for the interviewing panel was the famous mountaineer, Jack Longland. It didn't take them long to realise my lack of education and experience.

I even gained one interview for the position of a sailing instructor on a small gravel pit not far from my home in London. At this 'gathering' in the north of London there must have been about twenty-five people interviewing the seven candidates, all of us being men.

After waiting for an hour in an empty room for a decision, a nervous man wearing a black suit, made shiny on the seat by years of wear, came out and said, "Thank you, gentlemen, however the committee have decided to advertise for a lady."

We were all annoyed. Many of us had lost a day's wage or at least spent a long time in travelling to London when the committee could have made the decision to appoint a female beforehand.

One Scots lad was furious. He barged back to the interview room and shouted at the silent committee: "Yae didna have to drag me all the way frae Glasgow to find I'm no a lassie."

One interview was up on the north east coast in the council offices of Newcastle. The five of us candidates were confined to a dismal high room, paneled out in dark oak and smelling of damp and furniture polish. Round the walls were paintings of past mayors of the city, each somber picture mounted in a heavy gilt frame. We were in that room for five hours and nobody even thought to bring us a cup of tea. When it was eventually my turn the whole interview lasted just eleven minutes.

One man kept referring to me as Mr. Williams from Wales and a rather ferocious lady asked me only one question. "But…. But, Mr. Dyer, do I understand that you are not a qualified teacher?"

Every interview ended in the same way. After being seen individually the four or five candidates would wait together. I was always so nervous, and my heart would pound as one of the panel would emerge from the interviewing room.

The person would smile vacantly, look at another candidate and say something like, "Mr. Smith, would you come back please?"

My shoulders would slump, and a great tiredness set in. 'Mr. Smith' would be offered the job and I knew that I had failed yet again.

In the dark on a miserable train journey back from Newcastle I watched the rain streaking diagonally down the window, and for the first time I suddenly realised what might be the awful truth: I might never succeed in getting an instructor's job and leaving the city. I saw the future as it might be, working in London without seeing the sky for days at a time - perhaps traveling home on the underground train and living in a flat on the tenth floor of an apartment block. Some people might like that, but despite living there since birth, city life was not for me. I'd spent all my life in the shadow of a stinking gas works with coal dust blackening the buildings, and I knew that I wanted an open-air country life: a life where I could see the weather change, the seasons come and go, and be near mountains, rivers, forests and the ocean, and learn something of nature and the wildlife.

Without discussing these thoughts with Cath, I knew that she would not be happy living in a busy city. However, it was Friday and every Friday I lived with renewed hope. Fridays were special days for me because on Friday the Times Educational Supplement came out. In the back of this paper were the job vacancies and one small column had the heading 'Outdoor Education'.

*

Each week I desperately searched the advertisements. There were no jobs for a few weeks but then in early December I was looking down the vacancy column and my heart paused as I read: ---- Benmore Adventure Centre – Instructor wanted.

The advert was business-like but brief and I wrote off for the usual information to an address in Edinburgh. I had never been to Edinburgh, although I had done a little easy winter mountaineering in Glencoe. I took out an atlas of the British Isles and looked up Benmore. It was in the middle of Scotland and for the next few days I dreamed and schemed over the map and studied the area in detail.

Then the information came and I soon realised that Benmore simply meant 'big hill', and there were quite a few 'Benmores' marked in my atlas.

From the address I realised the adventure centre was not in the middle of Scotland but near the town of Dunoon. I found Dunoon in my atlas. It is on the west of Scotland and on the north shore of the river Clyde. On the atlas, just north of Dunoon, in small print, were the words, Benmore Botanic Gardens.

New dreams started again in my head, of mountains, sea and rocky islands. All the letters I wrote to Cath told of these interviews and she made few comments except to encourage me if things didn't work out. With no qualifications in the outdoor activities my application form was a bit blank in places. I had to try and justify my application with generalizations and my experiences. The form didn't look impressive, but it was the best I could do without lying.

It was nearly Christmas when I went downstairs one very dark morning. Mum, wearing her floral apron, was sitting with the usual cup of strong tea, and lying at my breakfast place was a buff envelope postmarked Edinburgh. This letter, lying by my porridge bowl, was not a thin rejection but was fat, and my chest went tight as I opened it.

I had been called for an interview and hope flooded back to me. "That's nice," was all mum said, but I knew she longed for my success. "Well, Peter, another chance, but if this doesn't work out there will be others," and she cleared my breakfast plate with brisk efficiency. As a true 'cockney', she was not about to show her emotions.

It was like the first time that I took my girlfriend Cath home. After a couple of days, when Cath was out of the room, my mum said, "she seems lovely, Pete." She paused to slowly look me up and down. "How did you do it!"

*

On interviews I had attended in the past, many of the candidates had beards. It seemed to fit the image of an experienced outdoor man. A beard, I thought, might make the difference between failure and success, I stopped shaving and waited to see the result. For the first few days it came on as I expected and lads at the youth centre made comments like "Eh, Pete, you've got a bit of fluff on yer chin." Some of them started to call me "Billy," as in 'billy goat'. But I laughed it off until my proud little beard seemed to stop growing. I'm not really the hairy macho type but I was hoping for a better beard than my threadbare tufts. Anyway, I persevered and eventually there was enough of a beard to show that it wasn't a mistake and at least it covered my acne. I pressed the trousers of my suit, studied the adventure centre details until I knew every word by heart. With thoughts of mountains, lochs and heather I dreamed away the few weeks before I would travel north to Scotland.

CHAPTER 11: INTERVIEW IN SCOTLAND

It was still dark in January when I left the warm, stale air of the London underground train and came out into the windy cavern that was Euston station. I stood with others looking up at the huge, green direction board with its clanking louvred signs. There, on one of the many columns was the information I wanted: Glasgow, platform 15. Through the smells of smoke, diesel oil and fried food, I weaved through the crowds, passed the chap wearing the usual drab uniform and flat cap to check my ticket and along the train until I found a non-smoking carriage.

I was wearing my dark suit, white shirt and polished shoes which I hoped would be appropriate for the interview. Over the top I wore my 'Gannex' coat which I thought made me look quite trendy. The information I had received from Scotland stated 'Accommodation at the centre will be provided', so I'd taken a rather large suitcase. Apart from the obvious pyjamas, towel and wash things, I had even packed some outdoor clothing.

"Better take them just in case," was mum's comment. "And don't forget a handkerchief." I heaved the case high onto the luggage rack, sank back into a seat and huddled to keep warm while I waited. Twenty minutes later the train was still half empty when doors were slammed in progression down the train, a whistle blew, and the carriage jerked slowly into life.

I was away on the long journey north. I had a book to pass the time, but my mind was too busy to read. Crowding into my brain were questions like, am I dressed to create the best impression? What type of people will interview me? What questions will they ask and who will be in competition with me? Never once did I think whether to accept the job if it was offered to me. I was desperate and would have accepted any instructing post.

Eventually I was grateful to fall asleep near Watford and only woke as the train groaned up the long incline to Shap summit. I felt awful; cold, with a stiff neck and a head that had been rattling against the glass window.

After staggering along two carriages I found the buffet car. "A white coffee please," I said to a weary man who never smiled. Sipping the drink as it splashed around the cup, I stood looking out of a window at the Lakeland fells, which I could see in the distance. The fells looked wonderful with a dusting of snow on the summit of each mountain. If I failed at this interview, I might get another chance to work in the Lake district which I thought would be nice.

The train picked up speed again and we thundered north, hour after hour through the rolling wooded hills of the lowlands. It was only four in the afternoon when the train pulled into Glasgow, but the light was already fading to leave a cold grey cheerless evening. I walked through the crowded station, over the legs of a drunk sprawled on the floor and found my next train. It was the more modern type with no corridors and a draught blowing its full length through open doors at both ends of the carriage.

However, there was no long wait and the train, still nearly empty, jerked out of the station on the way to the west coast. For a while we rattled rather slowly by tall grey apartment blocks, or what the Scots would call tenement buildings. They were about five floors high, solidly made and built straight from the pavement, with no gardens at the front or the back. With no balconies or decoration of any kind they seemed to be simply boxes in which to eat and sleep.

This was obviously a stopping train and as we stopped so often there was little point in trying to go fast between the halts. I was impatient to see the countryside and particularly the river Clyde, but any sign of it was hidden. Huge dockside sheds, tall cranes and the vast hulls of ships blocked any view of the river. Every few minutes the train would come to a weary halt and workers crowded in. Most were dressed in dusty boiler suits, open jackets and peaked caps, each one carrying an ex-army bag over one shoulder. They seemed tired and quiet, matching the flat-fronted tenements on the other side of the railway.

At one station we waited in that embarrassed silence that always seems to occur, and my eye caught sight of a faded wooden sign high on the side of a tenement block. It must have been painted many years before, but I could still read the words 'For Christmas - send your friends a box of Loch Fyne Herring'. I smiled at the thought of my bachelor friends, back in London, opening a Christmas present to find a box of dead fish. So, this was the river Clyde. A grey dusk had turned to a cold, wet darkness as the train squealed slowly to a stop in the station at the end of the line.

This was Gourock, and for me the place where I was to cross the river. From the tobacco smoke and warm air of the train I followed the small crowd straight out onto a windswept high dockside. This was not so much the river I had expected but a heaving cold ocean that glinted away into the blackness. Rain splattered in vicious gusts on the black tarmac of the dock and sparkled from one bare light bulb. I lowered my head against the rain and with a hand holding my collar I went over to a seaman standing in the shelter.

He was dressed in the usual heavyweight navy-blue jacket and trousers that always looked itchy to me. "Excuse me, is this the ferry for Dunoon?"

"Aye, it is." He nodded towards a discreet varnished board on the side of the wheelhouse that, I could now see, had a single word painted on it: Dunoon. I followed the confident passengers up a wooden gangplank, over a high doorstep and down a shoulder-wide staircase to a lower deck. There was a small counter in one corner where a plump lady, wearing a wraparound apron, was quietly serving tea and cakes, and I edged my way across.

"Tea please and one of those," I said, pointing to a flat pancake thing.

"The'r dropped scons," said the lady, with a charming accent and the patient smile that one might give when speaking to a child. I took the scone and mug of tea to one of the long, varnished tables, which were bolted solidly to the deck. I sat with elbows in, shoulder to shoulder with the other passengers.

These were not the same type of people that I might have met earlier in the day on the London underground, or even in Glasgow. These people moved a little more slowly, their shoulders seemed a little more relaxed and their faces would break into a quiet smile more readily. They spoke quietly to each other, and I had a chance to notice their clothes. The men mostly wore Harris Tweed jackets with a half-belt at the back and coarse trousers with heavy turnups. Without exception, they carried a long raincoat.

I had thought, in my south of England mind, that the kilt was something worn only on special occasions or by show business personalities. However, a number of men were wearing kilts with thick long socks, heavy brown shoes and a waisted jacket. Nobody took the slightest notice, except me. These people were not southerners or even Glaswegians. With the crossing of the Clyde I felt I was moving into the land of the highlander.

A shudder of powerful engines went through the small ship, and after a couple of minutes I knew we had left the shelter of the dockside as we rolled heavily in the first swell of the sea. I sat there holding the mug with both hands and grinning at the thought of living and working in this area. But like many of my dreams I knew it might all come to nothing.

After about twenty minutes the regular thudding of the engine slowed, and I could hear heavy boots on the deck above. We must be docking, and despite the wind and rain I was not going to miss anything. I turned up my collar, picked up my suitcase, and went up the steep staircase to a blast of ice-cold air on deck.

The ship had stopped and now rolled gently a few metres from a heavy wooden dock. I leaned on the polished rail and looked down at the few people waiting in the shelter away from the wind. The waiting area was the only part of the dock to be lit with a few yellow light bulbs. Further back I could see the lights of buildings and street lamps, which stopped abruptly at the end of the town. Everything beyond this feeble light was black.

Seamen moved about the ships deck and, in quiet confidence, threw lines to others on the dock. Heavier ropes were pulled across the gap and looped over oak bollards and we moved slowly alongside. The few people on the dock idled towards a place where a grey wooden gangplank was pulled up to our deck. Without hustle, passengers shuffled carefully down the slippery wood, and I followed them to the pier.

I was to be met with transport on the pier and I stood there looking vaguely into the darkness. People were dispersing until I stood alone. Then an elderly man wearing a flat cap and a brown tweed jacket over a boiler suit, eased himself from the support of a minibus and with hands deep in his pockets he moved over to me.

"Are ya foor Benmooore?" he said with a rather shy smile.

"Yes, I'm Peter Dyer."

"Aye." He spoke slowly and looked up and down at my dark suit and shiny black shoes. "Aye, I thought so. I'm Hamish, the janitor." He then walked over to the driver's side of the rather battered minibus and climbed up into the driver's seat.

It was obvious that I was expected to get in on the other side, but I couldn't open the door. There was only a hole on my side where a door handle used to be. I tapped on the window and mouthed the word 'Handle' to Hamish and pointed downwards. After a couple of seconds looking vaguely at me through the glass, he suddenly lifted his head in understanding and leaned over to open the door.

"Arr forgoot," he said. "Hasna been a handle there foor weeks."

When the motor started there was an immediate rattle from the engine, which was situated between us, and the engine cover slid sideways onto my leg.

Hamish struggled with the engine cover for a short while as smoke drifted upwards and then said, "See if ya kin hold that in place."

With me holding the cover we lurched, rather too close to the edge of the unprotected pier, and were soon on the road through the town of Dunoon.

Hamish shouted above the noise of the engine between us. "Do ya ken this part?"

I smiled rather awkwardly, so he shouted again in explanation. "Have ya been here befooorre?"

I leaned over and shouted. "Oh no, not here, but I have been to Scotland."

"Aye." After a few minutes we had left the lights and the town behind and continued on a road that edged the shoreline. As we passed through a small village Hamish leaned across and shouted, "Sandbank. This is Sandbank."

I looked out to the empty street where chinks of light showed through curtains of the houses. "Oh…. Sandbank".

"Aye." He leaned across and shouted again. "They make some fine big sailing boats here."

After passing a few dark fields we turned left along a narrow road that cut like a tunnel through dense trees. The beam from the feeble headlights bounced up and down as we negotiated potholes until we suddenly swung right through a pillared gateway, over a rattling cattle grid and went more slowly down a long gravel drive.

Silhouetted ahead was a castle-like building with conical roofed towers. It was dark except for two lighted windows shining through a break in the trees. We drove slowly round the back of the building, down a steep drive and into a small courtyard with windows on three sides, all of which were in darkness.

The engine spluttered to silence and Hamish turned to me. "We will go and find Miss Cameron. You ken Miss Cameron I understand?"

"Miss Cameron?"

"Aye, she says that she kens you." I must have looked stupid, so he said. "I believe you know Miss Morag Cameron when she worked in Wales."

"Miss Cameron?" I repeated. "Oh Morag! Is she here?" "Aye." He smiled.

"Miss Cameron is in charge of the hoose." I was surprised and delighted. Morag had been working at the National Mountaineering Centre in North Wales and we had come into contact many times when I was doing maintenance work on the house. She was a few years older than me and I knew she had a reputation of quiet efficiency and a ready smile. Hamish climbed out, slammed the door without looking and left me to follow him across the yard and through a side door.

With my large suitcase bumping against my leg I followed him where the only noise was our shoes on the stone floor of the corridors. "I think Miss Cameron will be in here." He opened a door into a brightly lit kitchen, which was stacked around with cardboard boxes.

Morag was there unpacking new equipment from a box and when she heard us enter, she straightened and turned. "Helloo Peter. It's grand to see you again."

She gave me a smile that made me think she really did mean it. She dusted her hands and removed an apron protecting her tartan skirt and brushed her dark hair back. "I was sure it must be the Peter Dyer I knew when I saw the list of those coming for interview."

I shook her hand warmly. "Hello Morag, so you're working here. You've returned to Scotland."

"Aye." She gave a short laugh. "I came here a couple of months ago in charge of the hoose. As you can see it's been a busy time of buying everything and sorting it oot." She stood with her hands on her hips looking at the piles around and then turned to me. "But you've had a long journey. You stay in London now don't you?"

"Stay?"

"Aye. You live in London."

"Oh yes. I stay in London."

"Right.... I'll show you where you're sleeping tonight." I followed her along dim passageways up a castle like circular stone stairway and into a turret bedroom. "I'm afraid it's a bit spartan yet," she said in her charming accent. "We've still not received most of the furniture. Anyway, you sort yourself oot and come doon to the kitchen. I've a meal ready in the oven and we can have a good blather."

I must have looked vacant again for she continued. "Blather.... A good talk about what you've been doing."

During the meal, we sat across the great kitchen table and I began to relax. The building seemed empty and I said to Morag, "It's all very quiet Morag, who lives in the centre?" She put her fork down.

"Well, I stay in a flat upstairs and next to me is Roger, the chief instructor and his wife Jenny. Vic, the principal, and his wife Jane live on the same floor but their flat has a front door from the drive."

"Just three, eh?"

"Yes, at present. They're all oot tonight but you'll meet them tomorrow."

My real concern was the other candidates, so I tried to speak casually when I said, "How many people are there coming for the interviews?"

"Three, I believe. Just you and two others. You might know them. They both came to instruct at Plas y Brenin National Centre at times."

"Oh, who are they?"

"Well, there's Rusty Baillie, who comes from Rhodesia, and the other one is Bill March who was at London University."

I shook my head. "I don't know the names."

60

"We'll meet them tomorrow. Rusty has arrived but is doon at the pub with Vic. Bill will arrive tomorrow morning."

My mind wouldn't stop going round when I got to bed. The other two chaps coming for interview seemed to be better than me. They had both worked at the national centre in Wales, so they had probably done more instructing than me. I fell asleep worried that tomorrow I would be on my way back home with all my dreams once again shattered.

*

Morag made me a fine breakfast, but I was pleased to eat it all alone in the large empty kitchen. To be alone gave my mind a chance to slow down before the tensions that I knew would be with me for the rest of the day.

I was trying to lick a spot of marmalade from my tie when the door opened quietly and in walked a man with soft-soled shoes, a baggy sweater and corduroy trousers. His brown hair was casually brushed to one side of a rather boyish face.

"Hello Peter." He spoke very quietly. "I'm Roger, the chief instructor."

I half struggled out from the solid kitchen table to shake his outstretched hand, but he smiled easily and waved me down again.

"Oh, finish your breakfast, I'll join you for a cup of tea." He brought a cup across and while he looked around for a chair, I poured tea for him. It seemed there was no other chair in the kitchen, so he sat on a plywood packing case with his chin only a little above the tabletop.

I felt rather awkward looking down at him but was already impressed by this man of authority who had the confidence to be so laid back. "Did you have a good journey up from London?"

"Yes, thanks."

"And Morag settled you in."

"Yes, fine thanks."

He took a sip of tea. "We were lucky to get Morag. She is a real gem. But of course, you will know her from the National Centre in Wales, won't you? It seems that all of us have worked at Plas Y Brenin from time to time."

I put my cup down. "You worked at the National Centre?"

"Yes. I don't think I was there at the same time as you."

It seemed that Roger was a keen climber, had a degree in geography and had been teaching at a private school in the highlands. I asked him about Vic, the principal. Vic had worked as the chief instructor at an outward-bound school in the Lake District and then been asked to head up an O.B. school in Australia. He had worked there for a year or two, but his wife was keen to return to Britain, so they had come to start up Benmore Adventure Centre for Edinburgh Education Department.

We talked easily for a little while about Wales and then Roger said. "Now, Peter, I will be showing you round the centre later. As you can see, we are still having deliveries, so things are a bit of a muddle, but we don't open with students for a couple of months." He poured himself another cup of tea and continued. "There are two other chaps coming for interview. One has arrived and the other, like you, is from London." He looked at his watch. "The fellow from London is due on the ferry in an hour and Hamish, the janitor, has gone to pick him up from Dunoon. When he arrives, I'll show you all around together and you will have plenty of time to ask questions. Then we'll have lunch and the formal interviews will take place this afternoon."

"Fine," I said and tried to look as relaxed as him.

"You might look around the gardens, they're beautiful. We're in a botanical garden. Apparently, it has the best collection of Rhododendrons in Britain."

"Oh, yes. I will.... Thanks."

"Good." He looked at his watch. "If you're back for ten we can all gather in the staff room for coffee."

"Yes, ten o'clock … right."

He stood up. "The staff room is on the left as you come in the big front door."

"Oh, right, thanks." When I was alone, I took a few deep breaths. I put the dirty plates by the sink and left, closing the kitchen door quietly behind me, which I felt appropriate in this seemingly empty mansion.

*

I found my way back to the turret bedroom, collected my coat and went out the huge front door to a frosty, still morning. I breathed in the clean, cold air deeply while deciding which way to go. In front were wide stone steps leading down to a glorious green lawn that was bordered on the left with great Rhododendrons. Beyond the lawn, fields, dotted with large trees ran away in the distance. That direction must have been the lower end of the valley for on either side steep hills rose from the level fields. I turned right and walked back along the gravel drive that Hamish had driven me along the night before.

On my right, tall Douglas fir trees crowded up a steep hillside. On the left it was quite different with the ground suddenly quite level. Tall Scots pines were spaced out to the edge of the gardens with bushes and plants weaving through this open forest. I could easily see beyond to the fields, which filled this lower part of the valley. I walked slowly on for a few hundred yards and came to the tall white marble pillars that I had notices in the darkness as we had driven across the cattle grid the night before. They supported great iron gates, which were painted gold, and these golden gates marked the end of the botanic gardens.

Set back on one side was a small house. This small lodge might have made a good prop in a pantomime with its steep roof and tiny windows with tall pine trees towering over it. Beyond the tall gates was a surfaced road, narrow, tree lined and completely silent. Silent except for the noise of a jubilant little river on the far side of the road that tumbled over boulders on its way from the hills. The road ran alongside the river and I strolled along gaining height, but the forest blocked any view I might have of the mountains. I looked at my watch, it was time to return. I marched along quickly to try and calm my nerves and all too soon I was back at the mansion.

I went through the wide front door and took another deep breath before quietly opening the door to the staff room. There was no sound anywhere and I was quite relieved to find the room empty. I walked across the deep carpet to look out of the huge window. The gravel drive ran across the front of the building and beyond a low stonewall the lawn could be seen with the flat fields beyond. The room was very light for this huge window was not the only one. Opposite the door was a large bay window, large enough to hold six chairs and a coffee table. This glorious house and gardens used to be a lord's home, very different from the homes where I had grown up in London.

I allowed myself to dream of working and living in these beautiful surroundings but then quickly forced myself to stop the dream and return to the fact that I was probably the least qualified of the people being interviewed and might soon be on the train back to the hustle of city life.

*

My dreaming and the silence where broken when I heard footsteps approaching down the corridor and in came Hamish, the janitor, in his blue boiler suit, who had picked me up from the pier.

He smiled and nodded to me, then turned to someone behind. "Aye, you'd better wait in here. I'll tell the principal you've arrived."

A very tall man with dark hair and wearing a smart, dark suit came in. "Oh, 'ello," he said in a London accent that was even broader than my own. He strode across the carpet and stuck out a huge hand. "I'm Bill," he said with a wide smile.

I smiled and shook his hand. "Hello, I'm Peter. Are you here for the interview?"

"Yeh, and you?"

"Mm."

He walked to the window and rubbed his hands together vigorously. "I came up from London overnight, awful journey, train was freezin'. Did you arrive this mornin' too?"

"No, I came up yesterday."

"Oh, wish I had." He rested his hands on a radiator and then turned and rested his seat on it. "The head wouldn't let me off."

"The head?"

"Yeh, the head of the school … I'm teaching." I gave a feeble smile, but my heart seemed to stop and I'm sure my shoulders slumped with disappointment. As a teacher he was already ahead of me in qualifications.

There was a rattle of cups and through the tall, white door came Morag pushing a trolley with steaming coffee pots and a large plate of dropped scones that I recognised from those on the ferry boat.

Bill threw up his arms in delight. "Morag you're an angel, I 'eard you'd got the job up 'ere." He went over and gave her a hug.

"Och, away with yer Bill." She laughed and turned to me. "Bill was also at the National Centre in Wales Peter."

Bill took a great bite from a scone and said, "Were you instructing at Plas Y Brenin as well Pete?"

"Well ... er, yes, I worked there, but not as an instructor. I was the maintenance man." "Oh, yeh. Great place, eh? Good food." And he took another dropped scone.

This must have been the regular time for morning coffee for Roger came in and Bill, towering over him, took his outstretched hand and shook it vigorously. "Hi Roger. Great to see you again." It seemed they knew each other quite well so I busied myself pouring coffee for everyone.

I was passing cups to everyone when the door was flung open confidently and in came a man in casual but well fitted clothes waving an ice axe. "Ah you're all here, good."

Roger put his cup down and stepped forward. "This is Vic, the principal." He turned to us "Vic, this is Bill, and this is Peter."

"Hello, Bill." Vic shook his hand enthusiastically. "Hello Peter." He held my hand as another man came in wearing muddy jeans, a sweater with frayed sleeves, and without shoes. "Ah, there you are Rusty." He turned back to the rest of us. "This is Rusty, we've been looking at the local crags."

Even without shoes Rusty was taller than me and broad in the shoulders with tight red hair and a red beard to match. He stepped forwards, wiped his hand on the seat of his trousers, and we shook hands. "Hi, Peter." Rusty had a deep soft South African accent. He turned his confident smile to Bill. "Hello Bill, nice to see you again. Been climbing much recently?"

So, they already knew each other. It seemed that I was the odd one out. I joined Morag to pour more coffee for everyone. Everyone talked easily. Everyone seemed relaxed, but I was pleased when Roger eventually took Bill, Rusty and me to one side and led us off for a tour of the house.

*

Some rooms had stacks of beds in them that would have to be assembled. Other rooms had chairs and tables, which were still wrapped in padding and brown paper. We followed Roger past the kitchen, out across the courtyard and through a door leading to a number of small rooms. "This," he said with a glint of enthusiasm, "will be our equipment store." Stacked high in every room were piles of boxes that held new equipment for the outdoor programmes, and these boxes were of more interest to us. There were new climbing ropes, chains of karabiners, harnesses, helmets in plastic wrappers and climbing kit of all types. In another room we could only look through the door at a high pile of shining fiberglass kayaks. In one corner were a stack of kayak paddles, and filling the remaining space were life jackets, still in plastic wrappers. Another room held neat piles of outdoor clothing. There were orange and yellow waterproofs, gloves, hats and even socks and sweaters. There were lumpy stacks of rucksacks and over everything was a glorious smell of new leather. Against one wall was a tall stack of boxes that contained about two hundred pairs of mountain boots. This equipment was all for the students.

By the time we had looked all over the house, looked at equipment and heard about plans for the future, it was lunchtime and Roger led us back through a wide corridor to the staff room. Rusty left to change and returned looking clean and smart. He was not dressed in the dark suits that Bill and I wore but seemed to be more appropriately dressed in casual trousers, checked shirt and a tie, which emphasized his broad shoulders and muscular physique.

Lunch was a pleasant, relaxed affair with people talking about shared experiences on the mountains, and I listened with fascination at the adventures. We already appeared to be a friendly team and I had to keep reminding myself that they had advertised for 'an' instructor. I was surely the least qualified of them all and would probably leave all this behind. Tomorrow I would probably be back on the long, cold journey south and to the crowded city of London.

Eventually, it was time for the formal interviews and Vic, still wearing smart casual clothes, stood up. "Make yourself at home. We shall call you in alphabetical order."

Roger smiled. "Stay close to this room so that we don't lose you," and he waived three folders he was holding marked R. B. and P.

Morag soon took Rusty along to be interviewed first, and Bill and I were left alone together in the empty room. Bill walked over to the window, crossed his arms and looked out to the lawn and trees beyond. Then, still looking out, he said, "seems a great place eh?"

"Yes. Seems a great area. All the equipment new."

Bill nodded. "Yeh, and only the best, too."

"Mm." I leaned back against a radiator. "Seems a very relaxed atmosphere. Everyone seems very friendly."

Bill appeared a bit tense and stood with his hands deep in his pockets looking out to the lawn and gardens. "Not much hope for us though."

I frowned. "Not much hope?"

He turned to me. "No, Rusty will be appointed I expect. Last year he was in the Alps and climbed the north face of the Eiger with Dougal Haston. He also climbed a serious new route on Mont Blanc with Chris Bonington. 'E's been instructing for the last year at the outward-bound school in Wales."

All I said was, "Oh … mmm." But I felt like holding my head and quietly moaning, 'oh, not again.' So Rusty would probably get the job and if he wasn't appointed then Bill, with his degree, would get it over me. I was probably there to make up the numbers.

Rusty wasn't away very long. Then it was my turn, and Rusty showed me the interview room. In the old days it must have been the laird's study, for it was large and beautiful. Deep bay windows looked out to the lawn. Three walls had full height book units with glazed doors and the window alcoves were paneled. All the timber was beautifully figured oak.

Quite unlike other interviews I had attended, there was only Vic, the principal, and Roger present, who sat relaxing in low chairs round a coffee table. Vic waved a hand at an empty chair. "Hello Peter, sit down."

I sat upright on the edge of the chair and he continued. "Now, Peter, we have your application. But tell us in your own words what you have been doing for the last few years."

I mentioned relevant experiences of mountaineering, kayaking and even the little sailing that I had done. From time to time they asked questions.

I never mentioned Cath and our hopeful life together. At other interviews, candidates had all been single and I suspected they always preferred single instructors, since they would have so much residential work to do; not always suitable for a couple or a family. They didn't ask about girlfriends and I never spoke about it. As the interview went on, I was conscious that I was rambling on nervously. Although they seemed very relaxed, some of the questions made me all too aware that they knew a great deal about the activities and could probably see the huge gaps in my experiences.

They eventually spent a minute quietly looking at papers in front of them until Vic suddenly looked up with a smile. "Any questions you want to ask us Peter?"

"Er.... No.... I don't think so. Roger seems to have told us everything this morning."

"Good.... Well, if you join the others, we shall be along shortly."

I walked back to the staff room wearily. Bill left for his interview and I smiled at Rusty. "I understand that you had a good season in the Alps last year?"

He grinned and in his soft, pleasant accent said. "Yes, I suppose I did for a first season in the Alps. I was just lucky though. I knew some good guys who asked me to join them."

I knew he was being very modest. My experience of the Alps was not that great but I knew even 'good guys' don't ask you to join them on the notoriously dangerous north face of the Eiger Mountain unless they know you are very good indeed. He seemed more interested in my work in the youth centre than his own adventures and we chatted on until Bill returned.

Bill and Rusty were talking about rock climbs they had both done, but I was very nervous and stood by the window looking out to the wonderful scenery. It wasn't long before we heard footsteps approaching and the door was flung open. Vic. Roger and also Morag came in smiling and laughing and went across to Rusty.

"Congratulations Rusty," said Vic with a great smile, and he shook his hand and slapped him on the shoulder. "It's a girl." The others congratulated him and they all shook his hand as he grinned shyly.

I looked on blankly. If he was being offered the post of instructor it was not quite the behaviour I had seen before. I turned to see Bill looking with an open mouth. He caught my eye and shrugged his shoulders. What was going on?

Morag turned to us and laughed. "Rusty's wife has been on the phone. She's just had a wee bairn, a baby girl."

We shook Rusty by the hand and said appropriate things but I was still on edge. What about the job?

When the congratulations had died down Vic turned to all of us. "Well now, we've made a decision." There was a pause when my breathing stopped and he smiled. "I would like to appoint all three of you. Is that okay?"

Okay! I felt weak and would like to have sat down but only nodded my head and smiled feebly. He continued. "We want you all to start as soon as possible but you will need a medical before we can send you confirmation. As time is short can you go across to Edinburgh for a medical tomorrow morning?"

The three of us all agreed to go for the medical so, it was all arranged. I was now free to go out into the gardens by myself to try and release the tension that had been building up all day. I put my Gannex coat on and left by the front door.

*

I had been on the gravel path to the left so this time I turned right and went round the mansion and along the edge of the gardens to shortly arrive at a row of very large garages.

The large doors had been renewed but it was easy to see that many years ago this building had been the stables, four in all, with accommodation above for the coachman and stable hands. The laird would have sent for a carriage and it would have gone round and crunched to a halt outside the main entrance of the big house. I could just imagine it all in the old days.

I continued on the gravel drive, which swung right again, and past three new bungalows. These, I suspected, were occupied by the full-time workers who maintained the botanic gardens for the public. Now, during the winter, there were no visitors and no workers to be seen. To my right was a high stone wall. I found a door and gently pushed it open.

Here was a formal garden with paths neatly laid out round lawns and flower beds. Clinging to the inside of the high walls that enclosed this wonderland were various creepers and clematis. I stood in the middle and looked around. I could hear no sound of people, traffic or human activity. The only noise was the calling of a buzzard that circled high in the sky and the twittering of small birds in the nearby bushes. Across the smooth lawn was the high wall and across this in the distance rose the mountains that were covered in snow down to about three hundred metres. Everything was quiet and peaceful; there was nobody to be seen or heard anywhere.

To think that I would be living and working in this wonderful area. All my tensions were suddenly released and I spun round and with my arms in the air shouted out "Yeehaaa!" I stood there grinning to myself then suddenly noticed a head appear over a thick beech hedge. This lone gardener pushed back his peaked cap, scratched his head and looked at me for a couple of seconds before returning to his work. He must have thought me crazy but I didn't care. I had failed many times before, but this time I had succeeded. I was to be a professional instructor of outdoor pursuits.

*

It was some years later that I asked Roger why they had appointed me, for on paper I seemed to be a weak candidate. Roger smiled. "Well, Pete, you had worked at the National Centre in Wales for a year but had not given the principal as a reference. So, we telephoned John Jackson and asked him about you. What he told us guaranteed you the job." So, John Jackson was another person that had a great influence on my future.

CHAPTER 12: THE MEDICAL

Morag arranged for Rusty, Bill and I to have an early dinner in the staff room. They talked and I mostly listened, but I didn't feel the odd one out. I felt very much part of the new team. "We can stay at Mary's house," said Rusty. "I've borrowed a van so we can all go in that."

"That will be great," said Bill. "You say her place is near Glasgow, so we shall be half way to Edinburgh."

Rusty grinned. "Mary's place is a bit strange. I stayed there on the way up. She knows many of the top Scots climbers."

"Perfect," said Bill, and he took another piece of apple pie." We stacked the plates in the empty kitchen, packed our kit and went out into the dark to Rusty's van.

It would have been much better for everyone if Rusty's van had been fitted with three seats, but it wasn't It was on old post office van which had been hand painted a brilliant yellow colour. Bill and Rusty were in the front and I tried to make myself comfortable in the back amongst a heap of climbing ropes, metal equipment, a rucksack and my incongruous suitcase. For me to travel in the back of a van was a mistake.

I must be one of the worst travellers in the world and become sick on the shortest journey. Either in the back of a car, a bus or a large boat it is only a short time before I start to feel ill. In the darkness we drove north on the winding road that boarded the fresh water loch. Rolling round the bends was asking for trouble. With a hot flush I felt a sickness coming on. I tried facing forwards and closing my eyes. Bill's voice faded into insignificance as I tried to control my rising sickness. What would they think of me, a professional instructor who became sick on the shortest journey?

We had gone less than ten miles, but it was no use. "Rusty," I groaned from the darkness. "You'll have to stop. I feel ill." I must have looked bad for after a quick glance he leaned away from me and swerved onto the side of the road. They both scrambled out quickly to let me crawl passed and I moved off as far as possible. The road was empty and I was grateful for the solid darkness, which hid my agony but not the noise of me being sick.

"Feeling better?" said Rusty, but neither of them wanted to get too close.

"Mm, thanks…. Sorry about that."

"Ah, don't worry about it," said Bill. "You sit in the front." And he bent his tall frame into the darkness of the back while Rusty and I sat with our long legs bent up in the front. Rusty had rather poor eyesight. He squinted into the darkness over the top of the wheel wearing a pair of glasses that made him look quite studious. We eventually made the high point of the road called the 'rest and be thankful' and the little engine raced as we coasted the few miles down to the end of Loch Long. Loch Long is a sea loch cutting deeply in from the river Clyde. The roads were lonely so that we made good time over the low hills to Loch Lomond and south towards Glasgow.

"I phoned Mary before we left," Rusty said. "She's a doctor, works with animals. She has a few other friends staying there as well."

I had fallen asleep and only woke when we were bumping over a rough track that led to our destination. I was tired from the tensions of the day and looked forward to this doctor's smart house, a hot drink and a long sleep. It was very dark and I could see nothing except the black silhouette of the house and the open hillside.

Rusty didn't ring the bell or anything, he simply pushed open the door and shouted into the darkness, "Mary.... Hi Mary." A door opened at the end of a long dark corridor and we shuffled towards it.

A lady, looking large and wearing a voluminous long dress and a tasselled scarf, greeted us warmly. "Hellooo Rusty. Come through, come through."

I got quite a shock as we stood there blinking in the light and taking in the smell of wood smoke and grilled onions. The room, which was obviously a vast farm kitchen, had only bare boards on the floor and flaking white paint covered the uneven walls. We were welcomed in a casual but friendly way by the crowd of people who seemed to be eating around an indoor barbeque. There were children and adults, mostly dressed as hippies, and Bill and I must have looked out of place in our dark suits.

The hostess, wearing an ankle length gypsy skirt, did her best to make us feel easy. "Oh now, put those cases in the corner and help yourself to a wee bite." There were no clean cups, but I used an empty one, and with a greasy sandwich in one hand and a mug of tea in the other I tried to keep a low profile.

I was just taking a bite of the sandwich when someone slapped me on the back. "Hello, Peter. Fancy seeing you up here north of the border."

When I'd finished choking, I turned to see a mountain guide that I knew from the national centre in Wales. "Hello, Chris. What in the world are you doing here?"

"Well, I finished at Plas y Brenin and I'm taking the children to live in the States." He waved a hand towards three of the fair-haired children around the stove.

"The United States, eh? That's a big move for you."

71

He shrugged. "Yes, but I understand that mountain guides can earn good money in Colorado, and the weather will be better than Britain."

I nodded. "Oh … yes"

Chris poured himself a mug of tea. "Rusty tells me that the three of you are to start at this new outdoor centre on the west coast?"

I grinned and nodded towards Rusty and Bill. "Yes, hope I'm up to it. We have to be in Edinburgh for a medical tomorrow morning."

"Edinburgh, eh? I have to go over there for a visa. I'll drive us all over." So, it was arranged that Chris would be our guide on the way to Edinburgh. We chatted on for some time until Bill leaned towards me. "Has anyone mentioned a bed he whispered? Where are we going to sleep? I'm whacked."

Rusty solved it for us. "Oh, you can use any room upstairs. Follow me." We slipped out quietly and up the bare wooden staircase to a spartan room of bare floor boards and a single bare light bulb hanging from the ceiling. There was only one bed, and this was covered with a rather tired looking sheepskin. Bill lifted the corner by the yellowed hair and looked underneath. "No sheets or blankets," he whispered.

I went over to a chair, which was the only other piece of furniture in the room. "Two blankets here," I whispered. "You can have the bed and the, er … animal skin. I will manage on the floor."

Before we fell asleep Bill's voice came across the darkness. "Funny house, Pete. Nice people but what a crazy place."

I slept badly, more because of excitement than the cold, and woke when I heard the children in the kitchen below.

Bill looked rough as well. "Christ Peter, what's the time? I feel awful." Downstairs the scene was much the same as the night before. People were getting a snack breakfast and were walking about with it. Although it was only 7-30 and still dark outside, the children were already busy. I was amazed to see them painting pictures on one of the lounge walls. This was certainly a free-living house and I felt the odd one out. People were friendly and made us welcome, but I was quite relieved when we eventually jerked away in the yellow van with Chris at the wheel.

Chris was the only one of us who knew this part of Scotland, so we were pleased that he was coming. It might have taken a long time to find the medical centre in a big city. Chris took a long drag of his cigarette. "Good place Edinburgh. Plenty of great pubs. Has a massive castle, stuck on top of a big cliff."

We had been driving for less than an hour when Chris pointed ahead down the straight road. "There it is. That's the castle up there on the rock." We swung off the main road and were soon amongst sandstone buildings and a busy little town. "What was the name of the street?"

72

Bill looked at the paper in his hand. "St. Giles Street."

"I'll ask this chap," said Chris, and stopped sharply against the kerb.

"St. Giles Street?" The man took off his cap and scratched the side of his head. "Ah'm sorry, I da na ken St. Giles Street."

We asked a few people, but nobody seemed to know the place. It was a small town so that we were nearly back where we had started when we saw a policeman. "St Giles Street ya say?" He stood there for some time looking at the ground with his thumbs in his pockets. "Noo, I know a St Giles Street in Edinburgh, but ah don't think there's one here in Stirling."

"Stirling!" Chris sat quietly looking down the road and around at the buildings. "Thanks anyway." He grinned nervously. "We'll find it." And he drove slowly off.

We turned back onto the main road and it was some time before anyone spoke. Then Bill broke the silence. "Stirling. That town was Stirling. I thought it looked small for Edinburgh."

Chris was quiet for an hour until we approached a large city with a castle perched high above steep crags. This certainly was Edinburgh. It didn't take us long to find the correct street but our diversion into Stirling had made us nearly two hours late. All three of us were in high spirits and I rather felt like one of the three musketeers.

We found the reception and Bill leaned on the counter and gave the receptionist a wide grin. "Allo, we've come for a medical. It's for work with the education department."

"Och aye, would you sit doon and I will call sister."

It took only a few minutes before the sister, walking with hard efficient steps, came along. I was in a flippant mood and happy with everyone. "Hello, we're the new instructors for Benmore Adventure Centre. We were told to report here for a medical to see if we are fit." I slapped my chest and grinned.

She didn't grin and wasn't at all put off by three tall men towering over her. "Yoor late. Your appointment was two hours ago."

I stopped grinning. "Oh yes, er sorry. We got lost on the way here."

Sister stepped back a pace. "Lost!" She exclaimed in a rolling Scots accent and looked at all three of us. "Are yer not mountain guides? That's no a very good start for your job, is it?"

After the medical we shook hands as newmade friends and departed in different directions. Bill was going over to the Lake District for some climbing, Rusty was going back to Wales to see his wife and new baby girl, and I made my way to the railway station. As the train thundered south, I was tired but at peace with the world. In only six weeks I would leave the crowds and hustle of city life. I was going to work and live in a wonderful area with mountains, rivers and ocean.

CHAPTER 13: FROM THE CITY TO THE LAIRD'S MANSION

Of course, the first thing I did when I got home was to telephone Cath. It was rather a one-way conversation from me as I was so excited, but she was lovely.

"It all sounds great," she said. "Is there a town nearby, with shops and things?"

"Yes, oh yes," I said. "Dunoon seems quite big and only about seven miles from the Centre."

"Oh good.... And does it have schools?"

"I should think so. There were plenty of people about."

Later, that evening, I realized that Cath was thinking more of our future than my instructing work and I shivered with delight.

*

I gave my 'notice' at the youth centre and spent the last few weeks preparing everything so that there would be a smooth transition for the new leader. The council even offered me a house to live in if I wished to stay, but my mind was only on Scotland.

On my last evening, the staff and club members called me to the main hall, and one of them gave me a present and gave a short speech of thanks. I was surprised and rather touched by everyone's good wishes for my future.

*

The day eventually arrived when I left London for my new life in the Highlands of Scotland, and this time I had to struggle with two large cases and a heavy rucksack. I eventually reached the same windswept dock at Gourock on the south shore of the wide ocean inlet. I staggered up the wooden gangplank to stack my things on the deck of the ferry that was going across the river Clyde to Dunoon.

Last time I did this trip it was dark and wet, but now it was daylight, and although there was a cold wind blowing, I was determined to stay on deck. I wanted to look at everything in detail not as a passing visitor but with the eye of someone who was to be a local. I would need as much knowledge about the area as I could get. The Clyde is very wide at this point, perhaps three miles across, and I tried to pick out the various lochs that radiated from it. I could easily identify the Holy Loch from the grey bulk of the United States' floating dock and the factory ship, still large although a long way off. The Holy Loch was the home base for the American North Atlantic fleet of nuclear submarines, which was still very active, watching with radar eyes and ears for the 'enemy'. To the right of the Holy loch were the steep wooded hills marking the entrance of Loch Long. I looked at all the navigation buoys, noting colours and shapes and assessing the dangers that each one might be marking. I was excited to think that in time I would know the whole area intimately. The ferry docked skillfully, and I followed the passengers down the sloping ramp.

Roger, the chief instructor, met me at the pier in his easy relaxed style. "Hello Peter. Good to see you. Welcome to the highlands." We chatted easily as he drove along the quiet roads until we reached the botanic gardens. He turned through the golden gates and as we passed the 'pantomime' small lodge house he said. "Rusty and Pat are well settled into the Golden Gates Lodge with their baby Rowan and their dog."

We crunched slowly down the gravel drive to stop quietly at the main entrance to the house. Roger turned to me. "Now Pete, you and Bill will have rooms on the staff landing. I'll show you the rooms. He helped me with one of my cases and I followed him through the very large, glazed door and up the wide oak staircase.

On the big landing he opened a door. "You can either have this room or the one in the corner there." I had a quick look in both rooms.

"I'd like the room in the corner please."

"Right. Bill can have the other one. The two of you will share the bathroom and toilet over there." He pointed to another door across the wide landing. "I'll leave you to settle in…. Dinner is at six and will be served in the little room next to the kitchen."

"Oh right. Thanks. I'll be there at six." I dumped my luggage in the middle of the room and went across to the French doors that also acted as the window. I carefully opened the doors and stepped out onto a narrow stone balcony that had a roof supported by stone pillars on the outside corners. I was looking south across the front terrace and to the lawn that stretched away to fields where a few Friesian cows were grazing. On the right, tall Douglas firs covered the steep hillside, and on the left the botanic gardens were crowded with the huge rhododendrons I had seen before. I took a long, peaceful breath. To think that this was to be my home.... I felt very lucky.

My room in the corner had the advantage that the bedroom door did not open straight onto the wide landing, as it had a small vestibule that had a deep cupboard. This would be handy for storing some of my outdoor kit. The furniture was plain but adequate. There was a bed and bedside table, a chest of drawers, a wardrobe and a tall bookcase. In the middle of the room was a coffee table and two easy chairs. With carpet and matching curtains, I was delighted with everything.

Building conversions were underway in the kitchen, and I was pleased to meet Morag again who showed me where I was to eat in a small back room. In the old days, when the Laird lived in this mansion, the back rooms would have been the servants' quarters, and the sunny front rooms facing south would have been used by the laird and his family. The front rooms were large and well-lit with wide corridors. The servants' quarters were cold north facing rooms with small windows, narrow stairs and dim corridors. The room where I was eating had a small window that looked out onto a high retaining wall made of rock. There was no view and little light. I was pleased that my large bedroom was one of the sunny, south facing rooms on the laird's side of the house. After a pleasant meal taken peacefully by myself, and leaving my dishes in the kitchen sink, I went up to my room. I spent the evening packing my things away and was pleased to get to bed quite early. It seemed wonderful to be now living in the laird's mansion.

CHAPTER 14: WOULD I BE GOOD ENOUGH?

Would I be good enough? I was thrilled I'd got the job, but now doubts started to grow that I had so little experience compared with the others. The next morning the whole house was still eerily silent. Morag brought a lovely breakfast through and told me that the principal, Vic, and Roger had left early for a meeting in Edinburgh. She told me that Rusty would meet me at breakfast and had, "a day planned out for the two of us." I was having a last cup of tea when footsteps approached along the corridor outside.

Rusty came in wearing gun boots, jeans and a padded jacket. "Hi, Peter." We shook hands across the table. "Did you have a good journey up?"

"Yes, fine thanks. Do you want a cup of tea?"

"Yes, thanks." He took the cup and sat down at the table with me. "You're settled in upstairs?"

"Yes, everything seems perfect. What about you? Is the Golden Gates Lodge okay?"

"Yes, a bit small, but Pat thinks it's great and she's soon made it cosy."

"And your little girl is fine?"

"Oh, yes. Rowan is great, and Pat seems so relaxed about everything - a good mum." We talked for a while with Rusty having another cup of tea, and after finishing off the toast he sat back in his chair. "Vic and Roger have gone to Edinburgh. A meeting, I believe. Vic said we could use the day to look at a crag across the valley. I don't think anyone has climbed on it before."

I put my cup down. "Oh, fine. Do you think it will give us plenty of easy student climbs?"

"Mm. It might be okay for students." He grinned. "Well advanced students." Rusty had only lived in Britain for a few years but already had a reputation as a talented rock climber. I began to think the crag he had found for 'advanced students' might be a serious undertaking. Desperate climbing was not what I was hoping for on my first day. I had fretted for some weeks about my abilities. Now, I had serious worries about climbing with Rusty who had such an awesome reputation.

I thought to myself, 'will I be good enough?' but all I said to Rusty was, "well we can have a look at this crag."

"Great." Rusty was suddenly full of enthusiasm. "I have everything we need in my van. It's outside."

So, I changed into outdoor clothing, packed my climbing kit into a rucksack, and met Rusty in the courtyard. The little yellow van he had bought from Chris struggled up the steep slope from the back yard, rounded the formal garden, went down the glorious tree lined main drive and over the bridge that crossed the river Eckaig. We turned left, and it was only a few minutes before Rusty pulled into a lay-by. On the left I could see through silver birch trees to the ruffled water of Loch Eck, the fresh water loch. On the other side of the road was a little sloping field, which swept upwards to a woodland of small oak trees and then up more steeply to the open hillside above.

At the steepest point, a cliff of vertical corners rose for about thirty metres. Rusty squinted through the window. "That's the crag. Thought we would have a go up that corner."

I bent forward to look up through the windscreen. "Mm, looks steep."

"Yes. Two pitches. We can take a stance on that middle ledge."

We got out into the cold air and sorted kit out from the back of the van. Rusty packed an assortment of karabiners and slings into his rucksack. "You okay with the rope, Peter?"

"Sure." I followed him across the empty road, over a rickety stile and up the hillside. He had the slow, confident gate of an experienced mountaineer and we made our way through the open oak woodland, round patches of yellow gorse and up to the foot of the crag. At this point a vertical wall rose straight up from the steep grass.

Rusty bent his head backwards. "I think this might 'go'." He shielded his eyes. "Up this wall and onto the ledge at the foot of the corner."

I put one hand against the wall for balance and looked upwards. "Mm. Okay." I was pleased he didn't ask me to lead. We put our rucksacks down and sat on them to put on our rock boots. The start was vertical and to make matters worse it was a bit wet. I only hoped that I wouldn't make a fool of myself in trying to follow him. I looked down the steep grass and decided to belay onto a small tree. I tied onto my end of the rope and held it ready to safeguard Rusty.

I noticed he had a quick look at my rope handling and then stepped up to the face. "Okay, Peter, here we go."

Right from the ground the climbing was hard. The holds for both hands and feet were small square-cut ledges. He moved up a couple of metres and then came down again. "Bit damp, Peter." He wiped the soles of each boot with his sleeve and started off again. This time he got a little higher but then stopped. He seemed perfectly in control but was obviously finding any progress difficult. At one stage he moved a foot up to a possible hold but eased it down again.

"Not much up here, Pete." His eyes searched the rock above for a decent handhold but after ten minutes of moving up, down and a little sideways he carefully climbed down. "I don't fancy it. It's a bit damp and there's no protection."

He started to coil the rope up but then suddenly turned to me. "Oh…. Pete. Do you want to have a go?"

While I had been standing there, holding the rope with my face to the rock, I had noticed a few holds that Rusty had not used. They were very small, but they might allow a very delicate progress up the face. I looked up to the top part of the pitch where it seemed that some protection might be possible for the leader. "Well … okay, I'll have a look."

So, we changed places and I stepped onto the rock. It was certainly steep, but by using the new holds I was able to just stay in balance, and moved up quickly before I fell off. Just above Rusty's high point I found a crack and placed a 'nut' for a running belay. I clipped the rope through the karabiner and with this runner I immediately felt more confident. The climbing became a little easier and I eventually pulled over onto the rock ledge that was to be our stance and belay. I tied on and shouted to Rusty to come up.

I'm sure he found the climbing much easier than he thought, but he was still charming enough to say, "A good lead Pete." He then took the kit and set off up the corner. By using hands and feet in the corner for jamming he was able to move up above my head. But it was in the corner that the rock was most wet. "Gosh, it's greasy Pete." He got a thread runner round a rock in the crack, but it was obvious that he was not going to risk injury in falling from this obscure crag.

He climbed down to join me on the belay ledge. "See what you think, Pete."

So, we changed places again. I had been able to see his problems and climbed up using wider and wider bridging. The runner he had fixed gave me extra confidence and soon I was past his high point. Here was a fine little oak tree leaning out over space and I was able to place a sling round it for a perfect running belay. I led on more and more easily to the top of the crag and once over the top I tied on to a solid little rowan tree. I peered down the rock face.

"Right, Rusty," I shouted. "When you're ready." As he climbed, I had chance to look around. Way below and stretching into the distance was the glittering Loch Eck and the beautiful glen. At this early time of year there was little colour in the vegetation except green, but what a glorious range of greens. The lush grass of the irregular fields bordering the lock was replaced higher up by a dark green of the Scots pines. Then, above them, the yellowing green of the high slopes was soon covered by the snow which still covered the tops. Dark grey nimbus clouds filled the sky to the southwest. A pair of ravens called to each other in raucous excitement and were playing in the sky above us. They had no difficulty in staying up by simply opening their wings, and were lifted up with the wind as it swept up the cliff face. When they were way above me, they would show off and fold their wings, going into a headlong tumble. After a few seconds they would throw out their wings and go soaring upwards once again. There were so many new things to see - things I would never have experienced in a city.

Rusty climbed up easily, but by the time he reached me menacing clouds had swept along the glen from the south and sleet was driving horizontally along the hillside. I was pleased when Rusty suggested we pack up and go back to his place for a 'brew'. We traversed the hillside easily and went down through the oak woodland where the twisted branches were still bare of leaves. Sheep, smelling of damp wool, had gathered amongst the trees to find shelter from the wind - but our shelter was in the van. It only took a few minutes to drive through the huge metal gates of the botanic gardens and along the gravel drive to the Golden Gates Lodge - now Rusty's home.

We dodged into the little porch to take our boots off and were greeted by a German shepherd puppy who tripped over Rusty's boots and weaved round my legs. His little tail wagged so frantically that it set off his bottom and even his fat little tummy. I bent down to pat him. "Hello, little thing. Is he yours Rusty?"

"Yes." Rusty gave a rather guilty grin and lifted him in the air with one large hand and we went into the lounge. They had only moved into the house a few days before, but already the little lounge was charming with a log fire throwing out heat and flickering light. A slight smell of wood smoke seemed to add to the cosy nature of the room.

Rusty sunk down on a settee and put his feet towards the fire. "Sit down, Pete. You haven't met Pat, have you? She must be getting Rowan to sleep."

Before I could sit down, Rusty's wife came in. I smiled and held out a hand. "Hello Pat, nice to meet you at last."

She shook my hand confidently. "Hi. You must be Peter." You both look wet. I'll put the kettle on." Pat was average height with a trim figure and short dark hair. Wearing jeans and a sweater she didn't give the impression of being a harassed mother with her first baby only a few weeks old. Her Yorkshire accent and ready smile gave her an air of confidence and open friendship.

She brought through large mugs of tea and a plate of warm rock buns. "So, Peter, you've been working in London?"

"Yes, all my life."

"This will be a real change for you, then."

I grinned with a mouth full of rock bun. "Mm." We talked on for an hour or so about their life at the outward-bound school in Wales, their move up here and baby Rowan, and by the time I left them the daylight had nearly gone. It was grey and wet outside and the tops of the trees were swaying with a strong cold wind coming along the valley. It was a miserable evening, but I was not miserable at all. I was very happy indeed and walked tall with the rain splattering on my face. I didn't care, for I was at peace with myself. I had shown that I could climb well. I had passed the first test. In the future, Rusty and I climbed a lot together but never again was I better than him. I learned a great deal about climbing from him on rock - but even more on snow and ice. He had so much more experience than me and seemed completely confident even in the most serious mountain situations. I walked along the gravel drive towards Benmore mansion with a sense of deep excitement. I now lived in a wonderful place, was working with fine colleagues, and from now on I would be confident of the future. I knew that I wasn't a brilliant climber, and I had worried I might not be able to do the job. Now I knew: yes, I would be good enough.

CHAPTER 15: BILL ARRIVES

There was a noise somewhere. I pulled the bedclothes over my head and tried to ignore this irritable noise, but I couldn't. It slowly sunk into my sleepy head that it was the telephone downstairs. My bedside clock told me that it was just after eleven, so I had only been asleep for an hour. As a 'resident instructor' I felt responsible, and I lurched quickly downstairs and tiptoed along the cold tiles of the corridor to the office. I grabbed at the telephone that was still ringing. "Hello, Benmore Adventure Centre."

"'Allo, this is Bill. Is that you Pete?" His cockney voice sounded relaxed and cheery.

"Yes, Hello Bill. Where are you?"

"I'm in Gourock. I've crashed my car and missed the ferry."

"Gosh, are you alright?"

"Oh, yeh. I wrecked the car a few weeks ago. Ran out of road on a bend going down the Llanberis pass. I've had to come up on the train."

"Oh."

"I've missed the ferry, but I can get another one. Can you pick me up?"

"Yes, sure. I'll come down straight away in the green minibus."

"No, no hold on. The first boat I can get is the mail boat. It doesn't leave here until two o'clock. If you can be on the pier at three that would be fine."

"Three? What, three in the morning?"

"Yes," he said cheerily. "Thanks Pete, see you then." The telephone went dead. I stood looking at the phone for a while and then stomped slowly upstairs and into bed.

Sleep came very slowly so that when my alarm rattled its call just after two o'clock, I felt that I had hardly slept at all. I dressed, collected the vehicle key from the hooks in the office and walked out into a cold, gusty night. I set off on the five-mile drive along the sinister empty road made darker by the tall trees on either side.

I could do without a cold drive at this time of the morning. Then I felt guilty when I thought of poor Bill. I imagined he had been waiting on the windswept dock at Gourock for hours. He would be cold, I thought.

The ferry was just leaving again when my headlights swung round the empty pier and there was Bill, cheery and talkative. "Hi Pete. Thanks."

"Hello, Bill. I bet you're frozen."

"No, I'm fine thanks. The mail boat skipper gave me a huge mug of tea."

"Oh good. Did it seem a long wait on the pier at Gourock?"

He grinned. "No. In fact if the copper hadn't woken me I would have missed the boat."

"Copper! What, a policeman?"

"Yeh, it was great. I went along to the police station and they gave me a cell. They even woke me with a cup of tea."

I stared wearily through the windscreen. It seemed that Bill had managed to get more sleep than me during the last few hours. I found out later that Bill's arrangement with the police station at Gourock was quite normal, and I also used the charity of a cell on quite a few occasions. The police on the desk were very friendly and put me in a cell with a couple of blankets. There were only two problems. One was that by law the door had to be locked, which gave me a queer feeling, being locked in. The other problem was that on two occasions the adjacent cells were holding drunks who either sang loudly for hours or snored almost as loudly when they fell asleep.

Bill's room was next to mine leading off from the main staff landing. Also, from this big landing a door led to Roger and Jenny's flat, and another door led to Morag's bedsit, which had its own en-suite facilities. Bill and I shared a bathroom across the landing. Bill settled in quickly over the next few days and we worked well together. We were the only bachelors living in the house, but only rarely did we spend time together in the evenings. When Bill was free, he spent most evenings in The Coylet, which was our local pub a mile away on the shore of Loch Eck. I rarely went to the pub for I had other aims.

Every evening I wrote a letter to Cath asking about her teaching and her life at home, but mostly telling her in detail of the new life I was leading. However, I also had other aims. I had left school at fifteen with little academic training, so I was delighted to have free time in the evenings to study. I studied the subjects that were necessary knowledge for my new career as an outdoor education instructor. I read books on the techniques of mountaineering, kayaking and sailing. I also studied subjects such as meteorology, geography, ornithology and the flora of the countryside, which, as a Londoner, I knew almost nothing about. I was very conscious of the fact that all the others had degrees and that I had lots of catching up to do.

So, Bill often went down the pub on his own and quickly gained a reputation as a generous drinker with all the locals. One of these locals was Bert, who was the laird's shepherd. We were all gathered in the staff room for coffee one morning when Vic turned to Bill. "Bill, I understand you were speaking to Bert last night."

"Yeh, we were drinking together."

Vic took a sip of coffee. "He phoned me an hour ago asking if we could help with the cliff rescue. Apparently, you were speaking about it in the pub. He said he would like us to rescue them fairly soon if it was convenient."

I sat up in my chair with a cup half way to my mouth. A cliff rescue? We will do a rescue but only if it's convenient'?

They hadn't noticed my alarm and Bill took another buttered scone. "Oh, yeh. Pete and I could go. Bert told me he thought there were two of them stuck on a cliff. I'd rather forgotten about it."

I looked at him in disbelief. They were stuck on a cliff and he had forgotten about it! Again, they hadn't noticed my concern, and Vic took a leisurely sip of coffee. "Yes, that's what Bert said. I told him you would go to his place straight after lunch. He tells me they're still eating."

I was amazed at their cool, professional approach. I knew that Vic had carried out a great many successful mountain rescues while at the outward-bound school in the Lake District, but I was still surprised at their carefree attitude.

I jumped up. "After lunch? We could get the gear together and be away in half an hour. Surely every minute is important?"

Bill looked at me blankly. "Relax, Pete. There's no hurry. They've been stuck there for three weeks. Bert doesn't want them approached until they're very weak."

I sat down again with my mouth open. "Two people stuck on a cliff for three weeks? I haven't heard about it."

Now it was Vic and Bill's turn to look surprised. They looked at each other and Bill laughed out loud. "No, Pete. We're talking about sheep, not people. Two of Bert's sheep have been stuck on a cliff and can't seem to get down."

So, Bill and I were launched on our first sheep rescue. We packed a selection of ropes, slings and karabiners and, wearing waterproofs, boots and helmets, we set off in the old green minibus. Bill gripped the steering wheel with eager fists, accelerated hard, and we spluttered up the steep drive. It only took us five minutes to turn off the quiet road and bounce across the potholes of Bert's empty farmyard. Bill jumped out and slammed the door so hard that the driver's door window slipped down out of sight.

He strode round the yard and shouted. "'Allo, 'allo? Anyone at 'ome?"

Out from a small barn emerged a relaxed Bert. He stood there, short and square dressed in metal-shod brown boots, khaki woollen trousers and a Harris tweed jacket. Round his waist, as an apron, was a Hessian sack, which was tied with binder twine. His hands were the things I noticed most. They were covered with blood and in one he was holding a blood-smeared knife.

"Hellooo Bill." He said in a quiet voice, and nodded to me. "The laird will be here in a wee while. I'm just working on a sheep."

He turned, and we followed him into the draughty barn smelling strongly of cow dung and damp wool. On a rough wooden bench was a dead sheep that had its throat cut, and blood was dripping into a galvanised bucket. I stood to one side looking sadly at the sheep, which had obviously been alive and well just a few minutes before.

There was the sound of a car stopping outside. "Ah!" Bert raised a finger. "That's the laird now. He's very deaf, you know."

Bert walked out of the barn and I was thankful to follow him. Lord Younger had arrived in a small shooting break, and he released three Jack Russells from the back of the car. He was dressed the part of the Scottish landowner in a lovat green tweed suit which had plus-four trousers. He had hairy woollen stockings to match, and on his feet were shiny brown boots. His hat was a deerstalker and he carried a knobbly wooden stick.

"Hellooo, sir," Bert shouted, and turned to us. "These here are the two mountaineers from Benmore." He made the words 'mountaineer' and 'Benmore' seem full and important with his strong Scots accent.

Lord Younger stepped forward. "Helloo, gentlemen." We shook hands vigorously. "Good of you to come out."

I smiled. "Hope we can help."

"Eh?" He raised a cupped hand to his ear.

Bill shouted, "'Ope we can 'elp you!"

"Oh, I'm sure you can. Good, good." He spoke very loudly. "They are on the edge of the crag, way over there." He pointed up the hill with his stick. "We certainly need your expert help with these two."

I was a little uneasy to be considered an 'expert' in sheep or any other rescue, but Bill seemed confident and we unloaded our kit. The laird put on a long gabardine raincoat and led the way, through a gate and up a rough track. I seemed to be carrying both of our climbing ropes and most of the karabiners, so I was getting a bit left behind when Lord Younger stopped. He leaned on his stick. "There!" He pointed. "Can you see them? On the big crag, way across the burn."

"Oh, yes." I shielded my eyes. "On the right side of the cliff."

Bert pushed his cap back. "Aye. They are both there together. I'm worried they might be a wee bit lively yet." It was a big cliff but mostly broken ground rather than vertical rock. However, the sheep were on a ledge about half way up with a serious drop below them.

Lord Younger turned to us with a friendly enthusiasm. "Now, do you want to go to the top or climb up from the bottom?" There was no question in my mind that climbing up could lead us into all sorts of trouble.

"What do you think Bill, from the top?"

"Yeh, I'll lower you down to them." I looked up at the crag. He was quick to offer his services, but I rather hoped that he would have been the one to be lowered down the cliff.

"Mind, now. Nothing dangerous," said Lord Younger. "Don't take risks. They're only sheep." He sat on a boulder on the side of the track. "I can see everything from here."

We scrambled down a wooded slope and used slippery boulders as stepping stones to cross the burn that tumbled noisily down a ravine. There was no path and Bill now went in front to lead across the yellowing grass hillside, which got very steep as it approached the cliff.

I caught up with Bill at the edge of the crag, where he was looking around. "Right, Pete. We can belay from here." He nodded towards a stunted little mountain ash that was still full of red berries. I went over and gave it a few slaps. It was rather smaller than I wished, but it sounded solid, so I took out the ropes. I have abseiled down big cliffs many times and one gets used to it. However, I shall never get used to being lowered down on the end of a rope. No matter how well you trust the person holding the rope, I find it an awful feeling to know your life is completely in their hands as the rope jerks out.

On this occasion, I took a subtle look at Bill's belay before checking my own harness for the third time. "Okay, Bill?"

"Right mate." He gave a broad grin. "Down you go."

Bert said, "Tek care noo," then sat down happily on an old army coat and lit a pipe.

I crouched over the lip of the cliff and looked at Bill. "You got me?"

"Yeh. Yeh, sure. Away you go." Then I was over the cliff face and suddenly felt very much alone. The trouble with being lowered is that you are never sure what is going to happen next. There was a tense silence as I sat in the harness going nowhere. Then, just as I looked up, the rope slipped. It was probably only half a metre but enough to give my heart a jump and I gripped the rope and looked hard at the rock and moss just in front of my face. And so it carried on, silence followed a jerk; an unsteady descent. By the time I was fifteen metres down I was gaining confidence in my new partner and could let go of the rope and look about the crag.

The two sheep were not far below me, and were taking absolutely no notice of the clumsy acrobatics above them. I continued to jerk downwards with my feet or hands against the rock to steer across to the sheep that were over to my right. When I next looked at the sheep, they were already level with me.

I shouted up to Bill, "Tight rope!" But I was still going down very slowly. "Bill…. Stop!" I yelled. I stopped going down but now I was a bit too low. I gripped the rope and with my feet on the rock face I swung and 'walked' easily across and pulled awkwardly up onto the sheep's ledge. The rope coming from above, was not now vertical, but coming across to me at an angle. I wanted to shout up to Bill to take in the slack. However, the sheep, with dirty and ragged wool, which had taken no notice of me when I was swinging above them, now found me on their ledge.

They looked at me in alarm and one of them took fright and dashed past me. Without thinking, I grabbed it by the scruff of the neck with my right hand while still holding the rope with my left. The sheep was amazingly strong and with powerful back legs it charged right off the edge of the cliff. I was immediately pulled off balance and out into space. This would have put a great strain on Bill, and more importantly on the little tree that was his belay.

I held my breath and instinctively held the rope with one hand as the sheep's momentum took us both out into space and in a great arc across the crag. I noticed now that Bert had walked down the steep grass to the side of the cliff and was level with me, although well over on safe ground.

As I swung out and away from him with the sheep dangling from my right hand, I heard him moan, "Good God. Good God, mun. Tek care, it's only a sheep."

As I pendulummed back across the face I passed the ledge and swung well across toward the grass hillside. I couldn't hang on for long to either my rope or the sheep and had to make a snap decision. As I swung to the end of the arc, I threw the sheep with all my strength into space towards Bert. As I gripped the rope with both hands and started to spin on the return journey across the cliff I could see, with relief, that the sheep had landed safely. Much to my surprise it shook itself, seemed completely unharmed and started to munch nervously at the grass.

Bill's voice came from above. "Peter? You okay Pete?"

"Hang on."

Bills shouted. "What? What did you say?"

I was still swinging and not too keen on a long conversation. I didn't answer, and his cry, more desperate now, came down to me with the odd bit of mud and grass. "Pete. Are you okay? Peter!"

My swing took me back and I managed to land on the far end of the same grassy ledge that I had left. The weight on the rope now eased for Bill and I was pleased to see the slack rope quickly snake up the crag as he took the rope in. The second sheep was still there on the ledge but was now shuffling about in alarm. I perched there, still trying to form a plan of what to do with this second ewe. I had no intention of making the same dramatic mistake twice.

The sheep sensed that it had to act before I could gather my wits. It stamped the ground rapidly with its front feet, looked towards me, then down the vertical cliff for a second. For a moment I thought it was going to jump out into space and I stood motionless. Before I needed to make any decision, the problem was solved for me. She took a mighty leap down and across to a short ledge only as wide as a shoe and in a continuous movement carried on to land on the steep grass not far from the other sheep.

Without waiting to be grabbed again, both of them galloped across the hillside with their thick wool bouncing out to each side.

Bert's voice showed relief and some urgency for me to get off the cliff and onto safe ground. "Aye, good work mun. Come off noo."

I scrambled up the rock, hand over hand on the rope, and sat down by the rowan tree. Bill let the rope go and stood up rubbing his back. "Crikey, mate, what was going on down there? I feel as if I've been cut in two."

When we got down to the farm yard, Lord Younger brought from his car a hip flask with a small silver cup on top. "I think a wee dram is called for," he said.

We stood in the yard with the glen stretching away in the distance, beautifully lit by a cold sunlight.

Bert pushed his cap back. "Amazing," he turned to the Laird. "Did you see it all, sir?"

"Aye. I did. You mountaineers," he shook his head. "You have some courage."

"Oh, it was nothing," I said, and smiled with false modesty. I knew that I had made a mess of it but thought it wise to leave them thinking the best of us.

In a cloud of exhaust smoke, we drove out of the yard, with a wave from Bert and a shake of the head from the Laird, who was pouring again from the whisky flask. I think they enjoyed the afternoon, but we never did find out if they knew the rescue had been a shambles.

There were just a few staff in for the evening meal and as we sat around chatting over coffee, Vic came in. He turned to Bill and me. "So, the rescue was a success?"

Bill stretched his long legs out towards the coffee table. "Yeh, Vic. It was easy."

"Yes, the Laird phoned me a few moments ago." He poured a cup of coffee. "Easy, you say. The word he used was 'dramatic'. Said that his nerves would take a few days to calm down, but he thanked us anyway."

I looked at Vic. I could not tell whether this was a compliment, but he said it with a slight smile of reproach. I didn't need anyone to tell me that it was only luck that had prevented a far worse fiasco.

CHAPTER 16: PREPARING TO START COURSES

We had five weeks to prepare before students would arrive for the first adventure course and there was plenty to do. Builders had come to do work on the kitchen and the students' showers, and this had been nearly completed.

The first work for Roger, Rusty, Bill and I was to sort out the equipment and make a practical store from the small rooms available. A corridor from these rooms led straight out to the quadrangle at the back of the mansion, and this entrance would be ideal for issuing kit to the students. I was asked to make a lifting counter in the corridor where students would come inside to be issued with their kit. I borrowed tools from Hamish, and after fitting the counter I started work on racks for all the equipment such as boots, waterproofs and rucksacks that would be issued to all students at the beginning of each course. I made wide shelving in one of the rooms for tents and other camping kit such as stoves and canteens. For the sixty sleeping bags I made racks with hooks that could be lowered from the ceiling.

Vic came into the staff room during morning coffee and sat by me. "Peter, we need a little shop to sell things to the students - sweets, post cards, drinks and things. I thought it could be made at the end of the common room."

I put my coffee down. "Mm. Yes, could do. The common room is big."

"Yes, put some thought to it, Peter, and let me know what you need."

I drew up plans for shelving and a counter that could be closed and locked, with a long roller hatch coming down from the ceiling. Vic was pleased with the plans, so I ordered the materials and went to work building the students' 'shop'. My building skills were obviously very useful, and I began to wonder if these skills were the ones that had got me the job in the first place!

Two more minibuses had been delivered, and a large canoe trailer. Twelve kayaks made of glass fiber had been delivered, so Rusty and Bill fitted them all with buoyancy and lines on each bow and stern. When I had finished my work in the stores, they were still busy sorting out and stacking kit. All the equipment had to be clearly numbered so students knew what kit belonged to them, and all one hundred pairs of boots had to be numbered and clearly marked with their size.

A small room behind the equipment store was the staff locker room, and each of us had two metal lockers and hooks around the walls. For the students, in their part of the ground floor was a drying room that was kitted out with hooks, seating and racks so the students could hang their wet clothing to dry after coming in off the mountains or water. Below the hooks were boot racks that were all numbered so that students kept their kit in the same place throughout the course and wouldn't get their equipment mixed up with other students'.

There was a nice lecture room that we fitted out with rows of chairs and I fixed a pull-down projection screen to the end wall. A slide projector and a cine-projector were delivered, and these were set up on a special wheeled trolley with cupboards underneath to hold rolls of cine films. Dining tables and chairs were delivered, and we set these up in the staff room and the students' large dining room. Also, in our staff room I fixed onto the back wall a large noticeboard for the course programme.

On this noticeboard I began to put up the daily weather forecast that I cut from The Times newspaper. Looking at this every day, we soon learned a lot about wind strength and direction and began to be able to forecast the weather quite well in our part of the west coast. I was also asked to fix a noticeboard in the main student corridor, where the students could see the whole course programme and any other information that might affect them. The student dormitories took a few days to establish, because the sixty bunk beds had to be taken up the winding stairs and put together with bolts. Then the visiting teachers' rooms were made ready - each with a bed and bedding, a side table with a lamp, a chest of drawers and a large wardrobe. These teachers' bedrooms were adjacent to the student dormitories, for night-time supervision of the students would be the responsibility of their own visiting teachers.

*

Eventually, everything was ready, and we had a final staff meeting on a Monday morning before the first bunch of students arrived. Teenage students from Edinburgh, with their teacher, would arrive on each course in a coach just after lunch on a Monday. They would be 15 or 16 years old, and would be divided into nine students per group. They would be introduced to their group instructor who would then be with them for the whole course.

Most course programmes were a mix of activities, and in the winter this would involve rock climbing, a low-level walk with some orienteering, and the ascent of a local mountain. On the last two days their instructor would take them on an overnight camp in tents. During the summer there would also be a day of kayaking on Loch Eck, and a day of sailing dinghies on the Holy Loch.

The school teachers who came with the students were free to join any of the groups or even have the day off. Every evening there would be talks to the whole course. One talk would be from 5:30pm to 6:15pm, and another would take place in the evening after dinner from 7:30pm to 8:15pm. Some talks would be technical – on such things as map and compass navigation, kit and clothing for the outdoors, and weather forecasting. Others would be illustrated with slides of trips that the instructor might have done – perhaps in the alps, kayaking or sailing.

All these evening talks would be given by the same instructor who was designated 'on duty' for the whole of that day. The 'duty day' was a very long one for the instructor. However, most days the instructors would arrive back after a day on the hills or on the water in time for tea and cake in the staff room, where we would chat about incidents of the day, often with plenty of laughter. I would then go to my room and change for a fine dinner and a chat over coffee in our lovely quiet staff room. Sometimes it didn't seem like work at all.

*

I felt like the lord of the manor myself, I reflected, as I lay in the hot, deep bath one evening. The bathroom that Bill and I shared was big – very big. It must have been the laird's when the mansion had been a family home. I had filled the bath almost to the top and lay there floating gently and drifting from one end to the other. What a wonderful life, with constant hot water, no expenses for heating, free accommodation and excellent food eaten in the best of company. Now, in the hot bath with nothing to think about except dinner in an hour, I had not a care in the world.

Then I suddenly realised that tomorrow it was my turn to be on duty. My peaceful thoughts changed, for our day of duty was very arduous indeed and started early.

*

At seven the next morning, the alarm clock rattled on my bedside table, and I rolled out of bed before I could fall asleep again.

Wearing my dressing gown and slippers I was still not fully awake when I went up and down the stairs to each student dormitory, switching on the lights. "Morning, everyone," I said, trying to sound cheery before going back to my room and making a cup of tea. After getting washed and

92

dressed I did another tour of the dorms to make sure the students were moving and all out of bed.

Then I went to our 'spare' dorm. In this room we would put any student who was keeping the others awake at night. With about eight teenagers in each dormitory, there was often one who would be full of life, even after midnight. Our solution would be to take the offender out, give him, or her, a sleeping bag, and make them sleep in the spare room, which had no light at all. I went along to the spare room and threw open the long curtains. Four sleepy heads emerged – but two were boys and two were girls. Obviously, a different instructor or teacher had put the offenders in the dark room not realising that we had created a mixed dormitory. The students hadn't realised either. Lucky that the 'gutter press' didn't know.

As the duty instructor, I ate breakfast with the students in the large dining room. Inevitably, there were things to do during the meal, so it was always a disturbed meal. One couldn't even relax later over a coffee, for straight after breakfast was 'surgery'.

Any students who was sick had to report to surgery which was a small room smelling of antiseptic, where the first aid and rescue equipment was stored. There was a bed behind a screen and two chairs. Most days there were only a very few students lined up in the corridor outside. However, when the weather was particularly bad, the idea of doing a mountain walk would not appeal to some of the students. On those days a line of malingerers would be waiting for the surgery to open. On this morning there were only two. "Morning. Come in," I said to a saucy fifteen-year-old girl who was in Bill's group. "Now, what's the problem?"

"I've hurt my leg," she said with a pained expression.

"Oh, where?"

"Here, look." She pulled her trousers down to reveal a beautiful bronzed leg, and pointed high on her thigh to a small bruise.

I felt my cheeks going red. "Well, it doesn't look very bad."

"Oh, it is," she grimaced. "Touch it and see."

I straightened up and coughed nervously. "Perhaps I will ask Morag for her opinion."

"Oh, doesna matter." The student pulled her jeans up. "I'll just suffer the pain," she said, with a martyred expression

The next patient was a girl in Rusty's group and I was relieved to see she had a teacher with her. "Morning," I said, with a casual smile. "What's the problem?"

Her teacher spoke. "Kate slipped over yesterday. Not a bad fall or anything but she hurt her shoulder." The youngster stood there quietly with both arms hanging by her side. I could see no difference in either side, so I said, "Which shoulder, Kate?" She lifted her left hand and pointed vaguely to her right shoulder. "This one."

"And you say this happened yesterday?" The teacher answered. "Yes, we were just coming down the hill and she slipped on the wet grass."

I smiled down at Kate. "Well, I think it's just strained."

"It hurt quite a lot in bed last night." She smiled apologetically.

"Oh." I thought for a minute. "Well, can you put a finger exactly where it hurts?"

"Umm." She put her left finger close to a spot on her right collarbone. "There," she said.

"What, exactly there?"

"Yes. Just there." This made me think more carefully. If an adult breaks a collarbone, it is very painful, and they stand in a particular way, supporting the weight of the injured side. Surely this girl had not broken a collarbone and slept all night with it like that? She stood in front of me with both arms hanging quite relaxed. But of course, children's bones are not brittle like an adult's. Perhaps it was a 'greenstick' fracture. However, if someone can point exactly to a painful spot, I have often found it to be more than a strain.

I didn't chance it. I arranged for Hamish, the janitor, to drive them both to the casualty department in Dunoon. The hospital was quite large for such a small town. Like the local secondary school, the hospital had to serve the wider population of people who lived far away on the distant offshore islands. That evening, Kate returned to the centre with her arm well supported in a sling. She had broken her collarbone and I was quietly relieved that I hadn't ignored it.

Straight after morning surgery I had to hurry along to meet my group to brief them for our day of activity, and although it wasn't yet nine o'clock, I already felt I needed a break. After the briefing I rushed off to change and pack for the day. My group and Rusty's group were climbing Benmore Mountain, and they went off to meet in the courtyard.

The students were already sitting in the mini-bus and I made a last-minute check. "Listen now, has everyone got waterproof tops and trousers, a hat, gloves and a spare sweater?" They had everything. It seemed that we had forgotten nothing. I drove up the slope and went a short distance along the gravel drive when the teacher who was joining us for the day turned to me. "The packed lunches, Peter. Have you got the packed lunches?"

"Oh." I stopped the vehicle. "Thanks." I hopped out and started to run back to the centre when the teacher called out to me.

"Peter, your boots. Have you got your boots?"

I looked down at my feet. I was still wearing my sandals. I grinned feebly and ran down to get my boots and, perhaps more importantly, the student lunches.

The drive was slow and bumpy. On the far side of the fresh water loch was the surfaced road, but on this side there was only a rough and potted forestry track. After two miles I turned onto smooth grass by a deserted croft. It was lovely to stop the noise of the engine and listen to the sounds of the countryside. A buzzard mewed high up and two crows pestered it raucously. A stream nearby gurgled along on its way to the loch and a little black and white dipper bird, bobbing up and down on a low rock in the stream and clicked at us. I breathed in deeply. It was peaceful to be away from the centre.

Before leaving the mini-bus I locked it and left the key in the exhaust pipe. Rusty had suggested he would do the same with his mini-bus. In this way we could do a more interesting walk, coming down from the mountain a different way and exchanging vehicles. We hoped to meet on the summit which Rusty thought would give extra interest for the students.

My group were a good bunch and we made slow but steady progress up through an open woodland of small oak trees. It was springtime and grass grew thick and emerald green in the clearings. Beneath many of the trees were glorious patches of bluebells and when the sun came clear of clouds the whole forest was made more beautiful with a dappled light.

The trees became more widely spaced until we eventually came up to the open hillside. We were lucky to disturb a hare. It looked up in alarm and for a few seconds sat high on its haunches, eyeing our clumsy line. Then, with no real sign of panic, it lolloped diagonally up the hillside and disappeared out of sight.

The weather was unsettled and getting worse. All morning the cloud became thicker and sunk lower on the hills. The wind increased and slowly 'backed' so that it was coming from the south west. As we gained height the visibility was very bad, and I told the group to stay close, with the teacher keeping at the back of the line.

When I found a little shelter from the wind, I stopped the group. "Now listen," I shouted above the wind. "I am giving you each a number. Remember it." I walked down the line and touched each student on the shoulder. "One. Two. Three. Four," and so on, until I reached the teacher, who was number ten. "Now, when I say 'number off', you shout out your number, all in order. Got it?"

Rusty had told me about this technique. I used it in situations like keeping a sea kayak group together when paddling at night. It helps in keeping the group together but also gives them a little amusement within the group.

95

I walked on for about fifty metres and then shouted: "We shall test the system. Ready…. Number off." It worked wonderfully:

"One, two, three, four," each student shouted out their number in order. Yes, everyone was present, and I plodded along happily into the mist. As we approached the summit the visibility got even worse, but I was not concerned for I knew all I had to do was keep going uphill.

The ground started to level out and then I heard a dog barking. It was Puck, Rusty's German shepherd, who greeted me like a long-lost friend. The dog was always keen to come out on the hill and even used to sneak into the mini-bus of another instructor if Rusty was not on the mountains that day. The teenagers liked to have the dog along and made a real fuss of him. The students enjoyed the reunion as we all gathered round the cairn.

It was also Rusty's idea to have a signature book on the summit. We opened the tin that was hidden under a nearby rock and everyone recorded their names. The mountain was not really very interesting, but these clever ideas gave the students a sense of achievement.

We found a place out of the strong wind and had some lunch, but it was not the sort of day to hang around.

Rusty stood up "Well, Peter, we shall be off." He shouldered his rucksack. "The mini-bus keys are left in the exhaust pipe?"

"Yes. And yours?"

"On the rear wheel…. See you back at the centre." He set off with his students all happy to be going downhill, and they soon disappeared into the thick cloud. The visibility was now so bad that it would be very easy indeed to lose some of the party in the thick cloud. Someone only had to stop to tie a bootlace or something, and when they looked up the rest of the group might have disappeared in the cloud.

I decided to employ the use of a light rope I carried to keep the group together. I tied a small loop every few metres and everyone put their right wrist through the loop and I tied an end round my waist. We were now all tied into the same rope in one long line.

Visibility was so bad that I could only see the first couple of students who were on the rope behind me. However, I could now concentrate on navigating over the plateau knowing everyone was on the rope. Again, it was Rusty who told me this technique. I was fortunate in working with someone of his calibre who could teach me so much and give us great ideas on making the most out of every day.

For nearly an hour we continued like this across the featureless plateau until we eventually dropped to a lower altitude and could see the bowl of the corrie below. I stopped the group and they gathered round. "There we are, everyone." I pointed down to a lochan. "That's where we go. You can take the rope off now and we will all stop at the lochan."

There was no need for a disciplined line, so everyone found their own route down, first on rough scree and then over grass with clumps of heather. The occasional beautiful little Rowan tree stood proud on the steep slopes. As the corrie levelled the ground became boggier and we picked our way around the alder forest and eventually through twisted oaks to the rough track by the side of Loch Eck. There was Rusty's mini-bus with the key as planned. What a professional he was.

Despite the poor weather it had been a good day and we drove happily back to the centre. The students went to clean up and I went to our staff locker room where we left our outdoor kit. I had a shower, dressed for the evening, and went down to the staff room.

It was fifteen minutes before our tea and cakes and I was reading a magazine when Sheena, our secretary, came in. "Oh, there you are Peter. Rusty is on the telephone. He wants to speak to you."

"Me? He wants to speak to me?"

"Aye. That's what he says."

I hurried along to the office. "Hello. Pete here."

"Ah, Pete. Good." He was speaking rather quietly. "Can you get a vehicle and pick me up?"

"Well, er … yes. What's the matter with my bus, has it broken down again?"

"No. It's still where you left it." There was a slight pause. "I've come down in the wrong valley. I'm in Glen Mason."

"Glen Mason?"

"Yes." He chuckled. "I must have been dreaming. We are by the gate leading to McNeish's farm."

I went out and as I drove up the tarmac road of Glen Mason I chuckled to think that even Rusty could make a mistake sometimes. His students clambered in the side door and Rusty got in the front with me. "Do you know Peter. I got right down to the road before I realised where I was." He raised his eyes in disbelief. "I thought to myself, when did they tarmac the road?" We had a good laugh but decided that it would be better if the principal and chief instructor didn't hear about his blunder.

*

At five thirty, between tea and the evening meal, the duty instructor gave a talk to the whole course. My lesson tonight was on using the compass. I took into the lecture room a box of compasses and our giant demo compass made of Perspex. After the lesson I just had time to clear up before supervising the evening meal, which, like breakfast, was always disturbed, for the duty instructor had to supervise the students in the dining room.

After the meal I had no time to sit in the staff room with the rest of the staff, chatting over coffee, for as the duty instructor I had to be in our little shop. We sold things like postcards and stamps, but more often cans of fizzy drinks and various chocolate biscuits that the students often took with them on the next day's activity. As might be expected, some of them had a can or chocolate before going to bed and were overactive for the next two hours. These were the kids that usually ended up sleeping in the dark spare room.

Starting at seven-thirty, the duty instructor gave the second talk of the evening and usually it was a slide show around some outdoor adventure. I always did the same one, which was a typical ascent of a mountain in the Alps. I had the slides always ready in order so that it wasn't too stressful for me. However, on this night the bulb in the projector failed and there was a delay for five minutes while I fitted a new one.

There was free time for the students after the talk but not for the duty instructor. I went to the kitchen and heated up a great pan of hot drinking chocolate that had been prepared by the cooks. This was the bedtime drink for the students and I served it in their common room.

By ten thirty I could begin to relax a little now the students were in bed, even if some of them were far from asleep. Finally, I walked round the whole building checking lights and doors, and when everything seemed settled for the night I went up to my room. I got ready for bed, relieved that my day of duty was finished.

Then I remembered with a silent groan that tomorrow I would take my group for an overnight camp. This would mean that after this very long duty day I would be working continuously with students, without a break for the next 48 hours.

I had probably been asleep for an hour when I woke up with a start. Was it my turn to stoke the coke boilers? Bill and I were the only instructors who were permanently resident, and we shared a special duty: to keep the boilers going through the night. The boiler system in the house was very old. To maintain the heating and hot water throughout the house a furnace needed to be stoked. Hamish, the janitor, did this work during the day, but at night the furnace had to be stoked up last thing before we went to bed. Bill and I were responsible. If we forgot to tend the furnace it would go out and the next morning all seventy students and staff would find the house cold with no hot water anywhere.

I fell out of bed in a panic and quickly put on a dressing gown and slippers. I stumbled downstairs and through the heavy fire door that led to the dusty cellars. As I went down the worn steps, I could hear a noise – the noise of shovelling. I went into the furnace room, which smelled of sulphur, and in the gloom from a dusty light bulb I found Bill in his pyjamas.

I made him jump. "Oh, allo Pete. I forgot the blasted furnace."

"You forgot it? I thought it was my turn tonight."

He looked as sleepy as I felt. "Oh, don't know. Anyway, thank god it's still alight."

We had free food and accommodation and many other little perks, but on days like this I thought we really earned our keep. Amongst the coal dust and gloom, I finished the very long working day shovelling coke. I didn't feel like the laird of the manor now.

Aunt May's house on the right

Peter in the Alps above Chamonix

The Matterhorn

The Swiss Alps

Crowberry Gulley, Glencoe

Sailing *Sisu* in the Clyde

Cath sailing in the Holy Loch

CHAPTER 17: KAYAK TRAINING

The laird, Lord Younger, was heir to the Younger Beer Company. He was a regular visitor to the botanic garden that he had given to the state with the great mansion that was now 'Benmore Adventure Centre'. He lived only a mile away in a lovely modern bungalow. Owning one of the largest breweries in the country had made him a very rich man and it was rumoured that he had two Rolls Royce cars in his garage.

However, one would never have guessed he was wealthy for he always visited the gardens on an old black bicycle. It was a woman's bike; very upright with the old-fashioned lever brakes. He always wore the same thing: a beige gabardine raincoat tied round the waist with a piece of string and a single cycle clip on his right trouser leg. Our adventure centre had been his home until quite recently and his garden was now the botanic garden, which attracted many visitors. He was very enthusiastic about the gardens and would cycle around the gravel drives. He knew everyone who worked in the garden and they all had great respect for the old chap.

As he was so deaf his voice could be heard clearly. "Hellooo Mrs. McClusky," he would shout when he saw one of his old members of staff.

Mrs. McClusky would shout back at the top of her voice, "Morning Lord Younger."

He owned the land for miles around: all the mountains and glens, the fresh water loch and the river Eckaig that ran four miles to the Holy Loch. We were free to take students over any part of his property: the mountains, the forests and the loch.

Everywhere except the river. The river he kept for himself. In the river were some of the best salmon anywhere, and fishing was the Lairds' passion. During the salmon season he could be seen prowling along the bank with his rod and a large box hanging from a strap over one shoulder. Two of his 'gillies' would regularly net the river where they stood in the eddies wearing chest high waders.

However, out of the fishing season, during the cold winter months, we were allowed to use the river for our own staff training. There was a fine little weir and we would carry our kayaks across the front lawn, then across two fields and down to the river. The weir proved to be great practise for our white-water skills, and inevitably we would capsize.

Rusty was no keener on cold water than the rest of us, and shortly after he had learned to kayak, he said to me. "Peter, I shall have to learn this Eskimo rolling business."

I nodded. "Yes. It's useful."

He sat there in his kayak, hunched up against the bitter east wind that was blowing across this open part of the river. "Well, how do you do it?"

I smiled indulgently. "Oh, it takes lots of practise. You couldn't learn here."

I slapped the cold water with my paddle. "Perhaps we could arrange a session in Dunoon swimming pool. I could help you there."

"Mm. Well, show me how to do it."

I looked at the river. Although we were wearing wet suits, I still wasn't keen to go in the river when I didn't have to. As I was not that good at rolling myself, there was always the possibility that I would fail and have to swim to the bank, which would be considerably worse in the cold water. "Well, er. It goes like this." I showed him how to hold the paddle and went through the motions without actually capsizing. "Of course," I said, "when you're upside down everything feels different. During your first attempts I would have to stand by and lift you up each time you failed."

He looked at me carefully and practised holding the paddle and sweeping it to one side. Then he said. "So, it goes like this." To my surprise, he capsized and all I could see was the upturned hull of his boat moving a little with his efforts underneath. The seconds ticked by and I started to paddle quickly over to save him. Then to my absolute amazement he rolled up on the other side. "Phew." He wiped the water from his eyes. "Something like that?"

I was almost speechless and simply grinned and shook my head in wonder. Never had I known anyone to roll a kayak after simply being told what to do. Rusty became a good and adventurous paddler, doing some of the dramatic rivers in America, and to my knowledge he never failed to roll up. So, we improved. But the water was cold, particularly in the spring. When snow covered the hills, the runoff made the river very cold indeed.

After a kayak session Rusty, Bill and I would stagger back across the field with our boats. Rusty would head for Golden Gates Lodge and his hot bath, but Bill and I had to share our bathroom so it became a race to get back first.

Still wearing his wetsuit, Bill would rush up the stairs and I could hear him singing above the rush of hot water while I would try to keep warm until it was my turn. What a wonderful sensation to lay with only my nose above the steaming water and feel the heat warming my blood. Glorious hot water, such a contrast to the dangerously cold water of our freshwater loch.

*

Our boss, Vic, had only recently returned from Australia, where he had been the head of an outward-bound school. Perhaps he had forgotten how cold the water could be in Scotland. After breakfast one morning Vic came in. "Kayaking," he said beaming. "For staff training this morning I thought we would cover the programme for a basic session of kayaking."

We were not entirely enthusiastic, but it was better than equipment maintenance, so we changed and loaded the boats ready for the lake session.

Snow was in the wind as we gathered by the loch, and Vic looked at us with a knowing smile. "You're all wearing wet suits. The students won't have wet suits." He laughed. "You're a bunch of wimps."

Wearing only a swimsuit and a thick sweater he got into his kayak and paddled a little way off. "Now," he shouted back to us. "First thing is a capsize so that everyone is happy in the water."

We looked at each other and then back at him in disbelief as he dropped the paddle and tipped to one side, disappearing under the upturned kayak. His head quickly appeared above the surface. His cheeks were puffed out and a startled expression, almost of panic, was in his eyes. He grappled with the kayak and seemed to be trying to claw his way up the side of the slippery hull. After a few frantic seconds he turned and swam strongly the few metres to shallow water and stumbled out.

He stood there with rigid arms and hunched shoulders. His mouth was moving but it was a few seconds before the words came out. "Christ...! Bloody cold."

We stood silent. What could we say? We knew it was cold; he didn't need to convince us. In the future we all wore wet suits during training in the winter months.

A few weeks later Vic marched into the staff room during our morning coffee break wearing a brilliant orange life jacket. He smiled. "What do you think?" he said, and spun round like a model.

"Bright?" said Rusty.

"You won't get lost," said Bill, through a mouthful of rock bun. There was always a good atmosphere in the staff room and Vic smiled. "Staff training this afternoon."

"Great." I was always keen on staff training. Vic took off the life jacket. "We can try out the new kayaks that arrived the other day." He looked at me. "Are they all ready, Peter?"

"Yes. They're all fitted out."

"Good." He took a rock bun. "It's still outside of the fishing season so we can use the river. Perhaps we can paddle the Echaig right down to the sea."

The Echaig started from the fresh water, Loch Ech, and ran through the botanic gardens to reach the sea at the Holy Loch four miles away. We had only been on the weir section of the river, but knew there were a few easy rapids and awkward trees to avoid higher up not far from the fresh water loch. With the boats loaded onto the trailer we set off straight after lunch for the Loch.

The shoreline had a bed of sharp little stones and we were keen not to scratch our shiny new kayaks. We followed Vic's example and waded into the water so that the boats were floating gently before we slid into the narrow seats. There were only a few minutes of paddling before we left the loch and felt the gentle surge of water as we entered the river.

On the right bank, fields came down to the water but, for most of the river, the banks were overgrown with quite a few trees and bushes. The water was high, but the river was not difficult. However, it is very narrow in places and we were keen to keep away from alder trees that overhung the bank.

The bank had collapsed on the outside bend at certain places and branches hung deep in the moving water. These 'sweepers' can be very dangerous as they can trap a paddler underwater, rather like an old-fashioned fish trap. However, everything went well until we came to a stretch of river where small trees were growing straight out of the river bed.

My experience in white water was not great but Vic evidently thought me more capable than the others, and after gathering together in an eddy he said. "Peter. Go on. See what you think."

"Mm." I wasn't that keen to be used as a 'test pilot'. "Trees are growing a bit close together," I mumbled.

Bill showed his usual confidence. "Go'on man. You'll be okay."

I pulled out into the river and back-paddled in a 'ferry glide' to control my approach through the 'slalom' of trees. I held my speed down and crabbed sideways through the first three little trees, but the ones in front were so close together that it was not possible to manoeuvre the length of the kayak across the river to miss trees below. There was no room and I was soon sucked amongst the trees and the kayak became stuck. I managed to clear that situation but in doing so I hit another tree sideways on and in a fraction of a second, I was upside down.

There was no question of doing an Eskimo roll and I spluttered out and was surprised to find that I could stand up. Although the current was quite strong the water only came to my chest and I tried to move the kayak quickly before it filled with water. But with an open cockpit the river poured in and within seconds the water pressure had pushed it below the surface. I struggled to free the boat but had to watch helplessly as it

107

crumpled around the cockpit and bent round the tree. I could do nothing by myself against the power of the stream.

The others stood on the bank shouting advice. "Pull it this way Pete." "Push it across Pete." "Lift it out of the water." All of this advice was useless as I could not move it forwards or backwards and certainly had no hope at all in lifting it clear of the river. As it was not necessary for them to swim, they very reluctantly waded into the shallow river and we all worked on the kayak together. Even with all our strength we couldn't shift it. Eventually the tugging broke the kayak right in two and the parts disappeared downstream.

We all gathered on the bank and stood with water dripping around us. I felt guilty that I'd lost a brand-new kayak but was thankful that Vic and Roger were there to see that we had done everything we could. Considering the boat was one of our brand-new fleet Vic took the whole incident very well. All he said was, "Well, that's that. No more paddling on this part of the river for the students or the staff."

Roger nodded his agreement and said, "We will call this bit of the river after you Pete. We'll call it 'Dyer's Downfall', and it was called that ever since.

Now that we were all wet and cold nobody wanted to get back onto the river. Working in pairs we picked up the kayaks and walked across the frosty fields for a hot bath. It was rather an expensive lesson, but we certainly learned what power the water has in just a small river. Rivers can be dangerous, but I was about to learn how serious the sea can also be.

CHAPTER 18: SEA KAYAKING

A few weeks later we were having a coffee after the evening meal. Bill was on duty, so he was with the students in the dining room, and Roger had gone up to his flat.

Rusty, sitting the other side of the coffee table, put his cup down and said, "Pete, now the salmon have returned to spawn, the laird won't let us use the kayaks on the river. But what about the sea? Do you fancy a trip on the sea?"

I had never done a sea journey. "Yes. Yes, I'm keen. Where could we go?"

"Well, I thought we could start at Loch Goil, paddle down until we get to Loch Long, and then round into the Holy Loch." We walked across the room to the large map that was on the wall.

"Oh yes, I see. Seems great. It should be an easy day. How can we get to Loch Goil Head?"

"Perhaps someone will drive us in the old mini-bus." Rusty gave a knowing smile. "I'll ask Roger."

The course came to an end and the next day when both of us were free was a Saturday. With Roger driving, we motored north along the beautiful glen road. On the right were a few hill farms with grazing fields at the lower level. Higher up, heather was the only thing growing in patches between the grass, which was broken by the rocky tops. Through the trees on the left, the dark loch was ruffled by a strong wind, and across was the wooded slope of Benmore mountain. We reached Loch Fyne where we turned right. It was only a few miles before we turned off on a road called Hells Glen. This quiet little road was lined on either side with gorse and broom, and the bushes were covered with dense yellow flowers.

The road had a number of sharp bends in its descent to sea level, and after three miles we reached the few quiet houses and the empty pier that was Loch Goil Head. After unloading the kit, Roger left us with the arrangement that we would telephone in the afternoon for a pick-up at the sailing club in the Holy Loch.

It was a pleasant morning, but the weather was rather strange. There was a strong warm wind blowing and in the sky were great streaks of high cirrus cloud with beautiful wispy clouds commonly called 'mare's tales' as they all look like horse tails kicking up as they gallop. We hadn't thought to get a weather forecast; we didn't think the trip would be serious. How wrong we would be … As we put on our life jackets and spray decks Rusty said, "It's getting windy, Pete."

"Yes." I looked around. "Should be okay. We're in sheltered water most of the way."

He looked up at the sky. "Umm, perhaps." As we paddled confidently from the shelter at the head of the loch the first gust of wind hit us. The gusts of wind could be seen as dark patches on the water as the wind funnelled down the glens and travelled across the loch. We had only been going for half an hour when the wind got much stronger and 'white horses' covered the sea. The gusts were now so violent that the surface of the sea was being picked up. It was these tremendous gusts of wind that gave me most concern.

"Gosh, Rusty, the wind is really strong now."

He shouted back. "Yes, let's keep close to shore."

But even keeping close to the wooded shoreline didn't seem to help. The wind increased still further and in one tremendous gust I was blown right over. I panicked and made a violent snatch with my paddle underwater and failed to roll up. I struggled from the cockpit of the kayak and was pleased that I had only a short distance to drag the kayak and paddle to the shore. There was no point in delaying and I got straight back and we paddled harder. Now the gusts were stronger than I had ever felt before and as each one passed, the spray from the surface was so thick that I lost sight of Rusty and just had to lay into the wind until the gust had passed. Despite his lack of experience, Rusty was handling the situation far better than me and it wasn't long before another vicious gust caught me, and I was upside-down again.

We continued close along the deserted rocky shore, struggling in each huge gust of wind and paddling, mostly only on one side, to try and maintain our course. The only advantage we had was that the wind was fiercely coming from the north so that we were being blown in the direction we wanted to go. For much of the time we were unable to paddle but were just hanging on and bracing against the gusts and lashing spray. But with the northerly wind we were still being blown along very quickly.

However, Loch Goil had nearly come to an end and we would have to turn right into Loch Long. In turning the corner, we would have the whole width of Loch Long in front of us and the wind was now so strong that we would probably get blown across from the shore and away into open water. It was so fierce there would be no chance of paddling back to shore against the wind, and there seemed every chance of being capsized in the large body of water.

"Rusty!" I shouted above the roar of the wind. "Let's go ashore." With his head down against the spray he squinted towards me. He nodded, and we quickly made for the safety of the rocks.

"It's too dangerous," he shouted into my ear.

I nodded. "Yes. Perhaps round the corner it'll be sheltered." He looked out to where the spray off the sea was dramatic.

"Yes, but how to get round the corner without being blown out to sea?" He turned around and looked up at the steep rocky headland behind us. "Perhaps we could climb up there and cut across the headland?"

I looked up. The hillside was densely covered in stunted mountain oaks, which were creaking with each gust. "Yes, perhaps.... It will be a struggle with the boats." We looked out to the sea that was completely white right across to the far side of the loch a mile away. As we watched, a tremendous gust of wind moved across the water and the spray it created filled the air to a height of about ten metres. "We can't go out there again," I shouted, and we lifted the kayaks and started the climb up through the rocks.

Without the kayaks it would have been an easy scramble, but the wind kept catching the boats and we were spun round one way and then the other. When we got higher amongst the trees the wind had less affect but now the kayaks kept getting stuck between the dense little oaks.

Rusty cursed and turned to me. "Pete, let's work together."

"Yes, okay. I'll tie mine to a tree and we can take yours between us."

This worked out much easier as one of us would scramble over any particularly steep part while the other held the boat, which could then be passed up. After leaving one kayak we would scramble down for the other one. It was quite a struggle but eventually we were on top of the headland and could look back down to Loch Goil. The sea was streaked with foam and in the gusts the sea would be lifted like a thick mist for hundreds of metres. The waves were not big but very steep. Even now, after many years of sailing across oceans, I have still never seen a more violent piece of sea. However, when we got down to an empty little bay on the shore of Loch Long it was much better.

Rusty looked down the loch. "Should be ok, Pete, if we keep real close to the shore."

"Yes, keep close to the shore. If we get blown out there we could never paddle back against the wind." So, we paddled on, nervously looking for gusts that might sweep us out to open water. But they didn't come.

After a couple of hours of hugging the deserted shore the wind, although still strong, seemed to be easing rapidly and we were pleased when we passed the wilderness coast to reach the part where a road was accessible. We carefully paddled the short distance to the small hamlet of Ardentinny and went ashore. The force of the wind was dropping all the time, but I still didn't fancy our chances in open water.

I turned to Rusty. "What do you think, Rusty? We could phone Roger and he might drive out to here." Rusty looked out to the sea.

111

"Yes. The wind is certainly dying off but when we turn into the Holy Loch we might catch it again. It could be desperate paddling into the wind, and we could easily get blown out into the Clyde."

A telephone cable on a tall pole stretched above the road to a house nearby. It was a stone house with windows set deep into the lime-washed walls. I knocked on the door and after a few seconds could hear approaching footsteps. An elderly lady, still brushing white flour from her hands, opened the door. I explained our situation and asked if we might use her telephone. "Aye, sure," she smiled. "Come through. The phone is right here."

Roger came on the line straight away. "Thank God, Peter. Are you okay? Where are you?"

"We're a bit wet but okay."

But before I could continue, he interrupted: "We've been worried. The wind here has been tremendous. Up to force 12 they said."

"Force 12! That's hurricane force, isn't it?"

"Yes, I think so. Everyone has been on alert. The American Submarines have all put to sea to get into deep water. The American factory ship was dragging its anchor. It's moved out into the Clyde to clear the land. "

"Gosh. We thought the wind was strong, but it was only the gusts that really upset us. We were probably sheltered from most of it."

Roger went on. "There has been serious damage in Glasgow too and lots of trees round here have blown down. You know the McClusky family, who live in the bungalow at the far side of the gardens?"

"Yes."

"Well, their whole roof has blown off and landed amongst the bushes."

I told him where we were, and he said he would come straight out. I turned to Rusty. "Apparently there's been a hurricane. Damage everywhere."

He grinned. "I thought it wasn't normal. I was thinking that if this is sea kayaking it's too dangerous for anyone."

We laughed together in relief. The effect of the storm in Glasgow was reported widely; it did millions of pounds worth of damage to buildings. Not much was said about the amazing affect the hurricane had on the west coast forests. More trees were blown down in that few hours than were felled during a normal year. They lay, like blown-down wheat in a field, lying on top of each other over great acres of the hills, and most roads were blocked for a few days. The hurricane gave us a respect for the sea that we never forgot. I learned that when the wind and sea are beyond our control the only safe place to be is on dry land.

CHAPTER 19: THE START OF SAILING

I had sold my little motorbike back in London and didn't own a car, so I bought a bicycle from a second-hand shop in Dunoon. It was very old, with lever brakes, but it was good enough to get around locally. Just a few days after my arrival in Scotland I was cycling along an empty road when I approached a man walking towards me. He touched his cap and called out, "Morning, Mr. Dyer."

I was very surprised for I had never seen the man in my life before. "Er, morning," I called back over my shoulder. This little incident made me realise that I now lived far away from the busy congestion of the London streets where nobody would do such a thing. I mentioned the incident to Roger at Lunch.

"Yes, we are in the highlands," he laughed. "The locals know us 'Sassenachs' and I'm sure they discuss everything we do." He poured tea and then continued. "I've put sailing on the programme next week, Peter. Each group can have one day, and you can work with all the groups."

Bill sat forward in his chair. "Sailing, eh. That sounds great. I'm keen to learn how to sail."

Rusty smiled. "Certainly be a change from climbing and being bitten by the tiny midge flies in the forest."

I looked at Roger. "Sailing?" I said. As we didn't own any sailing boats I was surprised. "What are we sailing in?"

"Vic has been in contact with the Holy Loch Sailing Club. They have four club boats we can use."

I was delighted. "Oh, that's great."

Roger smiled. "Yes. You and I can pop down to the club this evening and see the boats and look into the club hut."

"Okay," I said. "Where is the club?"

"Oh, it's in Sandbank. Do you know Robertson's, the boat builder?"

"Yes, with the slipways and huge sheds down by the Holy Loch?"

He nodded. "That's right. Well, the sailing club is the little wooden building just by their yard."

Instructors ate their evening meal in the staff room, so after I'd finished a slab of apple pie and custard, Roger and I squeezed into his white mini and set off for the sailing club. Along the gravel drive, past the glorious rhododendron bushes that were now in full bloom, and along the empty road the four miles to the sea Loch. Just before Robertson's Boat Yard he turned left, where a discreet little notice board read: Holy Loch

Sailing Club. He stopped the car on a large square of well-kept grass that ran down to the sea.

At one side was a shed-like building with timber weatherboarding on the outside. We walked round the end of the building where four sailing dinghies were neatly lined up. They rested on trolleys and were each covered with smart green canvas. We undid a couple of cords and lifted one of the covers to look inside the boat. The boats had apparently been made at the Robertson's yard and were clinker built in timber, with Gunter rigs and tan sails. The smart varnish showed they had been lovingly maintained. They had quite a large beam and would probably be stable. They seemed to be ideal for students and I was happy. "They seem just right Roger."

"Yes," he said thoughtfully. "The only trouble is that the younger club members use them most evenings. They must return in perfect shape at the end of every day when we use them."

"Oh, sure."

He smiled at me. "That means if they get damaged at all, we must repair them before a club member notices."

I grinned. "*We* repair them?" He slapped me on the shoulder. "Well, yes. *You* must repair them before anyone notices." He laughed. "Get anything you need from Robertson's Yard. Let's look in the club house."

Roger had a key and we went inside. There was a long open lounge with a kitchen set behind a counter. On one wall were pictures of sailing dinghies and on another was a glass-fronted cabinet holding a few silver cups and various trophies. Near the counter was a shipshape noticeboard, and opposite was a large display of all the knots that a seaman might use. At each end of the lounge were doors marked 'Ladies' and 'Gents'. We opened the gent's door to find a few toilets and handbasins with an area of bench seats and hanging rails.

This was obviously the changing area. "Looks fine, eh Pete?"

I grinned. "Yes, it seems perfect. We can use the kitchen to make a brew at lunchtime."

So that was how I became the instructor in charge of sailing; because I was the one who could best repair broken boats.

Each class of nine or ten students would come down with their group instructor who would lead one boat. We paid lads from the sailing club who were excellent sailors to help us instruct in two boats, and I took the fourth dinghy. Every evening I wrote to Cath about these new developments. We had done a little sailing together, so she could probably imagine my working days. Her teaching seemed to be going very well in her new Yorkshire school and she seemed to get on well with both the students and staff.

I think the instructors all enjoyed the change from mountaineering. All winter we were walking on the hills in snow and ice, or rock climbing, sometimes in the rain, so sailing made a pleasant change. Another very big advantage during summer months was that I avoided the midges. Rock climbing on cliffs surrounded by trees was a bit of a nightmare in the summer. The little biting midges collected near the trees in their millions, and their many bites gave everyone a bad time. Sometimes their attacks were so bad that even forest workers, with all their sprays, had to leave the trees. Yes, sailing in the summer was a great relief.

Even Rusty enjoyed the day on the ocean, and as he had done some sailing before he soon became very good. However, Rusty always wanted some excitement in the day, and if there was none provided by the elements, he would find some way of putting an 'edge' to a quiet morning. One of his stunts was to sail his dinghy under the enormous anchor chair that dropped from the bow of the American's massive factory ship that sat motionless in the middle of the loch.

He began to sail under the chain quite regularly, but the US navy was very sensitive about people getting too close to their machinery of war; even a little sailing dinghy. One day he sailed into the shore for lunch and I noticed that he, his three students and the boat were covered with vegetable scraps. There were bits of carrot in their hair. I leaned over to look at cabbage leaves and potato peeling squashed into the bottom of their boat.

"Huh. What's all this, Rusty?"

"Damn yanks … can't take a joke." He grinned and bent forward to shake his hair. "As we were sailing under their anchor chain one of the chaps on the bow emptied a big bucket of kitchen waste down."

Perhaps it was an accident, but I'm sure it wasn't. Rusty didn't sail under their anchor chain again.

We had no safety boat in those early days, so we usually sailed within site of the club. The other instructors seemed content to only sail in the Holy Loch, and there was a fair bit of extra interest for the students. Apart from the enormous, humming factory ship, there were usually two or more Polaris submarines skulking alongside it. There was a continual traffic of noisy landing craft going to the land base from the factory ship and from a massive floating dock that was moored towards the mouth of the loch. Sometimes the floating dock would be low in the water and at other times its tall sides towered high above our small dinghies.

At these times, the grey metal walls would be concealing a nuclear submarine that was in for servicing. More interesting for me was the collection of expensive sailing boats that were moored in a sheltered part of the loch, just off shore from Robertson's Boat Yard. Many of these one might rightly describe as millionaire's yachts, with polished woodwork and gleaming brass. Some were twenty-five or thirty-five metres long with two tall timber masts draped with white ropes reaching down to the deck. Some had a permanent skipper and perhaps a permanent engineer. On quiet days I would take my little crew of students alongside and we would take turns peering through the portholes into the plush interiors. Rarely did I ever see these yachts sail off their moorings and during the next few years a number were sold to rich new owners on the other side of the Atlantic.

The main damage to our sailing dinghies was to the rudders and tillers. I collected a few necessary tools and spare parts, and for most of the time I could do a small repair while the students ate their packed lunches. A couple of times I had to return after dinner in the evening to do work, and on one occasion I had to stay late into the night to make a repair that was vital for the next day of sailing. However, I wasn't complaining. After a winter of instructing mountaineering and rock climbing it was very pleasant to have a change of scene.

*

The thought that we were using other people's boats was always a concern for me, so I was pleased when Roger announced at breakfast one day, "Peter, the wayfarer sailing dinghies we ordered - they're arriving tomorrow."

"Oh, that's great." He went to the food trolley and poured himself a coffee.

"I've taken you off instructing for a couple of days so that you can sort them out, and I've asked Hamish to give you a hand."

The four sailing dinghies, all new and shining, were wayfarer class. Large, with a wide beam and plenty of room for four people so they were excellent for teaching the basics of sailing. We set four moorings out, just opposite the sailing club and usually left the large dinghies afloat as they were heavy to keep bringing ashore. We used the little club 'tender' to row out to them. Each student group of teenagers usually had one day of sailing with an instructor in each boat. We would all drive down together in a mini-bus to the sailing club. Then, split into 'crews' and with an instructor in each boat, we could teach all the basics of sailing.

Confidence amongst the instructors was growing, and we started to do more and more adventurous trips. My only real concern came late in the afternoons when the sea breeze might die off. On a few occasions our little fleet was left with a two-mile paddle to get back in time for tea and cakes in the afternoon. It is a slow business propelling a large dinghy with only a canoe paddle on each side.

One day I had been with Bill's group and the wind had died away completely when we were still a long way from the club. We were half an hour late for afternoon tea and Bill was appalled. "You gannets," he said to the staff sitting round the coffee table, "you've not even left us a scone."

That evening I met Vic after dinner. "Sailing is a bit of a problem without any rescue boat, Vic," I said, hopefully. "Is there any chance of getting one?"

"Well, Peter." Vic scratched the back of his neck. "I will be getting one, but not until next year. There's no money left for a big item like that."

"Oh, pity…. You see, very often the wind dies away in the afternoon and we're left stranded." Today we had to paddle all the way from Kirn."

"From Kirn!" He laughed. "That will keep you fit." He scratched his chin. "I shall think about it and let you know."

True to his word he came back to me the next day. "Peter, about that rescue boat you wanted."

"Oh yes?"

"Well, we just haven't the money left." I groaned, and he carried on: "However, we could buy a little outboard motor. It would mount easily on the back of your wayfarer."

"Oh Yes, I suppose so." I could see the possibilities. "Yes, I could tow the other three boats back if it was flat calm."

So, the next day a small outboard motor was delivered from Robertson's Boat Yard. I carried a large water tank into the courtyard and filled it with a hosepipe connected to a tap in the stores. The motor was fitted to the tank and after filling it with two-stroke fuel I tried to start it. I pulled and pulled the starter cord, but I could not get it to start. Roger came out to look, and I stopped to take off my sweater. "It's warm work. I'm beginning to think there is something wrong with this outboard."

"Mm." He examined the motor and smiled. "Well, Pete. If all else fails, read the instructions." He laughed and went back to work. I did read the instructions, but it seemed I was doing everything correctly. I removed and cleaned the spark plug and checked the air filter, but it still wouldn't start, and I was getting frustrated with it.

When Rusty arrived back from a day on the hill he saw me struggling and took over. "It's like one we had at the outward-bound school. Great little outboard." He pulled and pulled but not even a splutter.

By this time Bill had arrived with his group who had been climbing all day. "You just pull this cord, don't you?" He wound the cord round the head then stopped to put down his rucksack and roll his sleeve up. "Right – stand back." He gave a great yank on the starter cord and when it reached its full extent, it broke. "Damn it," he said as he passed the cord to me. "It's broken Pete."

117

"Yes." Rusty laughed. "We can see that, Bill."

I mended the cord and over the next few days we would stop whenever we passed the outboard, which was still attached to the water tank. We all tried to start the motor and although it sometimes teased us by spluttering a few times we could not get it to run.

I saw Bill one day, when he thought nobody was watching. He looked round furtively and gave a few violent pulls on the starter cord. When it didn't start, he kicked the water tank and walked off.

After a few days of trying, I eventually I took the outboard motor off the water tank, lifted it into the mini-bus and drove to Robertson's yard. I went into a long workshop with wood dust on everything and the lovely smell of timber that reminded me very much of my days as an apprentice. I was directed to the foreman.

"We bought this outboard motor from you but I'm afraid there's something wrong with it."

"Ach, noo." He seemed quite concerned. "What's the matter with it?"

"It just won't start, I'm afraid."

"Won't start, eh?" He patted the top of it. "Well, noo. Take it over there to old Cameron." He pointed to an old man at the end of the workshop.

I walked between the benches where men were working with hand tools on timber shapes that must have been parts of yachts I didn't recognize, until I came to an old chap who looked as if he should have retired at least ten years earlier. He was wearing a dusty blue boiler suit. On his head was a dusty tartan cap that he wore at an angle.

"Mr. Cameron," I said. "The foreman has sent me over with this outboard. It's broken." He didn't look pleased to see me or the motor.

"Broken? What's the matter with it?"

"It won't start." Then, with the confidence of one who had owned a two-stroke motorcycle for some years, I added. "Must be a fault in manufacture. We've tried everything."

"Woon' start." He looked at it suspiciously for some time but didn't seem keen to touch any part of it. Eventually he said. "Lift it onto there," and pointed to an outboard bracket that was mounted on a bench. "Won't start." He mumbled to himself as he fumbled with the choke and carburettor. Then he wound the starting cord a couple of times round the head.

He seemed to be ready to pull the cord, and I interrupted him. "You'll have to use all of the cord."

He looked at me blankly and didn't seem to understand, so I said. "You will have to wind all of the cord round the block."

He took no notice and gave the cord a feeble, half-hearted pull. To my stunned surprise and embarrassment, the outboard immediately fired into life and smoke enveloped the old chap as the motor roared and the propeller spun round frantically. He turned the throttle lever down and shouted to me. "Yer say it won't start? What's the matter with it?"

Completely embarrassed, I stuttered some feeble explanation, but he took no notice and stopped the engine. I was very pleased when I had loaded the outboard into the mini bus and, very embarrassed, was able to escape from the boat yard.

Never again did that little outboard fail to start. I would go off with my little fleet of sailing dinghies every day knowing that if the wind died away, I could confidently pull the starting cord and the outboard motor would tow us back to the sailing club. Vic's unscientific comment was, "outboards can be a bit tricky. Two-stroke engines can be very temperamental at times."

*

I was very aware that we lived in a small community and the local people found our adventure centre a most interesting new topic of conversation. Everything we did was noted by the locals. Even in remote places where we had never seen a soul, someone would have noticed us. We might have been inspecting a cliff and swinging on the end of a rope. Someone would quietly ask while I was in the local pub, "Having some trouble the other day? Problem, was there?"

"Problem?" I stopped drinking.

"Aye." They would look at me seriously. "I heard someone had to be rescued from the crag." My explanations never seemed to fully convince them.

Students often capsized while kayaking in the loch and no matter how quick our rescue, someone would have noticed. If we had been practising a capsize drill with the sailing dinghies it would be noted a few days later when someone, who probably sailed a huge deep-keeled boat, would casually remark to me in the sailing club,

"Your plastic boats. They go over easy, don't they?" and he would shake his head solemnly.

The sheep rescue that Bill and I had done had already been discussed at length in the local pubs, and now this embarrassing incident with the outboard motor would soon be round all the boating circles and cause much tongue-clicking and laughter. They would laugh, but in many small ways they showed that they quite enjoyed having us 'Sassenachs' around. They were always willing to help if we needed them; I was never shown

119

anything but open friendship. I soon lost my London ways and returned this friendship with a smile and wave whenever I passed someone.

CHAPTER 20: NEW INSTRUCTOR

We often had instructors working at the centre who were volunteers, and the one that I remember particularly well was Mark. I first met him when his car pulled up near me as I was repairing kayaks outside the workshop.

With a posh accent he said, "Hello. I'm looking for Bill. Is he around?"

"Yes, he's working in the stores." I walked across to the car and pointed down towards the courtyard. "You can park down there."

"Oh, thank you." He had a charming smile, which set off a relaxed face.

Before he could drive off, I said, "You must be Mark, then."

"Yes."

"Bill told us you were coming. I'm Peter, one of the instructors." We shook hands. "You were at university with Bill, I understand?"

"Yes, but a couple of years behind. We were in the university climbing club together. Your boss said I can do some voluntary instructing for my board and keep, so here I am."

"Great. We can always use help. I'll see you at dinner."

Mark settled in so quickly that I felt he had been around for a long time. He had dark wavy hair, which fell from a central parting. He dressed in a casual but smart manner and was always clean-shaven. He was very confident socially but managed to come across to people as someone who needed help. This quiet manner and his good looks quickly made him a favourite amongst the 'fair sex'. The students thought him wonderful, but this was nothing compared to the older ladies working in the kitchen. They mothered him, and he took full advantage of their generosity. He would be given all types of treats from the kitchen such as cakes for the evening, extra helpings of desert and more fruit in his packed lunch. I even heard Mrs McClusky, whose children were about Mark's age, offering to mend a hole in one of his shirts.

Rock climbing needed more than one instructor with each group, and Mark joined every group. He also led mountain walks and joined Bill or Rusty on the overnight camps at the end of each course.

We made each programme as interesting as possible, but in the winter it sometimes became difficult. The entire programme was in the mountains, and this didn't suit every student. Some of them got fed up walking, particularly if they developed a blister from wearing boots. It was okay if the weather was fine, but often clouds and rain would sweep across the hills for a week at a time. Sometimes we wished that we had an activity that could take place indoors.

One day in particular, it was bad. An occluded weather front had been sitting over the west coast since midnight, and dense cloud, pushing low down on the mountains, meant that we had seen very little beauty in the hills. Most of the day we had navigated by map and compass and cold rain had fallen wearily down upon us all since we left early in the morning.

We were sitting round in the staff room nursing cups of tea and moaning about the weather when Vic, no doubt feeling warm and dry from a day in his palatial office, swept in through the door.

He strode across the carpet with a wide grin, like a father giving his children a treat. "I am giving each group a break from the hills," he said. We could tell he was pleased with himself and stopped pouring tea and eating cake to listen. "I've arranged that each group can have a day in Rothesay swimming pool. You can take three kayaks and teach basic skills." He stood there beaming.

"Oh, good idea Vic." My feelings of envy at his day in the cosy office immediately passed and I thought what a fine boss he was.

Bill was nursing a cup of steaming tea with both hands. "It'll make a pleasant change from bog trotting."

Roger always spoke softly. "Perhaps we could take some snorkel kit as well. I have two sets that could be taken."

"Yes," said Rusty. "I have a set and Pete has a set as well."

I was getting really enthusiastic. "Yes. We could have kayaking at one end and snorkelling at the other."

In the next free day, I made a timber frame that fitted onto a van roofrack and would carry four kayaks. Mark joined me on our first swimming pool day. Our group of students were in good spirits as we drove up the winding road that led to Glen Lean. Lower down there was dense woodland but up here there was just the open glen with a few hill farms at a distance from the road. At the far end of the glen, we dropped down to sea level and along the shore of beautiful Loch Striven. Twisted oak forests grew down to the edge of the white-flecked ocean, and very few houses interrupted the empty landscape. We drove round the end of the loch and I selected a low gear for the long climb over Auchenbreck Pass.

Mini-buses in those days didn't seem engineered for a full load. There was seating for twelve but neither the engine, brakes nor bodywork seemed strong enough for the weight the vehicle was supposed to carry. The bodywork and doors rattled, and the poor little engine whined away getting hotter and hotter until we were over the top of the pass.

I cruised carefully down to sea level again and along the deserted, wooded shore of Loch Riddon. The narrow loch on our right expanded as it met other lochs, and we eventually stopped at a small village: the wee clachan of Colintraive.

Rothesay is on the island of Bute, so we had to get the ferry across the narrow stretch of water called the Kyles of Bute. I parked at the top of a wide concrete ramp that sloped down to the water's edge and sat looking through the windows at the wonderful scenery. The open rocky shoreline was completely empty of humans and the birds had it all to themselves. There were black and white oystercatchers in busy groups picking along the edge of the receding tide. A few cormorants were standing on the larger rocks with their wings outstretched and their beaks aloof as they stood facing into the wind. There were hundreds of sandpipers nearby but their camouflage was so good that we only noticed them when they took off together in a huge rippling flock. I felt very lucky to live in such a wonderful spot.

The noise of a throaty engine starting up brought me back from dreaming. The small flat-bottomed ferry had left the other side and was chugging across the water towards us. The heavy metal ramp was lowered to rest on the concrete, but there were no cars to come off, it was there just for us. I drove slowly aboard the open platform and it rolled gently with our weight. A man with a leather bag to collect money came over to me. I expected to hear a soft Scottish accent but to my complete surprise he spoke in an accent that I knew very well; he must surely come from the east end of London.

"Allo mate. Wher'r ya goin? Ow many of yer?"

"Eleven of us for Rothesay please. But what about you? You're a long way from home aren't you"?

"Yeh." He laughed. "My missis is from Bute. I'm from the smoke, never go back though."

As I looked around at the quiet water, the birds in the sky and the empty oak woodlands that ran along the coast, I thought to myself, 'Nor will I. I'll never go back to live in London'. And I never have.

With just our vehicle on board, the ferry 'crabbed' across the strong current, and soon we were driving the short distance to the little holiday and port town of Rothesay.

The pool was empty and we had a most successful day with me teaching kayaking and Mark looking after the students who were snorkelling.

The first part of the drive home also went well. Once again, we were the only vehicle on the ferry and I drove easily along the empty road and over the pass, which dropped down to Loch Striven. The road running down to the end of the loch is one long incline, but luckily, is fairly straight. I got into a low gear and went slowly down but our speed started to increase. I applied the brakes but we continued to gradually gain speed. I pressed harder on the pedal. "The brakes are pathetic," I mumbled to Mark. The engine was whining in second gear but I was too worried to change down again and stood on the brake pedal. "Don't know if I can stop it," I said, rising high off my seat in the effort.

Mark didn't reply and I had a glance at him. He was staring straight ahead and gripping the dashboard. The students had all gone silent in the back. We were not going fast but were still gaining speed. It was a bad feeling to realise that I could not stop and I just prayed that nothing on the road would get in our way. Luckily, the road was completely deserted and as we reached the end of the steep section and the road began to level out, I realised that we were slowing.

Eventually my effort with the brakes paid off and we eventually jerked to a stop. It was not much of a jerk, but enough to send the four kayaks and the metal roof rack sliding down the windscreen and over the bonnet to land on the road in front of us. The students peered over my shoulder to look with wide eyes at the boats and roof rack sprawled across the empty road.

During the days ahead, we all agreed that driving over the steep roads with a full load of students, their kit and kayaks was not very wise, and Roger had a much better idea: "We can leave the kayaks at the pool. Then Hamish will drive you to Dunoon and you can get the Mc Brain ferry to Rothersay."

So, on the next course my group of teenagers climbed into the mini-bus and Hamish tried to start the engine. The engine turned wearily but it wouldn't start. After doing this a few times the battery was flat.

"Right," I turned to the group. "All out to the back and push." With plenty of groaning and a bit of laughing, we managed to push it out of the courtyard and up the steep drive. After a brief pause to gather our strength, we pushed it along the drive in an effort to bump the engine into life, but it wouldn't start.

Mark was red in the face. "In future we should leave this vehicle at the top of the drive," he said.

We all pushed again and this time there were a few splutters, the engine started and out from the exhaust came a great cloud of black smoke. The students jostled back inside and we jerked along on our way to the ferry. We had lost about half an hour and it would be touch and go that the ferry was still there.

It was still at the pier but, even as the students were getting out of the bus, the ferry moved away from the dock and picked up speed on its way down the widening Clyde.

"Damn it." I turned to Hamish. "We've missed it."

"Och, no," he said. "If we hurry, we'll catch it at Innellan."

"Oh, it stops there?"

"Aye, its stops at Innellan." The students clambered back in again and Hamish put his foot down along the coast road. It wasn't far to Innellan and the ferry had quite a start on us. It seemed to be going surprisingly quickly, but the road was empty and we were gaining on it. When we got to Innellan I was relieved to find we had enough time to walk down the pier in a relaxed mood as if we had intended to catch the boat there all the time.

I made sure we never missed the ferry again, and this regular trip down the Clyde was a highlight of our week during the winter. The ferries on the Clyde are large as the sea can get rough, and during the summer they are full with tourists. However, during a winter morning, the ship was almost empty. I got to know the stewards well and they would bring me some free biscuits and coffee in appreciation of the young clients I had brought. It was a wonderful start to the day.

*

Our visits to the swimming pool stopped as the summer came on as kayaking and sailing could then take over. The weather got warmer and with the moist air the midges returned. Mosquitoes are bad but at least one can hear them. Midges are so small they can't be heard and even seeing them is difficult. However, we could certainly feel them. Luckily for me I spent a major part of each summer sailing on the ocean, where it was too windy for midges. But even on the grass by our sailing base the midges were sometimes a nuisance, so in the forest they were unbearable.

We rubbed on repellents and this helped a little, but around our local climbing crag they were impossible. On a still, moist day we could not use the cliff at all but had to drive to another crag along the coast. With a strong sea breeze, the little blighters were not nearly so bad. The bites itched for the rest of the day and little red marks could be seen on faces, necks and any skin that was exposed. We complained bitterly but by the next day it was usually forgotten; they were unpleasant but not serious.

They were not a real health hazard for any of us. Except for Mark. Mark suffered more than any person I have ever known. He plastered repellent onto his face and hands, but one day he wore climbing britches. During the day the midges found a gap between the top of his socks and his britches. The next day there was a wide swelling right round both legs. It was so bad that Vic made him go to hospital in Dunoon. They gave him an injection and a course of pills and from that time on he could not instruct rock climbing if the midges were really bad.

125

In subsequent years I often thought of the serious affect the midges had on Mark. Perhaps they could tell he had an illness long before anyone else knew.

*

That Mark couldn't instruct rock climbing didn't matter too much, for his time at the centre was coming to an end. He came in for afternoon tea one day in June and I said to him, "So, you leave in a couple of weeks, Mark?"

"Yes." "Are you starting a job?"

"No." He paused to take another jam scone. "I'm going on honeymoon."

I laughed. "Honeymoon! You'll need to find a girl and get married first."

He smiled in an abstract sort of way. "Jayne and I are getting married in July. The twenty-seventh." He hesitated. "Yes, it's the twenty seventh of July ... I think."

There was a stunned silence and everyone stopped eating, and even Morag, who had been reading a magazine, looked up. She was the first to speak. "Are you serious, Mark? Are you really getting married?"

"Yes. Yes, I'm getting married." He looked quite hurt.

"But you never even mentioned a girlfriend." It took us a while to take this all in.

Apparently, he had been courting Jayne for two years and the wedding had been planned long ago. He stretched his legs out contentedly. "She's just finished university. I'm going to ask Vic if she can come and stay for my last week."

When Jayne appeared, she was just what I would have imagined Mark's girlfriend would be like. She was very attractive, with red hair tied back, a good figure, a wonderful easy smile, and she was confident with all of us. Most of the time she wore jeans and a loose sweater and I never saw her use make-up.

Mark's last night was also the end of a course. On the last night of every course, we had a traditional ceilidh. The teenage students all knew dances like The Dashing White Sargent or an Eightsom Reel and even the awkward lads knew these traditional Scottish dances. Mark had made himself the compère of these last-night celebrations and became excellent at getting everyone involved. He played the guitar well, and Roger made up a song about the activities and staff for each course. So, during the ceilidh the two of them always had a duet with the students and staff joining in the chorus. When everyone was warmed up and the inhibitions of the teenagers had diminished, Mark would lead a conga. A long line of all sixty students and staff would conga all round the centre. Then, in true Scottish tradition, we always ended up arm in arm in a great circle singing Auld Lang Syne. This last night made a wonderful finalé to every course and Mark was a great inspiration. We would all miss him when he left.

Both Mark and Jayne seemed equally vague about their honeymoon. "I think we shall drive across Europe," he told me one day. "We would like to do some walking in Austria."

"Lovely scenery," I said. "Perfect place for some easy alpine peaks."

"Yes, Peter. You know it pretty well, don't you?"

"Mm, suppose I do, yes. I have a good guidebook. Do you want to borrow it?"

"Yes please." So, I went upstairs and lent him the book and thought no more about it.

As they drove off to get married, I thought they had everything. They both had university degrees, both were confident and bright, and both had that elusive ability to get on well with everyone they met. Apart from Mark's allergic reaction to the midges he also seemed to have excellent health. I thought no more about the guidebook until a year later, when I needed it. I wrote to him at the address we had on file in the office.

A couple of weeks went by before I had a reply, but the letter wasn't from Mark. The letter I received was from his wife, Jayne. She apologised for not returning the book but wrote, "Very sorry Peter, but I can't find your guide book. Things are in a bit of a mess at home. You see, Mark got cancer. He died six months after we were married."

It seemed the little midges might have known more about Mark's health than any human.

127

CHAPTER 21: CAROL McNEIL AND ORIENTEERING

It had been a long winter, but signs of spring suddenly appeared one day. Daffodils were out in dense yellow bunches throughout the gardens, and on the hills the mountain Ash trees were covered with young, green leaves. The sheep were all up high on the hills again, and the lambs were at that stage when they were testing themselves. A group of them would find a small rise in the ground and spend an hour or more trying to be 'king of the castle' by standing on top with others rushing up and trying to butt them off. At other times they seemed to be full of the joys of living and would spring off the ground with all four legs at the same time as if some hidden force had knocked them into the air. They would get quite adventurous, wandering across the hillside like a gang of teenagers. However, I was always amused to notice that when something worried them, they would all rush straight back to the side of their ewe mother.

*

I had spent the day sorting out kayaks and sailing boats ready for the summer season. It had been a glorious day and we were all in good spirits when we met at five in the staff room. We were sitting round drinking tea and eating Morag's wonderful cakes when Vic suddenly said, "I've been looking for a girl."

There was silence for a few seconds. Bill choked on a piece of cake and when he caught his breath he said, "A girl? Me as well."

When the laughter had stopped Vic said. "I am going to appoint another permanent instructor and feel we should have a female on the staff. Roger and I are going to interview a girl next week."

Roger took a sip of tea. "Carol McNeil. Anyone know her?"

Heads were shaken. "No."

Vic put his cup down. "She seems very good indeed. She's the current national orienteering champion."

"National champion, eh," said Rusty. "Can she climb?"

"Oh, yes. She also canoes well and has been teaching dinghy sailing during the summer."

It was six weeks before Carol joined us on the staff and she certainly was very good indeed. Becoming a new member of our little group might have been difficult for some girls, but not Carol. She was charming and completely confident. Never did she seem to feel it necessary to prove herself. She was always well prepared for any instructional session, and for work around the house she wore a smart tracksuit that seemed to fit well with her short bouncy hair. We silently assessed her as a fair climber and mountaineer. She could sail a dinghy well and was very confident in teaching kayaking. I was quietly relieved that she had not applied for the job when I was appointed for, she was more qualified and able than I was.

Carol's best skill, however, was in orienteering. Roger wanted to introduce orienteering as a winter activity and thought we could all learn a lot from Carol. He arranged for her to set up a few training courses for the rest of us. Rusty, Bill and I thought that our navigation was rather good so we didn't immediately agree with Roger that we needed a training course. However, it was a chance for us to show how good we were at navigation, so we went along happily with the plans. We were very much in a party mood for the first event that Carol had organized. Vic had the good idea of inviting Jenny and Pat, the wives of Roger and Rusty, to join us, and even Morag came along.

It was intended to be a simple course but as soon as we saw the maps and instruction sheet our jollity quietly faded. The maps were different to any we were used to and even the very smallest feature and detail of terrain was marked on.

"Where did you get these maps?" I asked.

Vic said in a nonchalant manner. "Oh, Carol knocked them off and we had them printed at a college in Edinburgh." We studied them in worried silence, for they were very professional indeed.

Even Bill, with his degree in Geography, mumbled, "Brilliant job, Carol." With each map came an instruction and mark sheet and Carol explained all about them. However, she probably spent half an hour patiently answering our questions, for it was quickly obvious that us five men had a great deal to learn about orienteering.

Eventually we were ready and Carol set us off at three-minute intervals. Even though I knew the area around the gardens I still made plenty of mistakes. However, I eventually managed to find all the markers and rushed along to the finish just behind Bill. I was panting heavily and Bill had a red face. Rusty was already back and so were the three girls who were already sitting on a garden seat chatting and seemed quite unruffled.

"Did you find the marks?" I said. "Yes, thanks Peter." The girls grinned happily.

They had obviously done a much quicker time than Bill or I, so Bill said, "Did you get them all?"

Jenny and Morag nodded and Pat said, "Yes," with an easy smile. "Did you find them all?"

"It's good fun, this orienteering," said Jenny.

Bill, Rusty and I tried to look nonchalant but we said no more. Carol had prepared a number of orienteering schemes for the students and we did them all. We started to improve on our first performance, but usually the girls finished ahead of us. What we couldn't understand was that the girls seemed to only jog round the courses and never seemed to break into a sweat, while us men ran off at a good speed. We would finally charge across the finishing line panting like Olympic athletes, sweating profusely, and with scratched arms and legs from the bushes. I must have run twice the distance necessary in correcting navigation mistakes. As we improved our orienteering skills, the courses became harder. Carol organized what she called a 'map memory exercise' and I did some studying to try and improve my performance against the girls. After all, we were the instructors who were supposed to have this expertise in navigation. But the 'map memory' course needed a special skill. Previously, we had a map and instructions to take round the course, and although I often went wrong, I could eventually find my way around. On Carol's map memory course we had no maps. There was a small piece of map clipped to a bench at the start of the course. It was only a small piece cut from the whole map and showed the way only to the next orienteering mark.

Bill was first to start and rushed off with the small piece of map clutched in his hand. "Bill, stop ... stop!" shouted Carol. "You can't take that piece of map with you. You have to memorise it. That's why it's called a map memory exercise. We all need to look at it."

"Oh, er, yeh." Bill rushed back, threw the map on the bench and quickly disappeared amongst the trees. At each mark, fixed to a tree, was another small piece of map, and this covered the next 'leg' of the course. After studying the tiny map carefully, we had to remember the way and run off to the next mark. Three times I blundered through bushes and into small stream valleys looking for a mark. Eventually I gave up and had to rush back to the last small piece of map. Even finding my way back took a lot of time. I passed Bill and Rusty a few times, both running in different directions, but none of us was laughing. Once again, Jenny and Pat beat all the instructors, with Vic coming in third.

The events didn't do a great deal for my confidence but it certainly brought everyone together. Not only did these little events bring the instructors together but it also made a happy extended family with the wives. In modern jargon it was an excellent 'team building' exercise that I was to remember in the years to come. We were lucky to have Carol on the staff.

CHAPTER 22: SAILING ... IN TIME FOR TEA

Instructors were not always on time. Sometimes we were late for breakfast. Sometimes we were a little late to meet our classes, and we often seemed to be a bit late for staff meetings. However, there was one thing we were never late for and that was teatime.

Five o'clock each afternoon was a favourite time for all of us. We would come in after a day of rock climbing or mountaineering and chat about incidents that had happened. Then, precisely at five o'clock, Morag would wheel in a trolley heavy with delicate scones, cakes and a giant teapot. Particularly after a day of wind and rain, teatime in the staff room was a haven of good living. The huge window faced the sun. It gave the white woodwork and delicate wallpaper a bright and clean atmosphere. There were no cluttered notice boards like one might see in the average school; only charming pictures were hung on the walls, and with fine mahogany furniture the whole room made me feel that I was wealthy. A thick pile carpet muffled the sounds of our laughter as we sat around in the vast bay window that looked across the lawn and towards the mountains.

It was during teatime that Vic came sweeping in with a book. "Here you are, Bill." He dropped the heavy book onto Bill's lap, which made him sit up with a jolt. "All you need to know about sailing."

"Oh, ta Vic," said Bill through a mouthful of sponge cake. "Any chance of some staff training?"

Vic poured a cup of tea and turned to me. "Peter, you are both off the programme for one day next week. You can work together on basic sailing."

I grinned at Bill. "Oh, excellent."

Staff training wasn't really like work for us but Bill and I took it seriously. We were away straight after breakfast and spent the whole day afloat covering all the basic techniques. He came on well and gained great confidence. Perhaps he gained too much confidence. He started to instruct sailing and things went okay until he became too enthusiastic one day.

The wind picked up and I could hear his voice across the water, shouting to his students: "You're doing great. Sit well out, everyone. Keep the boat level. Sit right out like this." With his feet under the tow strap, he leaned well out over the side of the dinghy but his weight was too much. The tow strap broke. He immediately toppled back into the water and as soon as his head broke surface I heard him shouting to the students. "Stop, STOP! Let go of everything ... let go of EVERYTHING!" The students were bright, but they had been told to aim at a buoy in the distance. It took them quite a while to cautiously let go of everything so that the boat slowly came to a stop. By then I had picked up Bill in my boat and all he said was, "Bugger."

Most people would not have thought Bill an academic, but he was. He had a degree and a sharp brain and was an avid reader. He studied the sailing book that Vic had lent him and took delight in knowing the names of all the parts of the boat and rigging. He would often tease me with obscure bits of information that he found.

"Pete," he said, while munching on a rock bun. "I feel that you should fit the boats with 'baggy wrinkles'."

I frowned. "Baggy what?"

He looked aghast. "Baggy wrinkles." He couldn't quite conceal a smile. "Baggy wrinkles, man. Surely you know what baggy wrinkles are!"

"Well … er … no." I made a mental note to find out what baggy wrinkles were.

"You're head of sailing and you don't know what baggy wrinkles are?" When the laughter had died down, he spoke more seriously. "Anyway, Pete, I've been doing a bit of reading, and to progress in sailing it seems that I need to do some racing."

"Oh … mm…. Yes."

"Rusty is keen too." He turned to Rusty sitting in the corner. "Aren't you Rusty?"

"Um … well. Yes. Okay." He didn't sound too certain but Rusty was a fairly good sailor.

"There," said Bill. "Rusty could helm and I will crew for him. We could come down and join the club races on a Wednesday evening."

"Mm," I nodded. "Yes. Okay. It's a good idea. Racing is certainly a good way of improving."

On Wednesday evenings I acted as the crew for a local man called Kenneth. It had given me good experience of more advanced racing techniques and would certainly help Rusty and Bill. Apart from that, I felt it good for us to get to know more of the local people in the area. They were a very friendly group at the sailing club. They were mostly professional people, a bit older than us, and very pleasant - the sort of people that one might meet at church on Sunday.

On Wednesday evening, before the sailing race I went down early and helped Rusty and Bill sort out one of our dinghies. Then I joined my own skipper, Kenneth, to prepare his boat.

All the boats were eventually on the water, sailing around, ready for the start. At the ten-minute gun the boats started to close up in an effort to make a fast start across the line. During these tense manoeuvres, Kenneth

132

put our dinghy onto a 'starboard tack' and was quickly approaching other boats on a 'port tack'. This meant that we had the 'right of way' over the other boats and they all turned away.

They all turned except one: the wayfarer sailed by Rusty and Bill. It was clear to me that we were on a collision course; we were sailing fast towards the side of the wayfarer. Kenneth called out politely, "Water," which was the command for the wayfarer to get out of the way. The two boats were closing fast and there wasn't much time for a change of course. I became alarmed when I noticed that Bill was helming the wayfarer and should have changed course, but he obviously didn't know the 'rules of the road' and kept sailing straight on.

Kenneth shouted urgently, "Water! Ahoy there, WATER!" It was a beautiful evening and sounds travelled easily across the sea so that all the other boats had heard the urgent shout of 'Water!'.

Bill steered straight ahead and only when Kenneth had swerved dramatically round the wayfarer's stern did Bill turn to shout in his cockney accent, "Bugger off! We were 'ere first."

My skipper turned to me with a shocked expression. "Are they from the adventure Centre?"

"Er, yes. New to sailing."

*

Despite these incidents Bill was a good and caring instructor and taught the basics of sailing so that all his students enjoyed themselves. However sometimes the weather and conditions meant that instructors needed more than a basic skill. Bill's group were sailing one day when grey clouds were chasing each other across the sky. His group of sixth form students were a pleasant bunch and as we bumped along in the old mini-bus on the way to the sailing club, he shouted to me above the engine noise, "Peter, the group would like to go on a trip if possible."

"Oh." I turned to Carol who was also instructing that day. "What do you think, Carol?"

"Well, they're a smart group." She peered out of the windscreen. "Make a nice change to go for a short cruise, if the weather seems okay."

"Okay," I said. "We can make for Dunoon. We'll take the sandwiches, warm clothes and everything with us."

There was a chilly wind coming from the east so everyone put on their waterproof suits with a life jacket over the top. With the wind coming straight onto the shore it was easy to hoist both the large Genoa and the full mainsail, and the other two boats were soon cruising around offshore and waiting for me.

I struggled down with the outboard motor and fixed it onto the transom of my boat while one of the students held the bow. "Right, I think we're ready." I had a last look around the boat. "In you get," I said to my three students, and we beat out towards a sinister black American submarine that seemed to be trying to hide in the depths of the loch. Once in clear water I eased off the sails and the students took control. We changed our course slightly to go on a 'reach' towards the Point of Strone. The Americans also had a huge floating dock near the mouth of the loch, and by the time we had made the short distance towards it the wind had certainly increased. The wind had also 'backed' quite a bit. With the sails eased further out, we were creaming along on a broad reach.

Bill sailed his dinghy close to me and shouted across, "Peter.... Wind is getting up."

"Yes, it's a bit strong.... We'll reef." I held three fingers in the air. "Three rolls and change the Genoa for the little jib."

It took a while to change the sails and by the time we set off again white horses had been whipped up across the water and the wind had backed even further. Now we were 'running'. I would normally have to gybe to make our course but I didn't want to chance this manoeuvre in the rough conditions.

I tightened the sails. "Ready to go about," I said to the crew and after a pause. "Lee ho!" and with flapping of the jib the boat rounded to the new course. We were now in a comfortable position to make for Kirn. The mountains that backed the small coastal hamlet were blocking the worst of the wind so there were no waves or whitecaps as we sailed close inshore. However, by the state of the sea offshore, it was easy to see that the wind was blowing strongly. It was getting too serious and I decided that we would go ashore by Kirn pier.

I sailed close to the other two boats, which seemed quite happy now that we were in sheltered water. "We'll go ashore," I waved an arm, "and have an early lunch." I pointed along the shore. "Kirn.... Go in at Kirn pier." The other two boats were making better speed than mine, and had already landed when I approached. However, they had landed on the near side of the little pier where they were finding that the shoreline was covered with nasty boulders.

Bill waved an arm indicating it was no good and shouted out, "No good, Pete. Too rocky for the boats."

"Oh," I let the sails flap while I shouted back. "It's okay on the other side. The far side of the pier is gravel." I sailed away from the shore and in a few minutes was on the west side of the pier and went ashore with my crew. With two on each side we pulled the wayfarer up the beach a little and looked back to see where the others were. Bill was walking round the top of the pier with the students and in a couple of minutes they joined me.

Although the morning had been short, the students were quite happy to have an early lunch and we all strolled up the beach to sit on the bank of grass that ran down from the coastal road. With the increase of wind, the morning had been enough of an adventure for the students and it was pleasant to be out of the wind and on safe ground. But although their adventure for the day had finished, mine was just about to start.

*

From my elevated position on the bank of grass I saw Carol and one student tie Bill's boat behind hers. She was a good sailor and evidently intended to move the two boats and bring them up on the beach by mine. It wasn't very far and would have only taken a few minutes with both sails up. However, this was a new experience for Carol and she only hoisted the jib at the front of her boat. With only the headsail, and towing another boat, it quickly became obvious that she would not be able to sail into the wind and get back onto this 'weather shore'. I sat helplessly as the two boats were swept further and further from the shore. The wind was increasing rapidly now, and the further out to sea the more they were away from the shelter of the land. Carol tried to get the mainsail up but with the boat tied on behind it was all too much. It only made the boats go faster and that meant faster away from our sheltered shore.

"Bill," I stood up. "I'm going out to Carol. I'll leave you with the group."

"Yeh. Okay."

I put my life jacket on and turned as I walked down to my boat. "See you in a few minutes."

I really did think I would be back in a few minutes, but even before I reached my boat, in the distance I saw Carol's boat tip to one side. I stood on the beach and watched as her wayfarer mast and sail slowly disappeared from view. They had capsized. Even with the help of all the students, it took me a few minutes to get my boat back on the water. I tied my sails down as quickly as I could, clambered aboard and lowered the outboard motor. The little engine started first time and I swung the dinghy round to head for Carol, but they were now a long way out to sea. The outboard motor was only small and although I was going as fast as I could I was still a long way from them when the Clyde ferry left Dunoon pier.

Going on its regular course would put the two little dinghies right in its way. The great ship slowed and then it stopped. I could see it way in the distance and to my amazement it launched a lifeboat. Not with an engine but with two fellows rowing long oars. Well before I was anywhere near,

135

they had rowed across, picked Carol and the student from the water, and rowed back to the huge ferry, which was rolling gently in the swell. By the time they had winched up the lifeboat I was alongside the two dinghies.

Passengers were lined up on the port rail looking down at me. There was a great blast from the ship's horn, which scared the life out of me, then the engines thumped into action and the ferry grew small on its way to Gourock on the far side of the Clyde.

I wasn't going to leave the boats in the middle of the ocean; they were two-thirds of my little fleet. I pulled round to Carol's boat, which was lying just below the surface of the water. Taking hold of the top of the mast I worked my way down the shroud and after a struggle, the capsized boat came up the right way.

Now I had chance to look at the situation and could see why Carol had not immediately righted the dinghy. The stern buoyancy hatch had come off and the locker was flooded. This meant that the back of the boat was underwater, so I couldn't bail it out. I could see no way out except to tow it like it was, up the right way but still full of water. Of course, there were two boats, one tied behind the other. The one at the back was still upright and fine, so I tied them onto the back of my boat so that we were all in a long line.

The wind was still increasing and rain blasted across the sea. Everywhere there were whitecaps. Although the waves were not particularly big, they were very steep, and as each one hit, the spray came over the boat, and more importantly, spray came over the outboard motor. I tried and tried but the motor had been soaked by the spray and I could not get it started.

I should have had a basic tool kit, but I didn't, so the only thing left to me was to sail. I tried to hoist the mainsail, but with the boats tied to the back, I could not get my boat pointing into the wind. The only sail I could hoist was the jib. With only a headsail I could not beat back into wind and the shore I had left. I looked around to get my bearings and was surprised to find that the visibility was so reduced by rain and mist that I could see no land in any direction. The only thing I could do with the little jib sail was head across the wind and try to reach a coast anywhere. "Hellensborough," I thought. That was my likely landing, but this little town was about eight miles away and also on the far side of Loch Long. I had no choice and settled to the course which I thought was the right direction, although I could still not see land anywhere.

I must have been rolling along very slowly for two hours when a fishing trawler came towards me through the mist. It passed me about fifty metres off my port side and two of the crew appeared and stared across. I was too embarrassed to shout for help and simply raised a hand as I wallowed in the steep seas. They continued on their course, but only for a short while. I was quite relieved when the trawler slowly circled and came back to stop, with its solid timber side of flaking paint close alongside.

The skipper and both crew members stood looking down at me for quite a few seconds and then the skipper shouted down. "Where the hell are ya goin?"

"Bit of trouble," I grinned.

"Aye, I ken see." He didn't grin.

I shouted across. "I'm trying for the Holy Loch. Can't get into wind though." The crew were pointing to the waterlogged dinghy and giving the skipper advice, but he seemed to take no notice. Then with a weary sigh he said "We'll tow ya to Strone."

Strone was the eastern point of the Holy Loch so I was delighted.

"Thanks very much. That would be great." The two crew leaped into action and one threw me a towrope that was as thick as my wrist.

I was worried. The trawler was so powerful and the dinghies so small and delicate in comparison, that towing them, with one full of water, might well break all sorts of things on my little plastic fleet. I stood there with the fat warp in my hand and shouted up to the skipper. "You'll have to be careful. Dinghies are not very strong."

"Aye," he raised his eyes as if asking God for patience. "Aye, I ken," and he returned to the wheelhouse.

The slow thump of the trawler engine changed note as the propeller turned and I took up the strain of the towrope. I was too concerned to tie it on but took one turn round the mast and held the end in my hands so that I could let it go if necessary. I waited for the great shock of the tow but it never came. I need not have worried for this skipper knew his boat and my delicate position far better than I did. He pulled away very gently and for the next hour towed me in perfect control towards Strone point.

Long before we got close to the shore the storm had passed and the coastline was clear. I was now well into sheltered water and the trawler stopped. One of the crew shouted down to me, "Close as we can go."

"Great." I stood up and released the tow. "I'll be fine now." As the crew pulled in the towrope the skipper came to lean over his gunwale. I raised a hand. "Many thanks. I'm very grateful. I could have been anywhere by now."

"Aye," was all he said, but this time he gave a wry smile. He went back into the wheelhouse and the powerful engine slowly gained speed and the trawler moved away, faster and faster into the distance. I waved towards the empty deck.

I only had a few metres to paddle towards the shore, but by the time I reached it a police car had stopped and from the back seat emerged the worried face of Carol. "Peter! Am I pleased to see you." Then with more concern, "The boats. Are they all okay?"

"Yes. They're fine. No damage." I joined her up on the shore road. "I think it easier if we contact Robertson's Boat Yard for a tow back to the clubhouse."

She nodded. "Yes. Oh, yes." "They have a small launch. Perhaps the police would contact them for us." Carol went off in the police car and they took her to our sailing base. I didn't have to wait long, for, by the time I had bailed out the boats and sorted and stowed the bits and pieces, the Robertson's launch had appeared round the point.

I was most embarrassed to recognize the old man at the tiller. I recognised the tartan cap pushed to one side, and his dusty blue boiler suit. It was Mr. Cameron, the same old man who had started the outboard motor a couple of months before! I'm sure he recognised me but was kind enough not to show it, which saved me more embarrassment.

By tomorrow the whole local community would be discussing how, "Those people from the adventure centre had to be rescued ... yet again."

The tow back up to our sailing club was smooth and uneventful, and Carol was there to meet me with the minibus. "How did you get back across the Clyde?" I asked her as we drove along.

"We caught the next ferry," she grinned. "They didn't charge us, either. As we were soaking wet, they even gave us a free tea and a bacon butty." She laughed. "Apparently Bill contacted the police, then spent a few hours in Dunoon." She raised her eyebrows. "Nearly caused a search and rescue incident until the coastguard contacted the police."

"The coastguard contacted them?" "Yes. Said that a trawler skipper had radioed them on channel sixteen." She threw her head back happily and laughed out loud. "The skipper said he had three dinghies in tow and one Sassenach." I was pleased to get out of my wet clothes and after a quick bath I changed and went downstairs to the staff room. Everyone had heard about our day and there was plenty of laughter with comments about pirates, single-handed sailors and air-sea rescues.

Then Bill's voice rose above the laughter. "What an epic." He took a great wedge of chocolate cake and grinned. "But Pete," he put his arm round my shoulders. "We're still not late for afternoon tea."

CHAPTER 23: WINTER TRAINING

It was coming up to Christmas when Vic surprised us. "We have no students for the week after Hogmanay. We shall be doing some maintenance work. But," he smiled broadly and sat back in his chair, "I've booked the CIC hut on Ben Nevis for a few days of staff training."

We were delighted. Staff training was always popular but this trip would be special. Ben Nevis is great for winter climbing, and the CIC hut is perfectly nestled in the great bowl of the northern corrie.

Much of our routine work was instructing at a fairly low level. Of course, there were times when we had to use all of our skills to bring a group home safely. Perhaps if the weather turned really bad, or a student became ill or even had a minor accident; it was during those times that we had to use all of our experience. However, most of the time the work was well within our capabilities. We were all keen to improve our skills and this had to be done in our own time or on the few days of staff training. These were the times when we could learn from each other and I always learned many mountaineering skills, particularly from Rusty.

At coffee time he came over to me. "Peter, we have a few days off after staff training on the Ben."

"Yes, I believe so." "Would you be keen to stay up and do some ice routes?"

"Keen! Yes, that would be great."

"Good. I'll take my van up then."

The morning we were due to leave for Ben Nevis, Roger stopped me in the corridor. "Oh, Peter. There's some ice kit in the store. We have to share it out. The others have already taken theirs and apparently the rest is yours."

"Oh, okay Roger, I'll pick it up." I went to the store and on the floor was laid out kit that we could use, such as slings, karabiners, ice screws, rock pitons and a rope. It seemed quite a mound for one person, but I crammed it into my rucksacks and loaded it into the mini-bus.

We drove off in high spirits. We had everything we needed including a huge pile of food from the kitchens. Morag had organized the food for us and in her usual efficient manner she had even thought to give us a few treats such as a great slab of fruitcake.

Roger drove, and in a couple of hours we had crossed Rannoch Moor, gone down to Glencoe Village and reached loch Leven. It was easy to see our road just across the short stretch of water, but in those days, there was no bridge. It was another twenty minutes before we drove round the end of the loch, through Kinloch Leven and headed north towards Fort William.

The engine eventually spluttered into silence when we stopped at the end of the forestry track where our footpath began. We shared the food between us, shouldered our packs and started up the hill. I tried to keep up but got further and further behind, so by the time I eventually reached the CIC hut it was nearly twelve o'clock and the others were well established with a kettle boiling away.

Bill helped to take my rucksack off and said, "Christ, Peter. What have you got in here! It weighs a ton."

"Just my share of the kit."

"Your share of the kit! You have far more than the rest of us. You should have said something." He laughed and slapped me on the back. "Anyway, you're here now. Have this." He handed me a huge mug of tea.

The hut is always left with solid shutters over every window, so after undoing the nuts on the inside we went outside, brushed away the blown snow and removed the shutters. The few candles could now be blown out and I could look around. The CIC hut, deep in the bowl of the corrie and right below the huge buttresses and gullies that were now plastered with snow, is perfectly situated for climbing. Inside was just one large, dark, timbered room which had a mixed odour of damp wool, leather boots and paraffin. Bunkbed shelving ran the full length of one wall, and on the opposite wall a large cubicle rack had been made out of timber to store personal kit. At the far end was a worktop for stoves, and in the ceiling a rack to dry clothing. Standing right in the middle was a long table with bench seating on either side. With the deep snow outside, the whole room made me think of Scott of the Antarctic.

We sat round the table eating our snack lunch while Roger outlined the training he wanted to do. "There is no time to climb today but I thought we might do some survival practise." He grinned. "I would like everyone to sleep out tonight."

"Oh yes, good idea!" I was enthusiastic. "Perhaps work in pairs and dig a snow cave." He took a sip of tea. "You should have plenty of time to give yourselves a comfortable night."

Rusty and I teamed up together and after sorting out our kit we went outside and plodded up towards number four gully. Here in the corrie there were few colours, just the black and grey cliffs which were etched out more clearly in the winter by the whiteness of the new snow. We were looking for a steep bank of snow, but the slopes we explored weren't deep enough to dig a decent cave. We moved across to where a steep buttress reached down to the gully. There was a very deep base of snow here and although the slope was not very steep the wind had created a beautiful

140

hollow like a miniature canyon. On one side was the rock of the buttress and opposite was a vertical sweep of snow about six metres high.

"Perfect, Pete." Rusty pushed his ice axe deep into the vertical wall. "Just right for a snow cave." We placed our sacks well out of the way on a rock ledge and removed our warm clothing to put on waterproof tops and trousers. We only had our axes to dig with, and I followed Rusty down into the 'canyon' to the wall of snow.

"If we dig straight in like this," he said, marking out a tall but narrow doorway with his axe, "it will be easier to open it out inside." He started scraping away at the snow and I moved it back and out of the way. The snow was soft and we made good progress with Rusty being able to stand up in the doorway that he kept quite narrow.

Despite the weather being cold and windy we soon got warm and took turns until Rusty eventually said, "I think that's deep enough, Pete. Now we'll dig out the sleeping platforms on either side. Here … and here." He marked lines on the snow.

We were now digging deep into the cave and as we dug out and upwards a faint daylight filtered through the snow above. Eventually after two hours of digging the snow cave had been dug out and we stood together outside. "We need to lower the doorway to about here." Rusty marked a line that was probably level with the sleeping platforms inside. "We need some good snow blocks."

I poked the snow. "That might be a problem. It's soft round here." We explored nearby and eventually found a patch of wind-packed snow that was fairly firm. Rusty cut a large block out, but when we tried to pick it up it broke in two. However, with a bit of practise we managed to cut six blocks and carried them carefully over to the cave. Rusty prepared a ledge on either side of the doorway to take a 'lintel' and we carefully lifted a snow block into place. We gently placed the other blocks across and it wasn't long before we had filled in the top part of the opening. The doorway was now a low opening that could only be entered by crawling. The sleeping platforms were above the cold trough from the entrance. A perfect design.

We checked inside to make sure everything was ready for moving in and eventually shouldered our sacks and walked the short distance back down to the CIC hut. The others had been building an igloo and although it was finished, they realised the snow was not at all suitable. "The blocks were too soft," Bill laughed. "It got taller and taller and ended up more the shape of an old beehive."

"Good practise, though," Roger smiled. "But I think I shall sleep in the hut tonight."

While I was pouring tea for everyone, I thought about sleeping in our snow cave and decided it was so good it would be almost the same as sleeping in the hut. "I think I shall see what it's like just to sleep outside, on the snow," I said.

"Good idea, Pete," Bill said. "I'll join you. Let's just take the sort of things we would have if we were stuck out on a route." So, after dinner Rusty plodded off into the darkness towards his cave while Bill and I went off with our rucksacks to find a suitable place to lie down. We uncoiled two ropes and spread them out to act as a sort of mattress. Then on top we laid our rucksacks, which had inner extensions and were to act as a sort of sleeping bag, with our boots as a lumpy pillow. With all of our clothes on we squirmed as far down into our rucksacks as possible and then pulled our waterproof jackets over to cover the rest of us.

I pulled my woollen hat low down and lay there looking up into the night sky. There was a moon and I watched the clouds sweeping across the few stars that showed through. The rock buttresses and fine snow ridges were faintly lit by the moon on one side but totally black in the shadows. The mountain faces and snow filled gullies seemed to be painted in various shades of blue and looked particularly close and timeless. It was a glorious experience. My nose was getting cold so I covered my face and was soon asleep.

It must have been about two o'clock when Bill woke me. "Pete, you awake?"

"Mm."

"You cold?"

"Er - yes. Fairly."

"Well, we've proved we can do it but I've had enough." I heard him shuffling about. "I'm going into the hut."

I turned over and went back to sleep but it was a restless few hours. The cold was coming up from underneath and I was surprised how cold my legs were. I would wake, turn over in an effort to warm the cold spots, and go into a dose again. I kept looking at my watch: three, then four, then five and eventually at six I eased out into a cold wind, bundled everything up and staggered the short distance back to the hut. I was too cold to think of sleeping again, so I lit a stove and put on a kettle. By the time the water was boiling the others were shifting so I took them all a mug of tea.

"Oh, thanks Peter." Roger cupped the mug in his hands. "Just what I needed." He looked around. "Is Rusty back?"

"No. I'll finish my tea and go over and give him a shout."

It only took me ten minutes to reach the foot of the buttress but everything was different. The wind must have changed direction because snow had completely filled the deep canyon where the cave entrance

142

should have been. There was simply a snow slope running straight from the rocky buttress and no sign at all of the cave we had dug. Rusty was now more than two metres under the surface of the snow. I was a bit concerned for without ventilation of any sort it might be possible to use up the oxygen and become unconscious. I tried to picture exactly where the cave might be and after walking round in circles for a while, I came across a neat, round hole, about the size of a rabbit's burrow. Rusty had kept a small ventilation hole open.

I lay down on the snow and put my mouth to the hole. "Rusty," I shouted, and then listened. All I could hear was the wind blowing round the buttress. I shouted again. "Rusty, you there?" This time there was an answer deep down in the snow.

"Hi! That you Pete?"

"Yes. You're snowed in. The canyon has filled up."

"Oh." He seemed sleepy but completely calm. "I'll dig out through the roof."

"Do you want me to help?"

"No." His muffled voice came up to me. "The whole roof might fall in on top of me. I'll try and do it myself." I moved well to one side and waited out of the wind. It was probably fifteen minutes before an axe appeared from the hole, and shortly afterwards a gloved hand. There was quite a bit of mild cursing before Rusty's head, plastered with snow, appeared above the surface. "Good God, Pete. The snow has got right down my neck." He pushed his rucksack up to me and clambered out himself. After bending his head low and shaking as much snow off as possible, he walked back to the hut with me, to join the others.

Three stoves were purring away and the hut was full of steam from the damp clothes drying, but the smell of breakfast cooking was glorious.

After the meal we sat round the table drinking tea, and Roger outlined the training for the day. "I want us to cover basic instruction first, such as traversing with the axe, step cutting, and ice axe breaking." He turned to Rusty. "Rusty, in the afternoon I would like you to cover ice work such as cutting handholds and placing pitons. Is that okay?"

Rusty nodded. "Sure." Wearing hats and gloves and loaded with kit we plodded happily the short distance to the foot of Tower Ridge. Roger pointed with his axe. "Up there to the right is usually a bank of good firm snow."

We followed behind and in ten minutes came to the perfect place to practise. Roger was not the best mountaineer on our staff, but he was a fine instructor. He started right from basics, the sort of thing we might teach a group of beginners, such as kicking steps uphill and down again, then using the ice axe to cut steps up, across and down the slope. We put on our full waterproof suits and practised using the ice axe to stop a slip. He got us to slide down the slope feet first, head first, on our front and then on our backs. It was great practise and we got pretty warm walking up the slope each time.

Then Roger covered belaying by only using the axe. He drove the axe into the firm snow and tied a rope to it. Bill and I pulled on the rope and the axe came out easily. Then Roger dug a trench across the snow and placed the axe lying down into it. When the rope was fixed Bill and I pulled but it wouldn't shift. Rusty and Roger came behind me and all four of us leaned back. The rope stretched and we pulled harder and then all of a sudden, the axe came out and flew in a violent arc towards us. I spun round and bent double but I was saved from a savage blow because the axe hit Bill square on his buttock.

"Christ! Dangerous business this." He rubbed his seat. "That hurt."

When we had stopped laughing Roger took from his rucksack a flat metal plate that had a short wire loop fixed in the middle. "Now we will try this. It's called a 'Dead man'" He slide the pate into the snow at an angle and clipped a rope to the wire. He ran the rope down the slope to us and we gently pulled it but it didn't move. We pulled it harder and harder but we couldn't shift it. We walked up to look at the plate that had slide deeper into the snow. The Dead Man plate certainly was a better belay than anything else.

We moved to another spot for the afternoon session. Rusty led us up the gully a little way, where he had seen a slab of steep ice running along the foot of the rock buttress. It seemed perfect for instruction and we were soon busy strapping on our crampons. In those days there were no modern ice tools as there are today. To climb steep ice, one had to cut handholds with the axe, and these handholds usually became footholds as one moved up. Rusty gave us all sorts of tips on cutting the holds, and my years of experience as a joiner and using a hammer in both hands seemed to help. Then he covered placing ice screws and eventually spent some time in showing us how to place the new 'chrome molly' pitons. All of us had done snow and ice climbing before, but as we walked back to the hut, I certainly felt more confident about instructing this aspect at a higher level.

Roger and Bill moved about the hut collecting and packing their kit. In the fading light they set off down the hill and Rusty and I settled in for the night. There was no electricity, but a couple of paraffin lamps hung down and gave the whole hut a feeling of solid security from the snow, ice and wind outside.

The stoves purred as we cooked an evening meal, and the hut became fairly warm although we kept our down jackets on. I made a large pot of

144

tea and we sat round the table and thought about tomorrow. "So, Rusty," I passed him a steaming mug. "What route do you fancy tomorrow?"

"Well, if the conditions are okay I would like to have a go at Point Five."

Point Five gully had a reputation and I knew it to be hard. "Okay, if you think I'm up to it. I'm keen to have a go."

"It's a long route so we should have an early start."

"Yes. We don't want to be still on the route in the dark."

"If we get up at six we should be on the route by eight."

"Fine," I said. "Up at six o'clock." I liked the way that Rusty was so organized. I was always keen to be away in good time and we spent ten minutes sorting things out so that we were prepared for the morning. It was still early when I climbed up onto the upper bunk and wriggled down into my sleeping bag. I was happy and fell into a deep sleep.

We had no alarm clock and, as I expected, it was still dark when I woke up. I fumbled under the pillow for the torch and looked at my watch. It was rather difficult to see but with one hand to the top and one down below it was already six. "Rusty," I said in a coarse whisper. "Six o'clock."

"Oh." He sounded sleepy but I was impressed that he got straight out of bed and lit a candle. I primed the stove and soon had it purring away for tea. I started to prepare a pan of porridge but I felt very sleepy.

A candle was nearby and I looked at my watch again. Sure enough, one hand was to the top and one to the bottom but I had mixed up the hands. It was not six but only half past midnight. "Rusty. It's not six." I turned out the stove. "It's only twelve thirty."

Many people would have cursed me but all Rusty said was, "Oh…. Just after midnight?"

"Yes, sorry."

Without a word we put out the stove and candle and both got back into our sleeping bags and I fell fast asleep. The next time I woke it was seven o'clock and I quickly clambered down and lit the stoves to make up for my blunder during the night.

We made good time and, with our sacks already packed the night before, we closed the door of the hut and set off up the corrie in deep snow. It was an unpleasant grey dawn and windier than the day before although it seemed warmer. Rusty looked up at the clouds sweeping over the lip of the corrie that was way above us. "Wind is from the south west."

"Yes. Seems to be warmer."

"Mm." Rusty had looked at the route before and I followed him to the foot of the gully, which curved narrowly out of sight. We stamped a platform in the snow and looked up at the first pitch that I was to lead. "Looks okay, Pete," said Rusty, as we fixed our crampons.

"Mm. A nice slab to start with." I sorted out the slings and other gear for protection and cut the first handhold. With a kick to penetrate the front points of my crampons, I moved up. Then, with the left hand I cut another hold and moved up again. The ice was steep but I could stay in balance and I continued like this, left hand cut, right hand cut, until the angle eased and I was at the top. I found a thread belay and after I had chipped away some ice, I fixed a sling and tied on.

Rusty made short work of the slab and we soon stood together looking up at the next pitch. It was a steep and narrow chimney that was thick with ice but I could hear water running down the back and said. "Seems to be thawing."

"Yes." He took the slings, karabiners and pitons from me. "Just have to see." At first, he was able to bridge up, but then had to start cutting handholds. "Ice is really poor, Peter."

He managed to get a runner on and moved up another three metres, but even I could see from below that the ice was very bad indeed. He called down to me. "It's completely honeycombed." He stood in balance looking up the chimney. "I wonder if it gets better?"

After spending a little time placing another runner, he moved up a few metres and then stopped. "It's no good, Peter. The ice is completely rotten. I'm coming down."

If Rusty thought it too dangerous that was good enough for me. "Pity," I said. "It looks a good route."

He looked up the gulley. "Yes. Perhaps another time." We climbed down and walked back to the hut.

It took us an hour to pack our kit and tidy the hut. The last job was to replace the shutters and when I went outside, I noticed a real change in the weather. Strong wind was rushing in gusts down the corrie and the air felt humid. By the time we started down the hill the change in weather was more obvious. Rain and sleet started to sweep across the open hillside and we were pleased to reach Rusty's van before we got too wet.

As we drove down to the main road Rusty said, "It's early, let's call in and see Hamish." Rusty had worked as an instructor for Hamish McInnes, who ran mountaineering courses and was well known in mountaineering circles. Hamish had done remarkable things in the Alps and the Himalayas. He was also an engineer, and we pulled off the road at his little engineering workshop, which was half way up the rugged valley of Glencoe.

He was at a bench, and turned his wiry frame when he heard us come in. He gave a delighted smile and held out his hand. "Hi, Rusty. How's it going?"

"Hello, Hamish." Rusty turned to me. "This is Peter. He's also at Benmore. We've been on the Ben but the ice has gone rotten."

146

"Aye." Hamish looked out of a small window. "A thaw has set in. Probably be poor for a wee while."

When not running his climbing programmes, Hamish made ice axes with metal shafts, and there were many in racks at various stages of production. Rusty was looking at one that was lying on the bench. "What's this then?"

Hamish grinned. "My new design, mun." He picked it up. "A dropped pick. You see with the pick at this angle it will stay in the ice. You can hang on to it."

"It won't come out?" said Rusty.

"Och, noo. You can hang your whole weight on it."

Rusty took the axe and swung at imaginary ice above his head. "You mean when it's driven in you won't need to cut handholds?"

"Aye." Hamish nodded. "You have it. An axe in one hand and a hammer in the other. I've tested it out. It works great." That was the first time I had ever seen this new design that Hamish had invented in his little workshop on that grey winter day.

Now, climbers all over the world use an ice axe with a dropped pick. The ice axe that Hamish designed has raised the standards of ice climbing to a very high level. Cutting handholds, even in vertical ice, is now a thing of the past.

CHAPTER 24: ICE CLIMBING WITH BILL

Bill became a reasonable sailor and canoeist. However, he was never that interested in pursuing these sports to a higher level. His real interest was climbing, and in particular, ice climbing. However, when we were young bachelors and climbing together, he was only average. In fact, he was probably even less experienced at climbing ice than me. That was all the more reason why we were keen to get onto the ice whenever we had days off.

It was the last day of a course. The students had just left in the coach for Edinburgh and we were having a coffee when Bill burst into the staff room. "Pete, I've just come off the phone to Jim McCartney. He tells me that the snow conditions are good at the moment. Are you keen to go up to Glencoe?"

"To the Coe...Yes sure. We have two days, eh?"

Bill poured a coffee and sat down. "Yeh, I can drive us up there tomorrow. We can stay in the club Bothy."

I was getting keen. "The club Bothy at the foot of the Buachaille would be perfect. We could get a really early start tomorrow to make the most of the light."

"Um." Bill was never too keen on an early start. But it was still dark the next morning as Bill drove us north, along the winding road of our glen to eventually go round the shallow sea at the end of Loch Fyne. The small town of Inveraray was dark and quiet as we turned north again through the forests and hills to the clachan of Dalmally. Bill could now keep on the main road or take a short cut on the minor road through Glen Orchy. It is a twisting slow road, but very pleasant, even at this early hour of grey dawn. Rolling hills come down to the burn that tumbles through numerous small rapids on its way to Loch Awe.

We soon reached the main road again and drove across the windswept moor of Rannoch. This high moor of empty landscape stretched away on either side of the road. Blotches of snow highlighted the treacherous boggy terrain. The dark bulk of Buachaille Etive Mor rose up in the distance, appearing to be isolated above the emptiness. The mountains drew closer and then we were off the moor and descending into the deep-cut Glen Coe.

Rocky ridges, dropping from the craggy tops on the left, are cut off by an ancient glacier that has left great cliffs of truncated spurs. On the right the unbroken ridge of the Aonoch Eagach rises steeply and borders the road as it runs down the glen.

Two hours after leaving Benmore we pulled up wearily at the lower end of the valley and peered through the windscreen to a cold grey dawn. "My God," Bill stretched his long frame. "I'll be glad when I'm old and senile. I won't have to do this sort of thing."

I knew he didn't mean it, and after pulling on more clothes I went out on the empty road to sort the kit out. I swung my rucksack onto my shoulders and followed Bill to the bridge that crossed the burn. We were now on flat ground at the lower end of the glaciated valley, and for fifteen minutes we walked in silence towards the complex mountain of Bidian Nam Bian. Our pace slowed a little as we started up the steep path with the mountains gradually closing in on either side. It was an hour before we gradually eased over the lip of the corrie and could now see the dramatic rock scenery in this huge mountain bowl.

Like all of the corries, the cliffs at the back were very steep with buttresses and gullies rising almost to the summit of the mountain. In front was the dark amphitheater, but our interest was on the right: a classic grade three gully that cut up narrowly through icy crags.

"Looks a bit hard, Pete."

"Mm." The walk up had made me warm and I took off my windproof. "Probably not as steep as it looks."

"Perhaps." Bill put his rucksack down. "Look at that chockstone where the gully narrows. Looks really hard."

This grade of ice climbing is fairly easy nowadays but this was still the time before modern ice tools were developed. When the ice got steep, we would have to cut handholds. I lifted my rucksack. "Just have to see when we get closer." I kicked steps up the steepening snow cone that had slid from the gully. Then I moved a little to one side and asked Bill, "Shall we put the rope on?"

"Yeh." He stood looking up the rock face for a while and then kicked a flat platform. I uncoiled the rope and watched it snake down the snow below before passing the end to Bill. After fixing my crampons I tied onto the end of the rope, hung a few slings and karabiners round my neck and clipped three pitons onto my harness.

Bill had found a spike of rock and fixed himself on. He grinned at me. "Okay Pete, up you go."

It was not steep so I could move quickly and was rather disappointed at the short distance I seemed to have covered when Bill shouted up, "Pete, five metres."

Just ahead I found a dubious old sling that was fixed to a rusty nut. The nut had probably been there for ages and I yanked at it fiercely to test it. This was not very wise because the rope sling broke and I lost balance. I lunged at the snow with my axe and this gave me just enough purchase to swing gently back into balance. I glanced down the slope but Bill was looking out into space.

He hadn't seen my blunder and I took a mental note for the future not to put a blind trust in any gear, particularly old gear.

When I was belayed, I called down, "Okay Bill, when you're ready." He didn't take long to come up level with me. While taking the slings and other bits of protection from me he looked up the gully. "Gets steep, eh?"

"Yes." I pointed upwards. "You might be able to bridge over the chockstone."

"Hope so, but I'll have to cut handholds up this first steep bit." So, he moved up and started cutting.

His axe crunched into the ice and pieces of it flew into the air across me. I pulled my hood up over my helmet and bent forward. He cut a handhold and moved up but he had cut the hold in the wrong place and precariously moved down again. "Bugger," he said. "Have to cut another one."

Bill was always very vocal while leading. "Good hold this one," he would say, or more desperately, "Christ, that was a bit dodgy." His continual commentary was very amusing. All of Bill's emotions came out in his chatter, particularly when he was on the 'sharp end' of the rope. Rusty, on the other hand, was cool and calm all the time. He always seemed in control. He only called down to me if there was something I needed to know, like: "Peter, Loose block here. Watch your head."

By the time Bill had climbed the steep ice he must have cut about twenty handholds and used only half of them, as many were in the wrong place. But we were both learning and certainly had plenty to learn.

He stayed for a while under the overhang and then called down, "Great…. A good runner there, Peter." He started to bridge up over the chockstone with his long legs getting wider apart, and as he moved further out, he grunted down to me, "You got me? You got me, Pete?"

"Yes." And as a bit of encouragement, I added, "You're doing great, you can do it."

With a few more grunts and curses Bill eventually got over onto easier ground and shouted down to me, "Okay Pete. Safe."

As I climbed, he kept me on a fairly tight rope and by using the handholds he had cut, it wasn't long before I joined him. "Good lead, Bill."

"Ta. Looks easier now."

As I took the slings and other gear from him, I looked up. "Mm, that pitch was probably the crux," I said, and this proved to be the case.

Bill had led the only hard pitch and the rest of the climb went easily. We reached the top and coiled the rope. A strong but moist wind was blowing over the ridge but we were well equipped for bad weather, and as I packed my sack I said to Bill, "Shall we go over the top of Bidean and go down the other side?"

"Yeh. Over the top there's supposed to be a scrambling route down into the corrie."

As we gained height the cloud descended and it was only a short while before the visibility was very bad indeed. We were used to these conditions and by using the map and compass we kept going uphill until, through the thick mist, we saw the summit cairn just a few metres away. We knew the way down would be easy if we found the route, but finding the route might be tricky in this bad visibility.

Bill looked into the mist in the direction he thought we should go. "Better get the map out Pete." I set the compass to a course that would put us just to the left of the rocky ridge that was our descent route. With the compass in my hand I turned and looked in the correct direction. "Well, it's this way and should only be about two hundred metres before we hit the top of the corrie and then we move right to find the ridge."

Bill chuckled. "I can't see a thing. I'll follow you." We crunched over the snow and paced out two hundred metres then stopped to look around. I peered into the fog. "What do you think, Bill? I can hardly see where the sky finishes and the snow starts."

"Yeh. It's a real whiteout. Let's move on a bit." We moved on more cautiously and came to the edge where a rocky buttress dropped very steeply down into the grey void. In these bad conditions a descent always looks far more serious from the top than it really is. but I thought this buttress looked horrendous. "Surely this isn't the way Bill?"

"No, looks desperate, but I think we are at the edge of the corrie. Let's contour round to the right a bit." So, we moved further on until we came to the top of another sharp ridge. It didn't look easy and Bill said, "What do you think Pete?"

"Doesn't look like an easy descent, but perhaps it's not as bad as it looks." Bill squinted down into the thick mist. "If only it would clear for just a couple of seconds." We both realised that the map and compass were of limited help in these particular circumstances, where we had to find an exact spot at the top of huge cliffs in whiteout conditions. Again, we were learning.

After moving carefully along the edge of the corrie the ground started to descend more easily, and through the mist a cairn appeared. "This must be it, Pete."

"Yes. Looks more reasonable." We moved down and very soon the route became obvious and the terrain easier. The rock gave way to snow and eventually a rough footpath led to the floor of the corrie.

Although it was still early in the afternoon the daylight was going by the time we reached the car. The club hut we could use was at the top of the pass and we drove up the valley and turned off over bumpy ground to park near the river.

A footbridge led across to our bothy and Bill opened the locked door. "Blimey, Pete. It's cold in here." It certainly was. It was also black as a cave, for the shutters were always kept bolted when the place was not in use.

We were only going to be there for one night so I lit a candle and found the paraffin Tilly lamp. When this was lit we could see around. The bothy was just a single room, and a bunk bed ran the full length of one wall, so there was sleeping for about fourteen if people squashed up a bit. On another wall was a wide worktop with four primus stoves and underneath a shelf for pots and pans. In front of the bunk bed was a table and six chairs.

Bill opened the round stove which stood in the middle of the room. "Mm, no firewood left for us."

"Oh. I'll get some." I put my gloves on, picked up the hand axe that had been left by the door and went outside to the back of the hut where there was pile of wood. It didn't take me long to cut some kindling and I clattered indoors again with an armful of wood.

By the time the fire was roaring, Bill had lit a primus stove and passed me a huge mug of tea. "There you are." He stood with his back to the fire and grinned. "Not bad eh? Soon warm up."

I cooked a mound of rice and then into the same big saucepan I threw a tin of steak and a tin of vegetables. It was easy and quick cooking. I tipped half into a large bowl and Bill ate straight from the saucepan. We sat at either end of the table in happy squalor, still wearing our boots, hats and down jackets. Afterwards we each had a huge wedge of cake that Morag had given us from the centre kitchen. With a mug of steaming tea, we sat with our feet resting on a chair close to the fire, which was glowing red through the tin stove. It was the end of a good day and we had learned a few things on the way. It was still fairly early when we slid into our sleeping bags. The hut was warm and we were cosy.

However, when I woke in the morning the hut was once again like an icebox. I lit the candle and pulled on all the clothes I could find. It was seven thirty and there was already a faint greyness about the sky to the east. I lit the primus and put a kettle on.

From the gloom of the bunk bed Bill's voice said sleepily, "Is it that time, Pete?"

"Yes. Seven thirty. I'll get some breakfast going." Bill wasn't really keen on porridge but I made a huge pan of it and it went down well on that cold morning.

As we finished clearing up after breakfast Bill looked at his watch. "Half past eight. Jim should be here soon." Bill knew Jim and he was joining us today.

Jim McCartney had rooms at the Clachaig pub where he was the stand-in barman. However, most days he instructed snow and ice climbing and was one of a group of young Scots climbers who were quickly building a reputation as exceptional mountaineers. Like Rusty he worked for Hamish McInnes with a team of other instructors, which included Dougal Haston, who had climbed the north face of the Eiger with Rusty and later did exceptional climbs including Mount Everest. It was through Rusty that we knew Jim.

We were still pulling our gaiters on when footsteps could be heard crunching over the footbridge. "He's just on time," said Bill, and before we could get our boots on there was a double rap on the door and in came Jim.

"Och, it's dark in here. Are ye ready then?"

"Hi, Jim," said Bill. "This is Peter." I reached forward with my boots still to be tied and shook him by the hand. He was about my average height but broad, with a ruddy complexion and red hair.

"Helloo Peter." He turned to look out of the open door. "Not a bad day but windy. You fancy Curved Ridge don't you Bill?"

"Yeh. We thought so."

"It's pretty easy, you should romp up it." I was not as experienced as Jim and hoped that I would live up to his confidence in us. However, the guidebook said it was fairly easy so I should be okay although these were winter conditions.

Jim was well organized and within a few minutes we were out in a grey, cold morning, walking in line along the rough track. Ahead of us was the great bulk of our mountain. Buachaille Etive Mor seems to be quite isolated when driving across the moor, and in this half-light it looked much higher than it actually is. The ground was well frozen and the snow lay thick on the Curved Ridge, which stood out clearly as it made a fine line almost to the summit of the mountain.

We stopped briefly to look upwards. "Should be good," said Jim. "We've had a wee thaw each afternoon and the nights have been real hard." He was right. The snow was thick and solid on the face.

We tied on as a rope of three with Jim in the middle so that Bill and I could lead through. Bill and I were fairly slow and after a few pitches we had all gathered on a ledge when Jim said, "It's a wee bit slow with three, eh?" He looked up the ridge. "You lads climb as a pair. I'll climb solo."

153

The route is not hard by modern standards but I was impressed. Bill and I had no intension of climbing without the safety of the rope. Jim was so much better than us on this mixed ground of snow, rock and ice that he moved up with easy confidence. He even started to prepare each belay for us so that we made steady progress to the top. We scrambled up the last few easy pitches to the summit and stood to look around.

Thick clouds were sweeping across the tops by a strong wind but now and then we could see the sun shining through a grey sky. The raw wind tugged around our clothing. The day could never have been described as beautiful but to me it had a wild attraction. Way below, the moor of Rannoch stretched into the distance with the many frozen lochans highlighting the smooth areas of pure white snow. The rest of this bleak landscape was so rough that patches of heather and bog gave the snow a mottled effect. "We need to go this way," said Jim. He led off along the rounded summit ridge towards a huge couloir, and turned to us at the top. "It's easy enough if the conditions are okay." He moved cautiously towards the edge. "But sometimes the snow is hard as iron when you don't expect it." He prodded the snow with his ice axe. "Two lads were killed here last year. They thought the snow was soft but it wasn't. They fell five hundred feet onto rocks."

Bill and I stood well back from the edge. Jim moved down a bit and then he turned to look up to us. "Och aye, it's perfect. Come doon." The snow was deep and soft but we didn't have Jim's skill, so it took us a few tense moments to get down the vertical section at the top where a snow cornice had fallen away. Then things got easier and with growing confidence we charged down and down until we were below the start of the climbs. We looked up at the high crags and Jim pointed out the more obvious gullies that were well-filled with firm snow. "You'll have to do some of these other routes." He pointed to one of the longer gullies, "Like Crowberry gully there. The left fork at the top makes a hard finish."

"Yeh," said Bill. "Looks vertical. Is there time to do it today?"

"Och, noo. It's a long route" Jim looked at his watch. "It'll be dark in a couple of hours and I'm working behind the bar tonight."

While we were walking back to the hut Jim told us about his girlfriend, Mary. "Now she's finished her degree we climb a lot together," he said. "She's very sound. She's keen to work at an outdoor centre." He turned towards us. "Have you any vacancies at Benmore?"

"Well, I don't think there are any full-time instructor vacancies."

"Um. Pity."

"But we have temporary instructors," said Bill. "Of course, we also have plenty of people who work for nothing."

"Oh aye," Jim stopped and looked at Bill. "Aye, she'd be keen to instruct voluntarily for a while. It would give her a chance to see if she'd like to do it full time."

We walked on to the bothy and as Jim shook hands Bill said, "I'll have a word with our principal, Vic, to see if Mary can join us. I'm sure he would be pleased to have her as a voluntary instructor."

"Aye, do that Bill. Ta."

Then with a grin Bill slapped Jim on the shoulder and said, "We could do with a few more girls around too." So that was how Mary came to work as a voluntary instructor at Benmore.

It was dark by the time we had tidied the bothy and packed our kit. We crunched across the frozen snow and up to the road where Bill's car was parked. Bill heaved his rucksack into the boot. "I'm knackered, Pete. You drive." So, I drove through the darkness and Bill, who was still wearing his gaiters, fell asleep.

*

Who would have thought the sleepy giant sprawled out beside me would become one of the best climbers on ice in the country? Bill put up many new routes and wrote the accepted textbook of the time on modern ice techniques. Not only that, but he progressed to be the principal of Plas y Brenin, the national mountain centre in North Wales where I had been the maintenance man. He then left the country to live in Canada and led their successful expedition to mount Everest.

He was married, with a small boy, when he had a severe headache and felt unwell at work one day. He drove home and collapsed in his driveway and died shortly afterwards. He was only about forty-nine years old, and the last person I would think of dying at that age. A terrible tragedy for the family.

CHAPTER 25: MARY, A NEW FACE

Our students at the centre arrived early on a Monday afternoon so we always had a staff meeting straight after breakfast. Breakfast on these first mornings, with no students to worry about, was a relaxed and special meal. Morag would spoil us with little extras like fruit and perhaps mushrooms, black pudding and two eggs, with the rest of a huge fried platter.

We were sitting round the table, finishing off the toast, when Roger came in from his lovely apartment upstairs. He poured a cup of tea and then said, "Right chaps, time for the staff meeting."

Carrying our coffee, we went along to Vic's office. His office used to be the laird's library when Lord Younger lived in the mansion. With alcove windows looking out to the lawn and the purple rhododendron flowers, it was a beautiful room.

But today it was made more pleasant for talking to Vic was a most attractive girl. "Good, all here eh?" said Vic. "First, let me introduce Mary."

The girl turned and with a slight nod of her head she gave us a confident smile. So, this was Jim McCartney's girlfriend. "Lucky Jim," I thought.

We sat down on the circle of leather chairs and Vic continued. "I believe some of you know Mary through Jim McCartney. She will be working with one group on this course." Bill sat upright and smiled across at Mary, but Vic turned towards me. "Peter, I want her to work with you on this course." Bill tried to hide a slight disappointment.

"The whole course?" I said.

"Yes. She can stay with you for everything so that she picks up all the details of running a group."

"Okay." I gave Bill a quick wink and he grinned.

The first morning of each course was the only time I could get for maintenance, and I spent a few hours repairing holes in a couple of kayaks. Mary did a complete tour of the house with Roger, but we met in the staff room for lunch. "So, Mary, you finished university last year?"

"Aye." She had a beautiful Scots accent. "Jim and I spent the summer climbing in the Alps. We were lucky with the weather. Did plenty of routes."

We talked on during the meal and I became more and more impressed. She was modest but I could see that she had abilities in many different fields.

"And what about the future?"

She gave a short laugh. "Och, I'm not sure what I want to do. Vic says there might be an instructor's job here so I thought I would try it out and work as a volunteer for a wee while."

"Yes, good idea." She seemed to be clever, intelligent and attractive. I felt that whatever she did she would be successful. A great future, I thought.

But then, we can't see the future and perhaps that is best.

When my group arrived and I met them for the first time she stood beside me. With her fair hair tied back loosely and wearing jeans and a patterned sweater I even felt that my own image was much improved!

The programme for the students was all land-based during these winter months. We did a few days of rock climbing, navigated through forests and traversed a couple of local mountains. During every lecture that instructors gave in the evenings, Mary sat at the back and even took notes from time to time. She was determined to make the very most of this opportunity.

On the last days of the course, we took the groups away from the centre. I decided we would all camp in the corrie of the Cobbler Mountain. The back wall of this great basin has a few easy snow gullies so we took ice axes and a few ropes.

The walk up to the campsite was rather slow as the students had quite heavy rucksacks with plenty of warm clothes and all the camping kit. Mary had a sack at least as heavy as mine but seemed to carry it with no problem at all. During the camp she quietly toured the tents helping students with stoves and organization.

As the course progressed, I had become more and more impressed with Mary. She could smile and laugh with the teenage students but had a natural authority. They liked and respected her. We were not always lucky with the weather during camps, but on this camp we were very fortunate. The sky was blue and although it was cold the wind was not too strong. We had a couple of days in glorious weather climbing two good gullies on firm snow. I think the students really enjoyed this new challenge and Mary seemed completely confident in leading one of the teams.

After a camp there was always the arduous task of hanging the tents and cleaning the cooking canteens. The students were not always very diligent on washing up, but even here Mary showed fine management skills. "Och, no Jackie." She smiled and shook her head at a girl who handed in her canteen. "I'm sure you can get it cleaner than that." The girl grinned and took the canteen back to give it another scrub.

"Mm," I thought. She has it all: ability and leadership skills.

The course had finished and the students had departed for Edinburgh when Vic called me into his office. "Well, Peter. How did Mary shape up?"

"Well, what can I say?" I smiled. "Brilliant. She is very sound on the rock, better than me on snow and ice, and handles the students as if she's been leading groups for years."

"Good. That's what I gathered from Roger." He leaned back in his chair. "Is she ready to lead a group on the next course?"

"Yes, sure. If it's a similar programme to this last one, she'll be fine."

"Great. Okay, I shall have a word with her before she leaves. She's going up to Glencoe to see Jim." He stood up. "She can take your group next week. That will give you a few days to maintain the boats."

"Oh, good." I was pleased because I enjoyed a break from instructing and there were quite a few small repairs to do on the little fleet of boats.

With the weekend off I went skiing in the Cairngorms, and the following Monday we all gathered in Vic's office for the usual staff meeting.

Vic turned to Roger. "Where is Mary?"

"She wasn't at breakfast," I said.

Roger stood up. "Perhaps she's in her room. I'll pop up and give her a call."

Morag had come in during this time and said, "Och, don't bother yerself Roger. Mary didna come back last night. Expect she will turn up in a we while."

Vic carried on with the staff meeting and afterwards we all went about our work until coffee time, when he came to see me. "Mary hasn't made a very good start. She still hasn't turned up for work."

I made a face. "Oh."

"You'll have to take her group if she lets us down. Phone the Clachaig pub, will you. Ask Jim McCartney where she is."

I got through straight away. "Helloo, the Clachaig Hotel," said a deep Scots voice.

"Hello, is that Monty?" Monty was the manager of the pub and Jim's boss.

"Aye."

"Ah, Hello. This is Peter Dyer from Benmore Adventure Centre. I'm trying to contact Mary. Is she still with you?"

"Och noo. Neither is Jim." He seemed a bit upset. "I expected them back last night."

"Back?" I said.

"Aye. They've been up on the Ben. Staying in the C.I.C. hut."

"Oh, I see."

158

"They will probably turn up in a wee while with some unlikely excuse about the car breakin' doon."

I knocked on Vic's door and put my head round. "Mary is with Jim. They've been climbing on Ben Nevis."

"Oh." He leaned back in his chair and stared out of the window. "Well, if she isn't here by the time the students arrive you will have to show her group around."

It was nearly mid-day when Sheena, the secretary, came puffing up to my little workshop. "Ah Peter. You had a phone call from Monty. Mary and Jim are still on Ben Nevis."

"Oh, marvelous," I said dryly.

"Apparently they are stuck on an ice climb and a team from Fort William has gone out to rescue them."

"Stuck!" I was amazed. "Did he say what climb?"

"Aye." She looked at a piece of paper. "Green Gully."

"Green Gully!" I put my tools down. "Green Gully would be an easy climb for Jim and Mary. I wonder what stopped them?"

"Monty said there were two others as well. A team of four."

"Does Vic know?"

"Aye. He's a wee bit cross."

"I told him she was reliable," I laughed. "Anyway, it will all work out okay I'm sure." I carried on working and sang happily to think of Jim's embarrassment. He was a member of the rescue team and they would tease him for a long time to come, at having to be rescued.

It was during our staff lunch when the telephone rang again.

Sheena jumped up. "It always rings just when I sit doon." She came back looking serious. "Peter, it's Monty on the phone from The Clachaig Pub. Says he wants to speak to you, only you."

"Fame at last," I said, with a smile. We were finding it quite humorous that our friends, top climbers, were having to be rescued on a fairly easy climb. But my humour ceased immediately as Monty spoke.

"Peter, it's terrible." He was breathing very heavily and not too clear on the phone.

"What?"

"I say it's terrible. They're all dead."

"What?" I raised my voice. "What did you say?"

"All dead, mun. They're not stuck on the face. They're all dead. Avalanched, apparently."

"Dead! Who? Mary, Jim and the other two?"

"Aye. Dead." He corrected himself. "Well, not all. One of them, John, is okay and still on the face. He's the one that's stuck. Jim, Mary and the other lad are all dead. Swept off the face. They're being brought doon." He gave me the details that he had received from the police, but I didn't really know what to say. Eventually I put the phone down and walked slowly back to the staff room. I sat down quietly at the table but the others could tell straight away that any sign of humour had left me. "What is it, Peter?"

"They're not stuck. Mary, Jim and the others. They're not stuck in Green Gully. They're dead."

They had stopped eating and all spoke together. "Dead!" "What?" "Who?" "Mary and Jim?" I took a breath.

"Yes. Both dead. Swept off the face by an avalanche."

"Mary's dead? And Jim too?" They couldn't bring themselves to believe it, but then there was a stunned silence and I told them the details I knew.

Vic eventually stood up and spoke quietly. "Please finish your meal and then let's all meet in my office," he looked at his watch, "at one fifteen."

Not only the instructors but all of the staff were in Vic's office. Morag, with her cooks and cleaners, the janitor, the secretary and even the wives who lived on site.

Whispered conversations stopped as Vic spoke. "It's been a terrible tragedy. Particularly for those of us who worked and got to know Mary." He spoke very well on these occasions and after speaking about Mary for a few minutes, he paused. "However, we have a job to do. The students will be arriving in an hour. They know nothing of this terrible accident and will be full of fun and excitement to enjoy their course." There were mumbles of understanding from around the room and Vic continued. "For their sakes we must try and put this sad business behind us. Meet them in the usual happy and professional way. The course must go on."

Everyone left but Vic asked me to stay behind. "Peter. You take over Mary's group."

"Okay, sure Vic."

"Also, when you have a minute go up to her room and pack up all her personal belongings. Leave them here in the office and I will send them on."

I collected a few old cardboard boxes from the kitchen and went to her room. I packed away the few things that she had left behind: clothes, shoes, an alarm clock and a couple of books - now just objects that had so recently been part of a youthful life. I left the sad boxes tied up with string in Vic's office.

I was just in time to meet my chattering group of teenagers stepping down from the coach and all excited and ready for their adventure course.

With Jim's sad death we lost a lad who would have made a big mark on Scottish climbing, and with the loss of Mary, it was more personal. I had got to like and respect her. I thought she had everything. She was clever and wise with a youthful vitality for the future.

But none of us can see into the future. Perhaps that is best.

CHAPTER 26: GLENMORE LODGE AND ERIC

Snow and ice climbing on the west coast of Scotland can be a little frustrating. It seemed that horizontal sleet and rain would blast in from the Atlantic and often spoil the good conditions needed for winter climbing. Further inland, away from the sea and towards the east of Scotland the weather was usually more reliable for winter climbing, but here on the west coast, it was often too mild and wet. We all became a little weary of the mountains during a west coast winter.

We were therefore delighted at the end of a staff meeting when Vic told us, "Glenmore Lodge are short of instructors for one of their courses." He gave a long pause then a wide grin split his face. "I've arranged for you to go over there for two weeks and help on their 'survival' course."

We left the room in high spirits talking about the winter skills that were covered on these programmes. Glenmore Lodge is the national mountain centre in Scotland and is situated in the heart of the Cairngorm mountains. Being further away from the west coast the weather is different. It is colder and there is a more regular buildup of snow and ice in the mountains, which is ideal for teaching winter mountaineering. To instruct on their survival course would give me good experience and be a pleasant change of scene.

Each morning I always cut out the synoptic chart and weather forecast from the Times newspaper and pinned it on the noticeboard. We would gather round it before breakfast, but now we had more reason to study the weather in the Cairngorms. "Plenty of snow over there," said Bill.

"Yes." Rusty looked closely at the temperatures. "It needs to thaw a little now for the best conditions."

*

Our kit had been packed the night before, so with Roger driving we left Benmore straight after breakfast. Going north and then east we went over the 'rest and be thankful' pass where a grey ceiling of cloud was so low that it nearly reached the road. A short while later we came to Loch Lomond and turned north towards Crianlarich. The stone buildings of Crianlarich always gave me the impression of a hamlet that everyone drove through, but at which nobody stopped. At the junction we turned east and past the tiny little clachan of Benmore, with the mountain of Ben More climbing up behind it. I smiled to myself to realise that this was the

Benmore I had found on my atlas in London before the interview - the Benmore where I thought the centre might be. It seemed such a long time ago that I was applying to be an instructor. I was pleased that I was now living near the sea as well as the mountains.

The west coast had been windy, wet and grey but now that we were inland the sky began to clear. It seemed colder and there was certainly far more snow on the mountains. We drove along the shore of Loch Tay where the wind was making short, black waves splash against the shore. A few trees gathered together along the lochside but the hills rising gently up on both sides showed nothing but yellowed grass. At the end of the loch our mini-bus rolled heavily round the bend and then we were over the humped back bridge at Kenmore.

Rusty leaned towards Roger. "Perhaps we could cut the corner off and go via Loch Tummel."

Roger turned his head slightly. "It's not worth it. That road is very slow and rough. At this time of the year snow drifts often block it." Roger had taught at Rannoch School and knew this lonely part of the country well, so we carried on until hitting the main road and went north through Pitlochry.

The stone-built houses looked severe but prosperous and I always wondered how people earned their living in this little town. We slowed round the bends through the Pass of Killecrankie. What wonderful names they seemed to me: Calvin, Struan Clachan, Dalnaspidal and Glen Garry. I almost felt like a patriotic highlander and started singing quietly, "by Tummel and Loch Rannoch and Loch Arber I will go... Oh, you've never smelt the tangle of the Isles."

There was plenty of snow on the Pass of Drumochter, which is so often closed, but the plough had been along and we made our way carefully down to eventually reach the small town of Kingussie. We were now in the wide-open glen that takes the river Spey and not far from Aviemore and the end of our drive. Only a few years before, Aviemore had been a small hamlet of solid stone houses that straddled a road of little interest. Now it was the centre of the Scottish ski scene with hotels, restaurants and all the facilities required for après ski. There was even a swimming pool, ice rink and cinema. We turned right, over the river Spey and past a few guest houses until we were amongst the trees.

These were not the dark green conifers around our Benmore centre on the west coast but an open woodland of Scots Pines that one could walk through easily. Underneath them, in the large clearings, the ground was covered with snow. On the right I could look through the lovely trees to Loch Morlich, now covered with ice and beyond to the rounded mountains, completely covered in snow, that are the Cairngorms.

After a short while we forked left on a narrow forest track and there below us was the flat roof buildings of Glenmore Lodge, the National Mountain Centre.

Snow covered everything and a very cold wind blew down from the open hillside. The path was icy and we tottered with our kit to the reception desk.

*

I was sharing a room with Bill and as we sorted our kit out he said, "Good timing eh, Pete. We're just in time for lunch."

Only the staff were in for Saturday lunch and we spent a pleasant meal talking to old friends. We would be teaching more advanced adult clients, in an exciting new area. With no lectures or evening duties for us to worry about, I felt that I was on holiday.

There were about twenty instructors and shortly after lunch we had a staff meeting to brief us on the details of the course. Working on a new programme in a new area meant that I had to do more preparation. I spent the rest of the afternoon looking at maps and guidebooks and checking equipment in the stores before having a shower and changing for the evening meal.

For the first part of the course I would be teaching snow and ice climbing. Each group had two days, the first learning basic techniques and the second day doing an easy climb. There was a good snow slope in the huge bowl of Coire an t-Sneachda, so I took my group of adults there on the first day.

The nine of us were taken up to the car park in one of the mini-buses and we walked across the bottom of the ski runs and gradually made height over the ridge; called a 'fiacaill' in this part of Scotland. It took us about an hour to get well into the corrie. The back wall of steep, black cliffs, are cut by well-formed gullies that were filled with snow. It was a fine day with a rather weak sun shining through some high cirrus cloud. In the bowl of the corrie we were sheltered from wind and this would make a good place to work from. I led the group across to some flat boulders where the wind and sun had cleared the snow. "Perfect," I said to the group. "We'll stop here for a break but I think we shall work in this area all day."

I took out my flask, poured a coffee and looked around. What a wonderful 'classroom' it was for us. To the north we could look down from our high ground, past heather slopes and down to the forests and lochans in the wide Spey valley. On one side of us a rounded ridge blocked any sight of the busy ski area and on the other side a fiacaill of spiky granite dropped steeply from the plateau, way above us. And behind us, still in shadow, was the dramatic back wall of rock and ice where, later in the week, we would climb.

Between us and the climbs, a wide slope of snow swept up, getting steeper and steeper until it ran into the vertical rock and deep gullies. It was perfect for instruction, being steeper as it went up, but having a gentle run out of soft snow at the bottom.

For the rest of the day, I covered the basics of winter mountaineering. Walking with the ice axe, cutting steps up, across and down and stopping a slide by using the ice axe. The adult students learned to belay on snow using the ice axe, and later used a 'dead man' belay plate that was a new technique. With everyone pulling on a long rope we tested the different methods. The 'dead man' plate was a far stronger belay than the axe. For lunch we returned to the flat rocks and lay around looking up at the wonderful craggy scenery. In the afternoon we covered the use of crampons and finally walked across to a little icefall. Water had been running down a rocky slab and a thick layer of ice had built up. I was pleased to see that snow had been blown to form a soft bank at the bottom. It was just what I needed to teach cutting handholds and using crampons on steeper faces. The whole day was very successful and I decided to use the same area for the next couple of days. Although it was only three thirty the sun was already low in the sky as we walked back towards the car park.

When we came over the rounded Fiacaill I could see Bill in the distance with his group. "Okay, everyone, I said. "I'm going to leave you here. You can see the car park I shall meet you by the bus." They went off talking together and I contoured across Coire Cas to where Bill was sorting out kit.

He had been teaching rescue techniques and although his students had departed with most of the kit, there was still the stretcher. Bill was standing in the snow looking at the stretcher as I came up. "Hi, Bill. Had a good day."

"allo Pete. Yeh, great thanks."

"What are you thinking about?"

"I've got to get the stretcher right down there." He pointed to the car park that was a long way down at the bottom of the ski hill.

"Oh, do you want a hand with it?"

"Er, no ... we'll slide it down." The stretcher, designed and made by Hamish in Glencoe, had runners underneath. After dragging it for a short way he stopped, looked around furtively and said, "Come on Pete."

He sat down on the front of the stretcher. "You sit on the back." I was a bit dubious but it would be more interesting than dragging it, so I sat behind Bill and we set off cautiously. As we gained control our confidence grew and we went faster and faster. Soon we were on the ski slopes and overtaking skiers with Bill shouting to them at the top of his voice. We went flying by lines of skiers having lessons and eventually hit a deep bank of snow just to one side of a queue of people who were waiting to get onto the chair lift. The stretcher went upside down and we fell about in the snow laughing like idiots.

I'm sure the Scots watching Bill would not have thought this happy clown would become the chief instructor of their National Mountaineering Centre.

For the next two days I taught two other groups the basics of snow and ice climbing. Then, on the fourth day, they were all ready to tackle an easy climb and I was given two men to teach. Adam and Steve had done quite a bit of mountain walking and seemed fit and keen. We made easy progress across to Coire an t- Sneachda on a route that I was now familiar with. We eventually stopped at the foot of a snow slope that became steeper as it gained height to weave a way through the dark crags above.

"Right, guys. Here we are." I pointed with my axe." That's our route: Aladdin's Mirror." I placed my rucksack down. "Let's have a coffee." I sorted out the two ropes and by the time Steve and Adam had put on their crampons, helmets and harnesses we were ready to go.

We tied onto the ropes and started up the snow slope but as we moved into the gulley it soon became steep. It was too steep for us to move safely together and I found a good spike of rock for a belay. "Right, fix yourselves on. Adam, you can belay me as I climb and then when I'm safe, you can bring up Steve."

It was easy climbing and we made good progress on snow that soon became so hard that only traces of our crampon points were left behind. At about half height the route traverses sideways across the face and it was here that we had our first incident.

Adam was belaying to safeguard Steve as he traversed sideways. I was way above and saw Steve coming across the traverse when he suddenly fell. The face was only steep snow but I immediately braced myself and watched Adam, who was holding the rope, get pulled onto the belay. After sliding down in a long arc Steve came to a halt.

He kicked a good step and when the tension had gone from the rope I shouted down. "Steve. You okay?"

"Yes." He looked up to Adam and called. "Phew, thanks." I was relieved because Adam was fixed to a dead man plate that I had placed, but it had held two of them well, so we had all learned something.

In a couple of hours, we came to the last pitch and I led up the steep snow that became vertical below a cornice. I pulled my hood over to stop snow going down my neck and hacked a way through the overhang, pulling myself onto the level plateau. I belayed, and while the others came up, I had a chance to look around.

The plateau looked wonderful with the bright afternoon sun casting long shadows across the snow. The sky was a milky blue with just a wisp of high cirrus cloud and although the wind was cold it wasn't strong. Adam's snowy head appeared through the break in the overhanging cornice and he pulled himself onto the plateau. He used my belay to safeguard himself and I moved back for him to bring up Steve. We eventually took off our crampons, coiled the ropes and packed our kit away. "A good climb, Peter," said Steve.

"Yes, and the snow was perfect, eh?" We shouldered our rucksacks and set off in the direction of Cairngorm Mountain.

*

Visibility was excellent and there were quite a few people skiing across the plateau.

As we crunched across the snow, I was just thinking what a wonderful day it was with everything going like clockwork when a man, not far away, stood up and waved a hand in the air. "Hey, can you help?" he shouted.

We changed our course and getting close to them we realised that a girl was lying on the ground and the chap was supporting her foot. He looked at us. "We were skiing back across the plateau and my wife had a fall."

"Oh." I put my rucksack down. "Let me see." The girl was resting on one elbow and smiled apologetically at me. However, I could tell from the way she was biting her lip that she was in real pain. Because her foot could not support itself, I was fairly certain she had broken her lower leg. "I think you might have broken it."

I stood up to think what should be done. If we left to get help the rescue team would not be here until well after dark and it would certainly get very cold up here high on the plateau. It was only a mile to the top of Corrie Cas and we could carry her if we had a stretcher. In training I had made emergency stretchers from all sorts of things but never from skis and poles. However, with all the kit we had it should be simple. I smiled down at our patient. "We can make a stretcher and carry you down." I looked towards the husband. "What do you think?"

"Yes. Fine … thanks." He seemed relieved.

I grinned at Steve and Adam. "A real live rescue, eh? It will be good training for us. Get out the ropes and jackets and sweaters." The husband was still holding the foot and I said to him, "We shall be together for a while. I'm Peter."

167

He smiled anxiously. "I'm Andrew and this is Dawn."

I used our tape slings to tie both boots together and Dawn said she was more comfortable. Then by lashing their ski poles and skis together in a frame and using the ropes as a woven base we made a fairly sound stretcher. We fixed slings to each end that made halters to help us take the weight. With spare jackets and sweaters for padding we carefully lifted Dawn onto the stretcher.

After taking a corner each, we were ready to move off. "One, two, three ... lift!" I said, and after a few jerky steps we settled into a rhythm and headed for the top of Coire Cas.

We stopped from time to time to change places and eventually reached a point where we could see down the steep back wall to the skiers on the piste far below. "We could now get a rescue stretcher," I said. "But it would be about two hours by the time I got down and brought them up." I looked down at Dawn and smiled. "How do you feel?"

"Well ... I'm not too bad on this stretcher."

Andrew pointed across to the far side of the corrie lip. "It's not too steep over there. We could probably carry her down to the top of the chair lift."

"Yes. Okay, let's do that." So, we carried her down to eventually reach the top station. Dawn moved over to sit on a chair and we took the stretcher of ropes, skis and poles apart. The chap supervising the big wheel allowed us all a free ride on the chair lift, right down to the car park.

When they were organized with transport, we left them, and as we walked towards the mini-bus Adam said, "Well, it's been a great day. A good route climbed and a real rescue. It's a great job you have Peter."

"Yes," I grinned. "Better than work!" They laughed. More seriously I said, "Of course, we have to go out in all conditions and the weather isn't always this good."

*

The weather certainly changed, and on the day, we left for our three-day expedition it was bad. I didn't have a group of my own but was helping Eric. Eric Beard and I had first met at Plas y Brenin in Snowdonia. We had worked on a few courses and did some mountain walking together. He was safe on rock but not the best climber I knew. However, he was the very best at one sport, and that was mountain running. At this gruelling activity he was the best in Britain. He held the record for many of the mountain challenges around the country and I particularly remember when he broke the record for the Snowdon Three Thousanders.

This challenge is to run over all of the mountains higher than three thousand feet, and at the time John Disley held the record. A few years before, John Disley had also worked at Plas y Brenin and had also become famous as the European cross-country champion. To break his record a runner had to be very good indeed. Eric broke John's record by more than an hour. Eric was well known for his running, but perhaps just as well known for being a happy outgoing person. With his Lancastrian accent and extrovert character he was always the life and soul of the party. He always struck me as a sincere man who was able to get on with people from all walks of life. So, I was delighted to be working with Eric again during this two-night trip.

*

We didn't take tents but were going to sleep in snow shelters and had everything, except food, packed the night before. We collected our rations straight after breakfast and eventually left the Lodge in a mini-bus, reaching the car park at nine thirty.

There were plenty of skiers joining groups for instruction or making for the chair lift but we walked past and up the path. As we passed the top chair lift station Eric turned to me. "Weather is poor, eh Peter?"

I looked upwards. "Mm… It will be a lot worse on the plateau." It was worse, with snow stinging my face, blown by a strong south-westerly wind. However, we had a good team and excellent clothing, and Eric, in his happy manner, seemed to give everyone confidence. We felt that whatever the elements threw at us we would be able to cope.

It was early afternoon when Eric led us across a shallow valley to a snowy bank. With his ice axe he poked about and eventually turned to the group. "Come close," he shouted above the wind. Everyone had their hoods up and with a hand held to stop the snow driving onto our faces we drew into a tight circle. "This is Coire Domhain. It's a good place to dig snow holes."

Eric marked the entrances of four snow caves with his axe and we all went to work. Each group had a snow shovel so it wasn't long before people started to disappear into the bank. Eric spent his time supervising while I worked on our snow hole. I eventually cut sleeping platforms and lowered the doorway with a solid lintel cut from hard snow.

Although we had started early the winter light had already started to fade by the time we finished and had all our kit safely inside. The storm outside had increased and the wind was howling across the open plateau, but deep inside the snow hole there was silence and peace. Eric had

169

checked the clients were settled and organized to cook for the evening and eventually he crawled through to join me.

He took off his outer clothes and very carefully shook the powder snow outside. We shuffled into our sleeping bags with the cold air trench running between us. I set the stove down in the trench and filled up a pan with snow cut from the wall. We listened to the familiar purring of the stove and it wasn't long before I had made two great mugs of tea.

We lay comfortably drinking while our meal was cooking. With the still flame of a single candle giving excellent light around the white walls, I felt secure and completely insulated from the arctic conditions outside. Eric went out again to check on the students and then we settled in comfort for an early night.

We could tell when it was morning as a defused light lit up our white dome. I lit the primus stove and put on a big brew. Eric rolled over and said, "Is it that time, Pete?"

"Yes. Shall I wake the others?" The stove had taken the chill from the air in our little den and I was very cosy deep in my sleeping bag. I was quite pleased when Eric said, "It's okay. You make breakfast." He put on more clothes and finally his boots and crawled down and disappeared outside. I made a great pan of porridge that was just ready when Eric crawled back inside the cave.

"Gosh Pete. It's wild out there." He slid awkwardly back into his sleeping bag and we had a fine breakfast in the quiet peace of the snow hole. I dressed with difficulty under the very low ceiling and packed the kit into my rucksack.

It was quite a shock when I eventually crawled outside to find there was an icy wind howling across the open white landscape. The students were all fine and had a good night.

We shouldered our heavy packs and crunched off across the arctic landscape in a line behind Eric. He was walking on a compass bearing, and with the visibility so bad he paced out the distance we had to cover.

Eventually, after an hour or so, he led us right to our first stop, which was the emergency shelter at Lochan Buidhe. The snow had built up around the corrugated shell and it took us a while to clear enough snow to open the door. We crowded inside but it was like being inside a freezer. "My God," said one of the group. "I wouldn't like to stay in here for the night."

"Perhaps." Eric pursed his lips. "But much better than outside. I'd be pleased to find it in a storm." A couple of years later I remembered this comment of Eric's when a terrible tragedy occurred near this spot.

We went out into the wind again and navigated to the top of the March Burn, and by following the shallow gulley we were soon down below the ceiling of clouds, in the Lairig Ghru. This deep valley gave us some shelter and we stopped for lunch. Afterwards, Eric led the way up the steep side of the glen, going with a slow easy pace on a rising traverse. We reached more level ground on a high ridge and plodded on to the summit of Braeriach.

It was now two in the afternoon and we started to look for suitable snow to make a shelter. Eventually we stood together and Eric shouted in my ear, "Not enough snow for another cave Peter, not deep enough."

"No." I leaned towards him. "The wind's blown it all off."

"Right." He looked in different directions for a while and then pointed with his ice axe. "Perhaps on the lee of the hill. The snow might have built up over there." We plodded on along a rounded ridge until Eric led us down a short distance to a more level area that was sheltered from the wind.

The snow was not deep enough to dig a cave but Eric walked about thrusting his axe in the snow until he eventually turned to me. "We can build igloos."

"Oh. Yes, that would be great. I've made them before but never slept in one."

Eric poked his ice axe in the snow. "There's good firm slab here." He drew a circle in the snow and while he helped the group plan their igloos, I cut snow blocks. The students gathered round to watch as we lifted the first course of blocks into place and shaved the top off to make a rising spiral. "Right," said Eric. "That's how you start. When you've got to this stage give me a shout and I will tell you what to do next."

They went off full of enthusiasm and the two of us carried on with the spiral construction until Eric left to help the groups. I finished with the key block in the top then cut a trench for a low entrance where the doorway lintel was lower than the floor inside. We moved in and weak sunlight showed through the joints in the blocks and it was very cosy and quiet. Eric went off to check on the clients and I cooked a big stew in the igloo.

The storm raged most of the night but we slept so well that it was nearly eight o'clock when I woke Eric. "Eric. It's time for the radio check."

"Oh … is it?" While I lit the stove and sorted breakfast, he unpacked the radio and poked the extended aerial through a weakness between two snow blocks. "Glenmore Lodge. Glenmore Lodge. Eric calling. Can you hear me? Over."

They replied straight away. They told us that because of the severe weather some of the groups had returned after one night and another group, apparently not far from us, had broken camp during the night and were now walking back in a rather poor state. "How are you?" they asked.

"Grand," said Eric in his Lancashire accent. "Still in our sleeping bags with a mug of tea."

When we eventually left our camp most of us glanced back at our little hamlet of igloos. They had served us well.

The wind had eventually died away and the sky was clear. Our walk back, down to the Lairig Ghru and east over the rocky pass to the ski road was a happy stroll. We arrived back at the Lodge in good time for a shower before afternoon tea.

Our clients were rather surprised that other groups had taken such a battering from the weather and their camps had failed to protect them very well. I'm sure that our group had enjoyed a relaxed and carefree expedition. We had plenty of time to wander at leisure over the mountains, stopping frequently to look at the view or stop for a rest. A few of the group were speaking to me in the bar that evening. "The other groups seemed to have caught far worse conditions than us," said one man.

"Yes," said one of the girls. "They seemed to have had really bad nights. It all seemed so easy on our trip."

"I think it was," I smiled. "But I'm sure it was Eric's leadership."

"Perhaps you're right," one of the group said. "Eric laughed and joked about everything but I always felt he was completely in control."
*

"Yes." I agreed with them. The weather had really been quite severe but our leader had always been in complete control.

*

However, not long after our happy expedition, Eric left Glenmore Lodge to return home. He had never learned to drive a car and hitchhiked everywhere. He was in a car travelling south when the driver lost control.

Tragically, the driver and Eric Beard were both killed instantly.

CHAPTER 27: DRIVING: THE REAL DANGER

"Very sad, Eric being killed like that," said Vic. He poured a coffee and took a dropped scone. "I've said it before: the most dangerous thing we do is not mountaineering or kayaking or sailing. It's driving." He waved the dropped scone at us all. "Most of you drive far too quickly, particularly with a group of students in the back."

We nodded and mumbled. In our hearts we knew he was right; we did sometimes drive too fast on the steep hills and narrow roads around Benmore. However, I wasn't driving too fast the night I took the secretary home.

Vic had given a staff party in his flat and, as I had not been drinking alcohol, he came over to me and said, "Peter. Would you give Sheena a lift home?"

"Yes. Sure."

Vic gave me some keys. "You can use my car."

It was a black night, cloudy, no moon and it was also raining. However, Vic had a good car with excellent headlamps and windscreen wipers. I was soon to be grateful for his good braking system as well.

It was about eleven o'clock as Sheena and I went through the coastal village of Sandbank and approached Dunoon where Sheena lived. The roads where wet, shining in the poor street lamps and completely deserted except for a single chap walking on the far side of the road.

I could clearly see him in the distance with his shoulders hunched up and hands deep in his pockets, walking slowly along. He leaned briefly on a high wall and as we approached, he turned and looked down the road at us. Then he moved away from the wall and went to the kerb, where he stopped.

He was not on our side of the road so I didn't take a great deal of notice of him, except to realise that he had clearly seen us coming. As we got closer, he suddenly lurched across the road right in front of our car. I braked hard but he just kept coming until I hit him, then he disappeared from view.

"Oh my god," said Sheena. "We've hit him."

I clambered out and went to the front of the car. There he lay, groaning, and when he saw me, he said, "Och. My bloody leg."

Sheena had got out the other side of the car and she peered down at the chap. "You must be crazy or something. Fancy trying to race us across the road like that."

The man took no notice of her but only reached for his tartan hat and perched it on his head. I looked around but there was nobody about at all. There was just the three of us and the car in the empty road.

"I must phone for an ambulance," I said.

I was looking round, desperately hoping to see a phone box, when Sheena said, "The police station." She pointed along the road. "The police station is just round the next corner."

"Right. You stay with this chap. I'll go round there." Perhaps I should have been more sympathetic, for Sheena didn't look at all confident as I drove away. After all, there she was, alone with this unknown chap groaning on the ground on a dark empty road.

I rushed into the police station and the policeman behind the desk looked up at me. "Quick. Um … I've knocked a man down. Just round the corner."

He slowly put a large mug of tea down on the counter and said, "Now, sir. Do you mean you have had a traffic accident?" He seemed very calm.

"Yes. Chap ran out in front of me. He's lying on the ground. Groaning."

"Alright sir." He picked a telephone up. "Now, exactly where is he?"

"Just opposite the gas works. On the main road." He gave directions to the person at the other end of the line and eventually put the telephone down.

"Ambulance will be there in a minute sir." He lifted his hat from a table and as we walked out of the station together, he said, "Just by the gasworks, eh?"

"Yes."

"A man, eh?"

"Yes."

"Ran out in front of you?"

"Yes. Yes. I couldn't miss him."

Then he stopped and looked at me. "Was he wearing a baggy suit and a tartan tammy?"

I must have looked puzzled. "A tammy?"

"Aye. A hat, mun."

"Eh…. Well … yes, I think he was wearing a …tammy."

He shook his head wearily. "McLeod…. It'll be McLeod again." I stood there with my mouth hanging open. In a small community the police seemed to know everyone by name. It took us only a couple of minutes to walk briskly round the corner. The policeman stood with his hands on his hips looking down at the poor chap on the floor. "Aye. McLeod." Then he bent down lower and shouted, "Drunk again, Jock."

We waited until the ambulance had taken McLeod away and the policeman had taken my name and address, but it was all very casual. Sheena phoned the hospital the next morning and we found that the man had a broken leg and was already up and about. I was relieved it was not too serious.

It was a few weeks later that I had an official looking letter saying that the 'Procurator Fiscal will not be laying any charge'. I suspect I had nearly stopped before I hit the man because there was no damage to Vic's car at all, and he took the incident in good humour.

However, he was certainly not in a good humour when he came into the staff room one evening a couple of weeks later. He had been to Edinburgh for a meeting and he sat down wearily. "Who was driving the Land Rover this morning, Peter?"

It was Bill, but I thought it best to be ignorant. "I'm not sure, Vic. Why?"

"I was going down that long hill the other side of the pass, doing nearly sixty miles an hour, when a Land Rover passed me."

I frowned and clicked my tongue a few times. "Some of these farmers drive too fast."

"That's what I thought." His eyebrows went up. "But there were teenagers hanging out of every window, jeering at me as it passed. When it drew level, I saw the sign on the side door."

"A sign?" But I guessed what was coming.

"Yes. Our sign! Benmore Centre. It was our Land Rover filled with students."

"Oh." I could just imagine the scene and had to stifle a smile.

However, I was saved because Bill came through the door, whistling happily. Vic turned to him. "Ah, Bill. Were you driving the Land Rover this morning?"

Bill's face was a picture of innocence. "Um, the Land Rover?"

I used the pause to make my excuses and left the room, so I never did know what Vic said.

Bill was an excellent mountaineer and a very fine instructor but driving was his weakness. It wasn't long before he was in trouble again.

He was driving my group one morning, and after motoring carefully round the gardens and down the gravel drive, he stopped cautiously at the main road junction.

It was a glorious winter morning, peaceful and quiet, with not a person or vehicle to be seen. Bill must have forgotten where he was taking us, for he started to turn left.

"Right Bill…. Turn right, we're going to Ardentinny," I said, to remind him.

"Ah. Yes." He had only gone a few metres and in getting ready to turn right he backed the minibus. The main road was completely empty with not a car in sight, and the gravel drive behind us was hardly ever used by vehicles. But Bill was unlucky.

The postman in his little van had come down the drive and stopped right behind us. There was a sound of breaking glass as Bill reversed right into the front of the post van. The postie regarded us wearily through his windscreen and shook his head in disbelief.

*

Instructing was no real challenge for Rusty and he found all sorts of rock-climbing problems round the building. It was good training to try these desperate little problems even though they might be only a metre above the ground. Rusty had developed a challenge for us that used the molding on a gothic arch. The arch went across the entrance to the courtyard where we kept the vehicles. It had a decorative stone edge and with straining fingers it was just possible to hang onto the moulding.

"I'm in training," said Rusty. "I'm going to try and climb right up and over the arch." Each time we passed the arch we would have a little go at the problem and were getting further and further off the ground. We were in the yard one morning with a crowd of students, waiting for a latecomer, when Bill thought he would try Rusty's climbing challenge.

He got quite high and then fell off. We always fell off, but Bill fell rather awkwardly on this occasion. We laughed when he complained about his wrist hurting, and he went off to take his group on a mountain walk. Evidently it must have been hurting Bill all day for as soon as he finished work, he went straight to the hospital in Dunoon.

Late that night he came into my room with a snow-white plaster on his arm, supported by a sling. "Gosh Bill, so you did break it."

"Yeh … and you all laughed." He said it like a wounded hero and then smiled.

"Colle's fracture apparently. The doc said I couldn't drive." After a few days Bill was back instructing but could only do mountain walking, and even for this, Hamish had to drive him out.

*

Transport was always a problem. Very often one of the mini-buses would be in the garage for a service or repair and Hamish often needed some form of transport to go to Dunoon for food.

Vic must have been moaning to the transport department in Edinburgh, for one day he announced at the staff meeting, "Oh, I've

176

managed to get us another vehicle. It's only a small van but it should be good for shopping runs. Next time I go to Edinburgh one of you can come with me and bring it back."

I was free on the day needed to pick up the new van and as Bill couldn't do much with his arm in plaster, he joined me. We set off with Vic, like kids going to the seaside for the day. It had been a cold night and Vic had spent some time cleaning ice from the windscreen.

He now had the heater full on and we bowled along like kings. We were in the middle of a high-pressure system so although it was cold the countryside looked beautiful. The trees were covered with frost and our fresh water loch was frozen round the edge. The mountains looked so much better with a dusting of snow on the summits, and they stood out in a clear blue sky.

There was obviously a temperature inversion, for smoke from the scattered farms rose straight up for a while and then curled slowly downwards to settle as a layer in hollows.

It was a pleasant drive over to Edinburgh but I could not fully relax because Vic drove so fast. I was concerned as we rounded sharp bends at great speed, particularly where trees hung over the road to create damp, cold areas where frost could clearly be seen.

Bill must have been feeling the same tension, for, after a lengthy silence in the car he suddenly said, "Are we late, Vic?"

"No…. Why?"

"You're driving a bit fast." I smiled. Perhaps it wasn't only the instructors who drove too fast.

On arrival in Edinburgh, we went straight to the transport section to pick up the new van. I suppose it was new to us, but we were rather disappointed to see it was a very old van indeed. It had wire spoke wheels, two small, round headlights and a rounded bonnet that hinged along the centre line which was held down by two straps on each side. The back section was rounded with two little doors that wobbled with the movement of the metal shell. It was dark green and reminded me of a delivery van. In fact, it was just like the small bread van that I had seen as a child in London and forever afterwards that is what we all called it: the bread van.

Inside it had low seats so that even tall people appeared to peer over the dashboard and out of the flat windscreen, which was jointed down the middle. The gear lever wobbled around by my left elbow and to use the clutch pedal my whole foot came well off the floor. I got in and turned the key but nothing happened.

"You have to pull the starter knob," said a plump chap in a brown smock coat who I assumed was the foreman. I pulled the starter knob and the engine wearily turned over for a few seconds and then stopped.

177

"Och. It hasna been used for a wee while." The foreman reached under the seat and brought out a starting handle. "You'll have to use this."

With Bill at the controls, I turned the handle tentatively a few times. It was a long time since I had used a starting handle but with growing confidence I swung it sharply and the engine purred into life, sounding rather like a sewing machine.

We left Vic in town and set off cautiously on our way home. The van was so old that when I wanted to turn left or right an indicator arm flicked out from the side.

The first time I pulled away at traffic lights, Bill's seat fell backwards and him with it. His feet pedalled in the air and he had to pull on my shoulder to drag himself upright. When the need arose in future he held onto the dashboard with both hands. It was a very light van, perhaps made worse by being completely empty, and I felt it might roll off the road on a sharp bend. However, I gained confidence as we went along and we picked up speed when the road was clear.

Bill rubbed his hands together. "It's freezing in here. Where is the heater?"

"Don't know. See if you can find it." He searched around the dash but it was soon obvious that the van didn't have the luxury of any heating. It was going to be a cold journey.

There was not much ice on the main roads but puddles had built up near the kerb. The first time we went close to one of these a jet of slushy water squirted up Bill's trouser leg. He snatched his knee up to his chin. "Oh, damn it." He peered down at the floor on his side. "Look, there's a big hole here. I can see the road passing underneath."

I couldn't help laughing, but as the time passed, we both got so cold that we eventually had to stop in a lay-by. "I've got to get my blood moving again," I said. We got out and with stiff legs did some running on the spot. Then I got down and did some press-ups.

Bill said I looked ridiculous. "People driving by must think we're religious or something. Mecca might be this way."

As we got into the hills the roads became worse with patches of black ice under trees. I drove slowly round some of the bends but perhaps not slowly enough. On one bend, where a bridge crossed a burn, we slid smoothly across the road and only missed hitting a stone wall when the wheels ran along a muddy bank at the side of the road. I managed to straighten up and looked across to see Bill with staring eyes sitting back stiffly in his seat. "Phew. That was close," I said.

"Yeh." Bill stopped bracing himself against the dashboard. "Vic was right when he said the most dangerous thing we do is driving."

CHAPTER 28: THE CAIRNGORM TRAGEDY

Most of our work was not adventurous for the instructors. In fact, it was even a little boring at times, but of course there are dangers in the activities we taught. Bad weather could also make things difficult in the winter. It was still winter when I heard about John Harlin.

Rusty and Pat had been married in the Alps and the famous American mountaineer, John Harlin, was their best man.

Mountaineering was never a big news item but there was more interest than usual on the radio as a team were attempting to climb the north face of the Eiger. Rusty had been the first from Africa to climb this extremely dangerous alpine face, but this new route was to be a direct line in winter and the leader was the American, John Harlin. I was keen to follow the progress of this international team of top mountaineers and listened to the radio every morning. It was at one of these early morning reports that I heard John had fallen from the face and been killed.

When Rusty came in for breakfast I said to him. "Have you heard the news from the Eiger?"

"No."

"John Harlin has been killed."

"Oh…. That's sad…. Was it a rockfall?"

"No. I understand that a fixed rope broke. Frayed by the wind, they think."

"Oh, that's very sad." Rusty spooned porridge into a bowl. "It's a dangerous face. Poor John." He showed no great emotion, but mountaineers attempting the biggest challenges take the biggest risks and I suppose he was hardened to the possibilities of losing a friend.

It was only a few years later that he lost another friend, Dougal Haston. Dougal, who climbed the north face of the Eiger with Rusty, also died in the Alps.

However, Rusty was still keen to accept a challenge and went across to Norway to do a new route on the massive face of the Trolltind Wall. He also helped to make a successful television film about rock climbing. He was the cameraman shooting a live ascent of the Old Man of Hoy, the tall sea stack off the west coast of Scotland.

Most of our work was naturally at a very low level but even this could be dangerous if we made the simplest mistake, and I made plenty.

There was one day when Rusty and I had a group climbing in Glencoe. It was terrible weather and Rusty said to me, "Well, Peter, the only route for this sort of weather is Clachaig Gully. Have you ever done it?"

"Clachaig Gully? No."

"It's easy," he said. "We can do it in our walking boots and wearing our full waterproofs." So, with the rain pouring down we got to the foot of the deep-cut gully at the lower end of Glencoe.

I checked that all of the students were tied onto the ropes and were going to be safe. Then I led up the first pitch. It wasn't hard, but with the rain pouring down and wearing walking boots it was hard enough and not the sort of place that one wanted to fall from. I got over some tricky parts and was grateful to put on a runner.

I reached behind for the rope to clip it onto the karabiner but the rope wasn't there. I had been so keen to see the students were safe I had forgotten to tie myself to the lead rope. I did not fancy climbing down again and soloed right on to the top, then had to scramble down the side of the gully and do the pitch all over again, but this time with the rope fixed to me. The rest of this long climb went well and by the time we were at the top the ragged black clouds were breaking up to show blue sky beyond.

Another time, I was on the last day of a rock-climbing course with a group of good students. For the last climb of the week I chose a rather difficult climb of two pitches. It was a wonderful day and I had not a care in the world as I reached the top of the cliff and tied myself to a solid spruce tree. I pulled the rope in which was tied securely to the lad way below. He was on a ledge and still tied to the belay. I shouted down, "Okay Stephen, untie and come up."

I had been working with the same students all week and must have become too casual. Of course, what I meant to say was, "untie from the belay and climb when you're ready."

I started to take the rope in and as it was slack I pulled it in quickly. Faster and faster I took the rope in until, to my horror, the end of the rope snaked up to the top. The student had untied completely from the rope and was already climbing up to the top of an 80-foot cliff with absolutely no protection at all!

I could shout down to him to stop and go back to the ledge but this might have been impossible for him. It would take me a while to abseil down to him and during the wait on small holds he might have panicked and fallen to a likely death.

I simply held my breath and said nothing. He climbed closer and closer and seemed to be enjoying it all but perhaps he hadn't realised that he had no protection from a fall. It was only when he was on safe ground and stood beaming with pleasure that I slumped down on the heather and could release my breath.

*

Even on our own small training cliffs it was possible for the students to make a mistake that might have been fatal.

Each student had a karabiner fixed to their harness and I checked all of these carefully. I would then climb to the top of the cliff, belay and safeguard the students as they climbed up. After each student got to the top, I would throw the rope for the next person to attach themselves. I had a loop well tied into the end of the rope and the student only had to clip the bight into the karabiner on the harness. However, each student had a spare sling looped round their neck which had a second karabiner attached into it.

A girl was to climb next and I always positioned myself so that I could see the rope clipped into the karabiner. "Is the gate screwed up securely?" I shouted.

She looked down. "Aye."

"Right, climb when you're ready." She was correct. The rope was secured into the karabiner, but it was the wrong karabiner. She had clipped it into the one loosely hung round her neck. It was only when she was nearly up to the top of the forty foot of cliff that I realised the mistake. In future I carried the spare slings and karabiner so there could be no mistake.

*

We often had voluntary instructors who came for a week or more, and one of these was Craig. He was an excellent mountaineer and a gifted instructor and over the weeks he was given more responsibility until he was left to lead his own group for a whole course. A one-night camp was part of most courses and the students were given a half-day of instruction on all the equipment we supplied.

One piece of equipment was a cooking stove, and the stoves that Craig's group had were gas stoves. They are almost foolproof, but not quite.

During the dark winter evening at Craig's camp, two girls from one tent joined another couple of girls in their tent. Both stoves were alight and when one of the gas canisters ran out a new cylinder had to be fitted. The students had been told by Craig not to change the canisters but to bring them to him if they ran out. But students don't always listen. The night was wet and windy and it seemed a simple matter for the girls to change the gas cylinder for a new one.

However, they made a mistake in trying to fit the new canister. It was pierced but not screwed in place and the liquid gas squirted out in a fine jet across the tent.

This might not have been a tragedy except that the other stove was still burning. In an instant the whole tent became a fireball. Craig did everything he could and gave perfect first aid to the girls.

The results could have been much worse but all four girls were burned on the hands and parts of their faces. The girls were taken to hospital and it was early morning when I was sent to sort out the kit from the abandoned camp.

I was surprised the students were not burned more severely. There was nothing left of the tent at all and the four sleeping bags were burnt to a black crisp. Apparently, the girls had been lying in the bags and that saved them from worse injury, but all four were burned and two needed minor skin grafting. The students recovered extremely well in a few months and even those who needed skin grafting apparently showed little sign of their ordeal.

Poor Craig was really shaken and asked if he could have done anything differently. We assured him he did everything that one would expect, but I'm sure that we all gained valuable experience from these incidents. In future the instructor kept all the spare cylinders for the students and only the instructor attached a new cylinder if required.

*

Edinburgh Education Department had a real commitment to outdoor education. Apart from our residential centre on the west coast there was a centre in the Cairngorms mountains. This centre was only small and had no permanent instructors only a warden. It was often used by instructors who worked from schools in the city. We met these city-based instructors quite often as they would come over to Benmore for joint staff training.

One of these instructors was Alison. I worked with her on a number of courses and found her to be an excellent mountaineer. She was very capable but not brash; very experienced in the Scottish Highlands but not foolhardy.

I was sometimes envious of the city instructors. Although they worked from the city and didn't have the 'esprit de corps' that our team had in a residential centre, they did have some good facilities. They had good local crags for climbing, and quite a few of the schools had indoor climbing walls. No cold days in the wet and wind for them; they could teach climbing in the dry. Other schools had swimming pools and they had a fleet of short kayaks so they could even teach kayaking in cosy warm conditions at any time of the year. They also taught skiing. This was carried out on one of the best artificial ski slopes in Britain and of course, they had free use of this slope themselves during free time, so they all became good skiers. They worked in schools and developed special activity clubs. The instructors didn't have to teach the basics of each activity every week as we did, and the young people in these school clubs became good at the activities.

*

These students were taken on more and more adventurous expeditions. One of these expeditions was a traverse over the Cairngorm Plateau one winter. There were two groups, one group being led by Alison, the very competent instructor I had worked with. The forecast was poor, but they were all experienced and extremely well-equipped.

They left the cosy little centre and were driven to the ski car park. Each with a heavy rucksack they walked up to the top station of the ski lift and then headed for the summit of Cairngorm Mountain.

As they gained height the weather deteriorated, but the wind was behind them and they bent their heads to the challenge. At the summit they split into two groups, the faster group going with the male instructor and the slower group being led by Alison. They took a compass bearing and set off across the four miles of plateau with the faster group gradually pulling away in front. The weather started to get much worse, but with the very strong wind pushing them along and down the gentle incline for the first couple of miles, they made good progress.

The faster group made their way in deepening snow and after a few hours, eventually struggled up the gentle slope to the top of the March Burn. At this point they had a steep descent downwards and as soon as they started the descent they were out of the severe wind. They made good time down to the shelter in the deep-cut valley of the Laraig Ghru and eventually back to the outdoor centre just before dark.

The slower group were having trouble. The snow was getting deeper by the minute and it was being driven by a tremendous storm. As the snow got deeper the students were finding it more and more difficult to make progress and one or the other would slump down in the snow. Alison decided that they couldn't push on. They would retreat back to the Cairngorm Mountain and down to the car park.

They turned round to re-trace their steps but it quickly became obvious that they were now walking straight into the driving snow and a very strong wind that was increasing all the time. Progress was made more difficult as they were now going slightly uphill. It is only a very gentle gradient but with the hurricane force wind it wasn't possible. However, they still had a safe refuge.

This refuge was the mountain hut, a 'bothy' made from corrugated iron sheets that was not far off their original route. This was the same bothy that Eric had shown the group on our two-night snow hole expedition.

Once again, they turned with their backs to the wind and made for the Lochan Bhuie hut. Alison's navigation was excellent but in the severe weather anyone would have found it extremely difficult to find the small bothy. What Alison didn't realise was that the snow had now virtually covered the hut. It must have been a terrible few hours.

The students could not go on so eventually Alison decided there was no alternative but to sleep out overnight. The students were extremely well equipped with plastic survival bags and sleeping bags and they all settled down for the night waiting for the storm to subside in the morning.

But in the morning the storm was just as bad as ever. The students were now in worse shape and there was no chance of them walking out. They would have to be rescued. This would probably be straightforward for people knew the route they were taking. During the day the weather did improve a little and late in the afternoon they heard a helicopter searching overhead. Alison had rescue flares and she fired two off. However, in the severe weather and thick clouds, they were never seen and as darkness closed in on the group they settled down for another freezing night.

The next day the weather had cleared and after much searching the group were found. But it was too late. Only one student and the instructor had survived. The others had died of hypothermia. This was probably the worst tragedy that has ever happened to a student group in Britain.

*

There was a long enquiry but it was eventually decided that the instructor did everything anyone could have done in weather that was exceptionally bad - even bad for the Cairngorm plateau. One decision that came from this sad tragedy was that too much reliance was put in the refuge hut. I thought it a strange decision but the bothy at Lochan Bhiue was demolished.

A few years later, Alison took a mountain instructor's exam with twenty other instructors who were all men. After a week of assessment, she passed as the top instructor.

CHAPTER 29: KAYAK RACING

Although Rusty's first love was climbing, he had become more interested in kayaking and it hadn't taken him long to get very good. We would practise in the local weir and I was keen to get experience of other aspects of the sport.

So, one morning I said to Rusty, "I'm keen to do a few slalom competitions. Would you be interested?"

Rusty nodded. "Yes, sure…. We could go in my van."

Our first competition was a slalom course set up on a stretch of the River Tweed. As we had never been in a competition before we had been entered in the novice category. This meant we could practise as much as we wanted and we made the very most of the time. Time and time again we went down the course practising to get through each gate without touching the hanging poles on either side. With frequent rests, we eventually managed to get through all of the gates - all except gate number nine.

Time and again we failed to get through cleanly and eventually I pulled alongside Rusty who was resting in a large eddy. "This gate is difficult, eh? I think the key is to do a powerful hanging draw stroke."

"Mm. Perhaps. I've been trying a strong cross bow stroke; the water is so powerful at that spot." He pointed with his paddle.

"Yes. We're fit and we can't do it. I don't see how some of these skinny kids will manage it."

Just as I said this a girl with arms like matchsticks came down the course. We watched from the slack water and I smiled knowingly to Rusty. "Look at this poor little girl. She won't have a chance."

She plunged down the small fall above the gate and spun the kayak round with a couple of very basic strokes and looked so relaxed and elegant. Then, sitting confidently upright she paddled forwards into the current and, without any great effort, it seemed, she went cleanly through gate nine and swept down river again quite close to us. With an open mouth I watched her line up for the next gate, go through cleanly and disappear.

For a few seconds I was speechless, then I said, "That's the way to do it."

Rusty shook his head in disbelief. "As she went through the gate, she wasn't even looking at it. She was turning round to look for the next one."

"Yes, she was reading the water so well."

Rusty laughed. "We have the strength, it's the skill we lack."

We enjoyed the few slaloms we did and certainly we improved but I didn't have the time to specialize. I wanted to experience other aspects of the sport and was pleased to see there was a long-distance race on the River Tay.

Vic was very good at encouraging us to develop our skills and he allowed me to use the 'bread van' and a centre kayak to compete in the river race. The weather had been terrible for a week. Not cold, but very wet indeed and there was flooding in many areas. As I drove towards Loch Lomond the wipers could hardly manage to keep a small patch of the windscreen clear and I had to lean forward to see through. If I went into a puddle a jet of water squirted up through a hole where the brake pedal went through the floor. However, as I drove east the sky began to clear and it became a glorious autumn day. The yellowing oak leaves glistened brightly in the morning sunshine and the burns, tumbling from the hills, shone with patches of sparkling spray. Cumulus clouds floated across the sky majestically and their edges were so sharp it highlighted their whiteness against the blue.

I had left home very early and reached the town of Dunkeld just as a café was opening. I stretched and went in for a pot of tea. I felt better when I came out and walked across the quiet road. Below a grass bank was the river, which seemed to be in full flood. It swirled round the stone columns of Dunkeld Bridge where the race was to start.

The race was to start at eleven and other competitors were already arriving and unloading a variety of kayaks. There were plenty of slalom kayaks like mine, a few general touring boats, a handful of K1 racers and even two sea kayaks. It didn't really matter that the boats were all different for the race was to be run on a handicap basis depending on how fast each boat was. All of us would start together except the specialist K1 racers. The start time for the fast K1's was delayed so that most boats might finish about the same time.

I changed, sorted my boat out and got onto the river.

Eventually, we were all on the water and paddling slowly in the eddies so we would not be swept under the bridge; with the current so strong it would have been rather wearing to paddle back. The marshal called us to order and for just a short while we managed to keep to a line. It was just long enough for the starter to blow his whistle and we were away.

I had never been in any race before and this was a long-distance race of more than sixteen miles. As I didn't have any idea how fast I should be going a race plan was a bit of a problem. The river was also completely unknown to me so I wouldn't be able to judge how far I had gone or how far I still had to paddle. It seemed that the only reasonable plan was to stay on the shoulder of the leading group. If I was able to stay with them, I could follow them down the best part of each rapid. At least I would not be last, although it all depended on staying with the leading group.

The crowd of boats soon started to spread out and I settled into an easy rhythm at the back of the leading group. The river seemed exceptionally high with the brown water containing branches and even larger tree trunks. We were being swept along very quickly past the occasional tree and the odd expensive house and I followed round one bend after another.

The people in front seemed good and appeared to always find the fastest current and only moved from it when it ran through a tree. There were quite a few of these dangerous 'sweepers' lying at the surface, just ready to trap a person swept along by the rumbling river. These trees had fallen over as the strong current on the outside curve of the river had collapsed the bank. Time passed and I began to relax and look around.

There had been ten of us in the leading group but now there were only eight. Each rocky rapid that we came to would have been a problem for me. Not knowing the dangers, I would have had to slow in the quiet water above to inspect a route. But the others knew the river so I confidently followed them between rocks, around vicious little 'stoppers' and on through the crashing standing waves that tailed off after each rapid.

I began to enjoy the day and even had time to notice the beautiful banks of alder and willow trees with plenty of charming little flowers in the clearings.

There were now only four in our leading group and on a straight part of the river I looked over my shoulder to see that the others were well behind. We had definitely broken away from the rest, but where were we? Had we paddled a quarter of the race or half of it? Perhaps I was going too fast and would burn out; I had no idea so I just kept close behind the leaders.

At the next rapid one of the lads in a touring boat hesitated when he saw big standing waves. He fell behind and never caught us again. Then we were only three and all in slalom kayaks.

We went on like this for some time, sweeping along past trees, fields and small villages that had one or two bridges crossing the water. I could guess the names of some of these villages by looking at shop and hotel signs. However, as I was not really clear about their position along our course, I was still no wiser as to how far we had paddled. Then at one sharp bend a stocky chap steering near the bank went too close in and slowed at an eddy line. By the time he had corrected his course the two of us were well ahead and the chap leading grinned across to me.

So, now there were just the two of us at the front. I followed closely in his wake and every now and then he looked quickly behind. He paddled a little faster at times but it didn't last and I began to think he was tiring. I could go in front, but where was I?

My race plan had never got far enough to consider me leading the field and for a while I stayed just behind. A race based on a handicap system means that the person crossing the finish first does not necessarily win the race. On handicap, a competitor coming in later might win the race because the boat is assessed as slower. I now started to think that I might even cross the line first, but still I might not win the race. I would have to paddle faster if I was going to have a chance of winning. The chap in front had looked strong but I felt he was going as fast as he could.

I eventually decided that I could go faster and waited for my moment. It came as we went round a bend and crashed through some standing waves. I increased my paddle speed and he caught up with me but just as he settled I increased my stroke again. He got further and further behind and after half a mile I realised that I had dropped him. Now that I was by myself, I had to find my own way down the river. There were no particularly difficult rapids but I would have preferred to slow down and look for the best line. As I was in a race, I could hardly keep slowing so I plunged down the deepest water and hoped for the best.

From time to time, I glanced over my shoulder to see if anyone was catching up but the river was empty for a while. Then a boat appeared and in a short time a chap had caught up in his fast KI racing boat. He looked completely relaxed and the boat was slipping through the water beautifully. I wasn't surprised for I recognized him as the current Scottish sprint champion. I smiled across and nodded my head as he came level. "Hi. You're going well," he shouted, and I watched his powerful rhythm as he pulled away in front.

The only feature on the river that really worried me was Stanley Weir. I had seen it from the car and it stretched right across from one bank to the other. There were no obvious deep-water shoots and at the bottom of the weir was a nasty big stopper wave that was just the right shape to trap a boat or person. Far worse, I had read there are piles driven in below the weir that a kayak could hit at low water. Surely, I must be getting close to the weir by now but I had to paddle further before I saw the first worrying signs.

The water slowed and became quite smooth at a straight, wide section of the river. There was nothing to see - but then I heard the distant roar. The ominous roar of water got louder and I could see a thin line of spray but nothing below and ahead. Closer and closer I was swept to the shining curve of black water. I kept to the middle and thought about slowing to look over the drop but I knew it would not be possible to hold myself on the lip. I put my head down, gripped the kayak firmly with my knees and paddled hard and straight.

Then I was over and had a quick glance at the frothy standing waves below before I plunged down and through a great trough at the bottom. I flailed at the water churning round my ears but I could see nothing. I paddled frantically to move forward in the weir slot but I had no need to worry; I was not going to get sucked back into the trough. The river was in flood and the water so high that any dangers had been well covered. The kayak careered up and over the huge standing waves, cold water slapped into my face and I paddled hard to keep control. But I could relax for I was over the worst and I settled once again into a steady rhythm.

The banks were now less steep, and cows were grazing in fields on either side. I swept under the odd stone bridge and was surprised to get a wave and shout of support from the few spectators leaning over the arches. The river became more placid and I was just thinking that I was now in the lower part of its course when I saw a small group of people standing on the bank ahead.

As I approached, they clapped and shouted, "Well done!" They must be marshals, I thought.

I called across to them, "Is this the finish?"

"Aye, it is," they shouted back, and waved for me to join them. I paddled across, swung the boat round in a small eddy and leaned on the pleasant grass bank. A couple of guys, came down to help me. "You're the first," one said, and he took hold of the bow and helped me lift it up the bank and onto the level, grassy field.

I was standing with water dripping from me when a fellow, well wrapped up against the cold wind, came over to me. "You did a good time. Do you want a lift back to Dunkeld?"

"Well, er, thanks…. That would be great."

"It's a service we're laying on this year." He pointed across to the road. "Put your boat on the trailer."

Back at Dunkeld bridge it was pleasant to get into dry clothes. I had been warm and comfortable in the enclosed kayak but now the cold was getting through to me. After packing everything onto the bread van I went back into the cafe and treated myself to a large pot of tea and a huge fried dinner with four slices of toast. It was just what I needed and I was soon warm and cosy.

Although it wasn't late it would be dark in a couple of hours. Driving the bread van at night was rather nerve wracking, as the small round headlights were particularly feeble. I decided to set off for home straight away and make the most of the autumn daylight.

*

It was the middle of the next week when the phone rang and Bill went to answer it. We were sitting in the staff room drinking coffee after the evening meal when Bill returned. "Pete. It's for you."

"A phone call, for me?" I was surprised as a phone call for me was a very rare thing indeed.

"Yeh. A man. Don't recognize the voice."

I hurried through to the office and picked up the phone. "Hello, Peter Dyer."

"Helloo. My name is Duncan. I'm chairman of the Scottish Canoe Association and I organized the LD race last Saturday." He went on to tell me that on handicap, I had won the race. I was pleased but he continued, "You are now the Scottish long-distance racing champion."

I was taken aback. "The National champion?"

"Aye. The L.D. champion this year."

"Oh."

"Now, Peter, you drove off so soon we could not present you with the wee prize."

"A prize?"

"Aye. It's a painting. There's also a wee cup that you can keep for the year but it has to be engraved."

"A painting and a cup. That's nice."

"Aye, now," he continued. "We need to present them to you. We have a sprint regatta in four weeks. It's across the Clyde, here, near Largs. If you come over to race we can present you with the picture and the cup."

"Well, er … yes. I would like to come to the regatta but I have no racing boat, only a slalom kayak."

"Och, no problem," he said. "There will be the club K1 sprint boats that you can use."

So, it was all arranged and Bill decided he could also do with some flat-water racing experience, so we left in his mini. We crossed over the Clyde to Gourock on the ferry and drove south to the race site, which was a flat and completely calm stretch of river. Fields stretched away on both sides. A herd of young Fricsians lined the muddy bank opposite, intrigued by the large group of people milling about along the bank.

Bill parked in the field and as we got out a distinguished looking chap wearing green wellingtons and a Barbour jacket approached, "Peter." He

191

held out a hand. "You won't remember me but I saw you on the Tay. I'm Duncan. We spoke on the phone."

"Oh, yes." We shook hands and I introduced Bill. As we walked across towards Duncan's camper van he said, "I thought it best if we present you with the picture and the cup before we start racing today."

"Well. Okay. Whatever suits you."

The crowd of paddlers gathered round and Duncan presented me with the little silver cup and a picture, which still hangs on my wall. When the group of admiring canoeists had dispersed to prepare for the races Duncan said, "I have two club boats for you to use. They're over here." We followed him to where two shining and very narrow K1 racing kayaks were laying on the bank.

"This will be a good experience for us," I smiled confidently. "We've never paddled K1's before."

"Well, if you change you can have some quiet practise before the first race."

"Thank you," I said. "It'll be nice to paddle a boat that really can go fast." As I changed for the race I thought, 'what a nice polite chap and what a pleasant bunch of racers. They were obviously impressed by me, their new Scottish long-distance champion.' Bill stood back a little, and two willing helpers lifted my kayak gently into the water.

Quite a crowd had gathered along the bank to watch me. After all, here was the new Scottish champion: obviously an elite paddler from south of the boarder. I expect they thought they would learn something about the most advanced paddling techniques.

The kayak, long and particularly thin, rocked gently by a grass bank. I took the paddle, stepped in and sat down. Well, I think I sat down, but everything happened so fast it was difficult to tell. The kayak seemed to jump sideways towards the bank and I was upside down in the river. It wasn't a slow capsize but must have seemed more like stepping in one side and straight out of the other. For a few seconds I could not get upright and my legs kicked on the surface with my hands flailing. But it was only for a few seconds, for I quickly realised that the water was only a metre deep.

I stood up with long green weeds draped over my head and one shoulder. There was absolute silence for a while. I could plainly hear the gentle wind through the rushes and even heard the cows stop chewing as they lifted their heads to watch.

The faces on the line of people were a picture of embarrassment and rigid control. They were so polite they didn't even smile. Bill had no such inhibitions. The embarrassed silence was broken as he slapped his knee and through a burst of laughter said, "Marvellous, Pete. They do move quick don't they!"

192

As soon as I laughed the crowd broke into hysterics and kindly helped me out of the thick mud. I did eventually learn to stay upright in the boat and even managed one wobbly race, but it was clear that I was not the outstanding paddler they might have thought. I had only been famous for ten minutes but, even if it was only on the champion's cup, I saw my name in print.

CHAPTER 30: GLENMORE LODGE AND THE AVALANCHE

My name and picture were in print again and this time it was on the front page of all the national newspapers – and it wasn't for a kayak race.

Before the new group of students arrived on Monday mornings, we always had a staff meeting in Vic's office. We had each taken a coffee, and after talking about the coming programme Vic put his cup down and said, "Glenmore Lodge needs more instructors in February so I have arranged for you all to help out."

We were delighted. It was a change to work with adults and I always gained valuable experience.

Early winter that year was windy and January was wet and mild. There was plenty of snow but on the west coast it quickly washed away and ice didn't build so there was little good winter climbing for us. The winter climbing conditions in the Cairngorms always seemed better with deeper falls of snow and cold, clear days. So, a few weeks later with all our winter climbing kit we set off in our best mini-bus and were in high spirits as we drove along the shore of Loch Tay and turned north on the A9. It was a particularly cold day and the sky was completely clear. We could see for miles as we crossed the wide-open pass of Drumochter. The hills and corries, set a long way back from this bleak stretch of road, were deep in snow and it looked good to me.

However, Rusty put on his specs and peered from the side window. "Seems to be plenty of snow, but has it consolidated."

Bill polished the glass and looked out. "Certainly a huge amount of snow, and cold with it." He looked across the other side. "We don't need anything too hard. Perhaps the easy routes have been swept clean."

"Mm, perhaps," said Rusty. "But we don't want knee-deep powder. We can ask the instructors at the lodge what the climbing conditions have been like." I sat and watched the empty valley passing by and thought about what Rusty had said. Yes, I would ask the instructors at the lodge.

Perhaps it was because I always went to the Cairngorm Mountains in winter but as we motored along the open glen towards Aviemore I felt that we had come to a different country. We had left the damp west coast just as the gorse and broom bushes were covered in glorious yellow flowers. The blackthorn trees looked wonderful with all of their white flowers in full bloom set against the purple heather. Daffodils had started to appear in sheltered spots, and there were even newborn lambs in the lower fields.

However, here in the Cairngorms the landscape was still arctic. We turned south at Aviemore. Piles of dirty snow lined the ski road, and the water of Loch Morlich was completely frozen over. The deciduous trees were still bare and their dead branches showed black against the heavy grey sky. Roger eased the bus down the icy driveway of the National Centre, turned off the engine and stretched. "Looks cold out there," he said.

Without sunshine, the mountains in the distance looked dead and grey. Even the green conifers looked sombre and without life. We climbed out of the bus to a thin wind and carried our kit the short distance to the entrance hall.

The principal was there to meet us. "Hi chaps, nice to have you here again. I'll show you your rooms." Despite living in England for some years Eric Langmuir still had a charming Scots accent with every word spoken crisply.

I was sharing a room with Rusty and as he stood looking out of the window to the grey, colourless afternoon he said, "the west coast might be wet but I'm not sure I would want to live here."

We didn't know it at the time but a few years later Rusty and his young family did go to live at Glenmore lodge. He became the chief instructor when Bill left. However, he was right when he had said he might not wish to live there. After a year or so he left to join Bill in Canada where they worked at Calgary University.

We unpacked and joined Roger and Bill for afternoon tea in the staff room. Posted on the notice board was the two-week programme with the staffing details. I was pleased to see that I was instructing snow and ice climbing again. The first few days would be basic techniques and after that some face climbs before the final expedition. I looked forward to the snow-holing expedition. I didn't know it at the time but I was to miss most of this course.

John Cunningham now worked as an instructor at the National Centre. John had been a phenomenon in the climbing world. He had done new rock routes in Wales as long ago as 1947, but it was in Scotland that he was most famous. I remember going to one of his lectures about Mt. Everest, which he attempted with Hamish McInnes some years before its successful ascent in 1953. He told us there were just the two of them on the expedition and as they could only afford one tent they moved it up the mountain as they went - quite revolutionary at the time. The expedition came to an abrupt halt when they returned after a reconnaissance above a dangerous icefall to find their tent and everything in it had been wiped away by an avalanche!

I was in the staff room with the other instructors, munching a piece of fruit cake, when John came up behind me and tapped me on the shoulder. "Hi Peter. Back again for the survival course?"

"Oh, hello John. Yes, back again. I see that we're both instructing climbing."

"Aye." He shook his head. "Could be a wee problem though."

"A problem. Why?"

"Och, the snow conditions are terrible."

"Oh." I frowned. "Probably be something in Coire an t-Sneachda, won't there?"

"Noo, don't think so." He shook his head." We've had no snow until just recently. There's been no build up at all. It's either vertical ice or soft powder."

"Oh, that doesn't sound too good. Not good for students, then? Where do you think we should go tomorrow?"

He poured another cup of tea. "Well, I think the only place is in Coire Cas."

"Coire Cas, eh?"

"Aye." He nodded. "To the right of the corrie it's fairly steep. Last week there was a reasonable slope of firm snow. Not perfect but as good as we're going to get."

After dinner I met my group of clients, who were all men, and briefed them for the following day of climbing. I told them the conditions were not good and we might have to do a bit of searching to find the best spot for instruction. "Let's try and be away sharp in the morning," I said.

*

It was a cold windy night and a little snow had fallen but by the morning the wind had moderated, although clouds lay very low on the hills.

The group seemed excellent and we got the first minibus up to the car park. It was quiet as the ski schools would not start for another hour and we made our way slowly up the wide track that led to the top station. As we got warmed up, I took off one of my sweaters but had to keep on my weatherproof suit for snow was being blown around in all directions.

We reached the top chairlift station, and while the students took a break, I took the opportunity to look more closely at the weather and conditions. Above and across the far side of the corrie I looked for the slope that John had mentioned. It didn't seem very steep and as far as I could see there was no ice at all. Higher up the clouds were very thick indeed. They lay just above our heads in one solid mass as if the ceiling to the world had been lowered.

This was frustrating for me as I was hoping to see if the back wall of the corrie might prove better for instruction. I knew it was steeper and John had already mentioned there was no cornice. He had also told me there was very little snow laying up there either, which was rather unusual. I looked up and, although I couldn't see above the low clouds, there did seem to be plenty of snow on the face now.

We set off again, aiming to keep level, towards the side wall of the corrie, where I hoped to find the place that John had told me about. As we went the snow became soft and not anywhere steep enough for instruction.

I stopped after fifteen minutes and turned to the group who were in a line across the slope and called to them. "I'm trying to find a good spot for us to work but I can't see anything suitable at all. I was told there was a reasonable area over here but it's just soft snow."

One of the clients pointed down the slope. "Is that one of the other groups down there?"

"Yes." I could see three groups and pointed down the face. "That one to the right is the group led by Ross. They're learning avalanche rescues. Finding bodies in deep snow. That sort of thing."

The chap near me laughed. "Perfect conditions for them, then."

"Yes." I pulled my hood up tighter as the wind was blowing from above. "The group walking across below are doing the same programme as us today. They're with John. He was instructing here last week. He told me the only place that we could find a suitable face in these conditions is across there." I nodded my head to where we were walking.

We stood there looking down the great sweep of unbroken snow to the chair lift and the piste far below. To shield us from the wind we had our hoods pulled up tightly. Perhaps it was the hoods and wind that stopped us hearing the dull boom and noise above. However, it wouldn't have helped us.

My feet suddenly slipped down the slope. For a second, I simply thought the footsteps had collapsed and didn't even take my hands from my pockets. Then in an instant the whole mountain seemed to be moving. I was thrown forwards and over and for a while I was on the surface. I was on the surface tumbling over and over and it was then that I realised we were in an avalanche.

It had come from way above and we were swept downwards at quite a speed. We were moving fast but my thoughts and images seemed to have plenty of time to take things in. I had no real chance to control my fall and the possibility of 'swimming' to stay on the surface never existed. I had no more control than if I had been in a weir slot.

Then I was covered but still being tumbled downward. I clearly remember seeing daylight through the snow that appeared yellow. Until now I felt that I was just being swept along; my mind was clear and I wasn't injured.

Then everything changed. My whole body seemed to be violently struck, not by a sharp object, but by a hard, crushing force. I continued to be tumbled down inside this great mass of 'yellow' snow but now only in a semi-conscious state. Then the movement stopped and I forced myself violently back to consciousness. I tried to thrust an arm towards daylights but that was the only part of me that I could move. The rest of my body was held as solidly as if I had been set in concrete.

It felt like only a few seconds before people were touching my hand but I was later told it was nearly half an hour. I was drifting in and out of consciousness and remember feeling quite peaceful and not even cold. I only felt the cold when my face was cleared and it was John who first spoke to me. "Peter. We've got you. You okay?"

"Yes … yes." Even though I wasn't fully conscious, now that I was not buried alive, I was most concerned about my students. Apparently only half the people buried in an avalanche survive; the others are asphyxiated. John had probably saved my life.

"John." I croaked. "John … listen. There were eight students."

"Aye. It's okay Pete … relax." He brushed the snow from my face. "We have them all."

There seemed to be plenty of people about and they dug around me and eventually cleared most of the snow. They gently tried to slide me out of the icy 'cast' and it was only then that I realised I was badly injured. "Argh.... No.... My leg."

With Ross on one side and John on the other they carefully freed me and I was able to look about. The students and instructors, who we had been watching down below us only a few minutes before, were all around. Little groups were looking after the injured and I could see patches of pink snow around most of the bodies. It seemed that most had open wounds and some were groaning in pain. But I could relax. At least all my students were out of the snow and alive.

As I relaxed, I must have slipped out of consciousness again for the next thing I remember was sliding down strapped firmly to a stretcher. I was placed inside the top chairlift station and it was here that a doctor bent over me. "Hello. How are you? Do you want a painkiller?"

"No, thanks." I mumbled. "I prefer nothing until I'm in hospital." As they transferred me to a snow rescue sledge, I must have groaned for the doctor came over.

"Och. I think we had better give you a shot. Aye, a shot of morphine."

I remember nothing else until I woke up between crisp white sheets in the hospital at Inverness. They kept me well sedated and it was only after a couple of days they could tell me I had a crushed pelvis. All nurses seem attractive when one is in pain, and my nurse with her lovely accent told me, "Och, you've been lucky but you have lost a lot of blood."

"Oh. Lost blood. But I'm not cut anywhere?"

"No. You're in shock from the blood lost within the injury." She tucked the sheet in. "We might have to give you a transfusion."

After three days I was aware that other members of my group were in the same ward. There was a chap with a broken spine, but thankfully this turned out much less serious than it sounded. Another man had two black eyes from a cracked skull. In fact, everyone in the group had broken at least one bone. However, most had already been discharged with only minor injuries.

They hooked my right leg up for traction and a cord went from my foot, over a pulley on the end of the bed and down to a heavy weight. The rope seemed to keep falling off the pulley and I was put on a course of pills. "Now, what are these pills for?" I smiled at my lovely nurse.

"Och, doesne matter. You just keep tekking them."

"Seriously," I smiled. "What are the pills for?"

"They're tranquillizers. Och, you're far too active. You're wriggling aboot and the rope at the end of the bed keeps falling off the pulley. It's supposed to keep your leg in traction."

We laughed and I did as I was told. After a week lying flat on my back I was no longer in pain and it was decided I could do some physiotherapy. I was delighted about this but when the doctor came to see me he made it quite clear that I was still going to lie flat on my back. "Now, Mr. Dyer," he placed his hand just above my right toe. "Can you lift your leg to touch my hand?"

I rolled my eyes. Of course I could do that, I thought. I need some real exercise. They took the traction off and I tried to move my leg but to my utter amazement I could not even lift it one inch off the bed. In fact, my brain seemed unable to work out what muscles I even needed to use for the exercise. The doctor lifted my foot just clear of the bed. "Now try."

My brain seemed to get the message and by a great effort I did nearly take the weight. "Very good," he said. But I was shocked. "You have a serious injury," he said consolingly. "You won't be walking properly for three months. No mountaineering for six months."

After about three weeks lying on my back, I was instructed never to put weight on my right leg, but was allowed to get up. By using crutches, I was able to hobble round the ward and chat to the other patients who were older than me. On one occasion the matron came in and said, with a patient smile, "So Peter, I can see that you're doing my ward rounds."

*

The doctors seemed pleased with my progress so a few weeks later I said goodbye to all the hospital staff and left Inverness. In an ambulance I was taken back to the west coast and Benmore Gardens. I was given strict instructions that on no account must I put weight on the leg as this would strain the mending pelvis. However, it wasn't long before the doctors allowed me to do more and I soon managed to do plenty of exercises and was back at work in two months. That summer I went to France and had a very good season of climbing in the Alps. Once again, I had been very lucky.

*

Poor John, who had saved me in the avalanche, was not so lucky. A few years later he was climbing on the sea cliffs in North Wales. A great wave hit the cliff and he was swept off and down into the sea. John was never a strong swimmer and with heavy climbing kit attached to him there was little hope. John's body was found a few weeks later in Liverpool Bay.

John was there when I needed him and it was a pity that I was not there when he needed me.

CHAPTER 31: ROB AND ANOTHER CENTRE

John Cunningham was unlucky - and so was Rob. Rob was an instructor at the Derbyshire outdoor centre who came to us for two weeks of winter training.

We were at the usual staff meeting before a new course arrived when Vic said, "Would any of you like experience of working in another centre, perhaps for one course?"

The others didn't seem very interested but I was very keen. "Yes, that's a good idea Vic. I could do with experience of other centres."

A few weeks later I was returning from a day of sailing. The students had all gone to the drying room to leave their wet gear and Vic met me as I was sorting out the minibus. "Ah, Peter. Had a good day?"

"Yes, thanks Vic. The wind was perfect today. It's getting a bit cold for the students though. I shall have to get them to take more sweaters."

"Mm. Nearly October I suppose. We shall have to stop sailing in a few weeks." He leaned against the minibus. "I've made some enquiries about you working in another centre for a course."

"Oh yes?"

"Well, there's an instructor who works at Whitehall, the Derbyshire centre; an instructor called Rob Stone. He would like to spend a few weeks up here. Would you like to work at Whitehall for a while?"

"Yes. Certainly, that would be great."

"Well, Rob wants some snow and ice experience so I've suggested he comes up next February. You could go down there as soon as we finish sailing in October."

"Right. Great."

*

It was nearly November when I left Benmore in the 'bread van' that Vic had loaned me. I drove to Dunoon in a leisurely way and caught the morning ferry across the Clyde. I stood on deck as we cut across a silky, blue ocean. Scotland looked wonderful. The sky was unusually clear and the tops of the hills were covered with the first dusting of snow.

It was a long, rather tedious journey, down the main road to Carlisle. The back of the van squeaked and rattled. The engine kept going well enough, but it was my comfort that was the problem. A strong wind blew up through holes in the floor of the van. There was no heater but I was

201

prepared and wore my down jacket over a sweater. With a woolly hat and gloves my body was warm enough - it was my feet that were freezing.

I had to stop every hour or so to get out and run stiffly on the spot. I kept going south on the old A-roads, as motorways had not yet been built this far north.

I drove around Manchester and eventually east to Buxton in the Peak District. From the look of the countryside it still seemed to be summer down here. Oak trees had lost no leaves yet and the fireweeds and primroses along the edges of the roads were still in bloom.

Driving out of the little town I gained height onto the moorland and eventually crunched slowly along the driveway to the outdoor centre established by Derbyshire Education Department some years before.

The programme during my two-week visit was similar to ours at Benmore. I did a few days of rock climbing on the local 'edges', which were a big improvement to ours in Scotland. The outcrops the instructors used for climbing were either limestone or gritstone rock. This made a pleasant change from the rock of mica schist around Benmore, which had smooth friction holds and was very slippery when wet. There were days of walking through the countryside with little streams to cross, interesting paths through open forests, and small valleys alongside rocky crags.

There was plenty of interest for the young students and they enjoyed the walking. I can't say that our students in Scotland always enjoyed hiking up the mountains. Certainly, the countryside in Derbyshire seemed more suitable for teaching children outdoor skills.

However, as I drove north after my visit, I was looking forward to seeing again the craggy mountains and particularly the ocean.

Having left rather late in the day there was no chance of catching the last ferry. I would have to drive straight through Glasgow. It was after one in the morning as I rattled along Sauchiehall Street. I must have been going too fast, for a few blocks ahead of me a policeman stepped smartly into the deserted road and stood with a hand held up. He was unaware how poor the brakes were on my little van otherwise he would not have been so reckless.

For a few seconds I was scared that I might not be able to stop and would have had to swerve by him but I did stop and he walked up to my door. I opened the window and he said, "Where's the fire then?"

"Er. Sorry?"

"Och, you were gayin a wee bit fast, were ya not?"

"Oh, was I?"

He stepped back a pace and looked at the van. "Is this your vehicle sir?"

"Well, no … it's from where I work."

He strolled to the front and took out a notebook and pencil. "What is the registration sir?"

"Mm ... well, I don't know ...." He licked the end of his pencil, wrote something down and came back to my door.

I looked up at him. "You see.... My boss let me use the van to do some work down in England."

"England, eh?" The way he said 'England' I was not at all sure I had said the right thing. He walked slowly round the van. He looked at the wheels with their wire spokes and gave a couple of tyres a kick, then appeared at my door again. He must have thought anyone driving an old vehicle like our bread van could surely never be a criminal.

Eventually he said, "Now lad, drive more slowly." He looked at the van again and smiled. "Off you go."

Glasgow is a big city but even before modern roads it didn't take long to reach Loch Lomond. The feeble round headlamps did little to brighten a very dark night. The loch looked sinister and the mountains across the other side were pitch black, but I liked the timeless emptiness of everything.

I turned west, over the top and down to Loch Long and then made the climb over the Rest and be Thankful Pass. A new moon slipped out from behind clouds as I rolled round the bends alongside Loch Eck until I eventually arrived at the great gates of the botanic gardens. I drove slowly up the gravel drive, past staff houses that were all in darkness, and stopped in our courtyard. The engine juddered and became quiet. It was very late; I was weary but I felt that I was home.

I had not met Rob from the Derbyshire centre. He had been away on holiday with his wife while I was in the Peak District, so the first time I met him was in February. Vic brought him into the staff room just before dinner one evening. "Ah, Peter. This is Rob."

"Oh, Hello Rob." We shook hands.

"Show him around and sort out any kit he needs."

"Right, okay Vic." The principal left us and I smiled at Rob. "We'll have dinner first."

Rob rubbed his hands together "Oh, good. I'm hungry. The drive took much longer than I thought." He was dressed in corduroy trousers and a thick Norwegian sweater, and on his feet were well polished brown shoes. He was a good-looking chap, clean-shaven, with dark hair. He immediately looked the sort of chap I thought I would like, and I was not wrong.

We talked together long after dinner and the coffee had finished. He was a keen climber and enthusiastic about most outdoor sports, but I gathered he wasn't a fanatic. He was keen to learn as much as possible about our work but his number one interest was his new family. He had been married for about two years and his wife had given birth to a little girl just two months ago. I could imagine him being a great dad.

Rob joined groups for all the normal mountain activities, but the weather was rather 'normal' for the west coast. It was wet and windy most days and although snow had fallen on the higher mountains there was little solid snow around Benmore.

It was nearly the end of Rob's visit when Roger sat down beside me at teatime. He poured a cup of tea and said, "I feel rather bad about Rob's time with us here, Pete. The weather has been damned awful."

"Yes, pity. It's been worse than usual."

"He particularly wanted the sort of experience that's not possible in the Peak District."

"Yes." I scratched the back of my head. "I believe he was hoping to do some snow and ice routes with students."

"Mm." Roger gave a sly grin. "How would you like a day with him tomorrow? Take him up to Glencoe and do a decent route?"

I sat up and put my cup down. "What, just the two of us?"

He smiled. "Yes. A decent winter route. The sort of thing he could never get in Derbyshire."

"Sure." I was delighted. It was like being given a day off work.

I spoke to Rob and he was keen. "We should try and leave really early."

"Right," he smiled. "As early as you like."

The next morning, we had a huge bowl of cereal and made ourselves some toast and tea. The centre was still silent as we drove off into the darkness at five o'clock.

We were in Rob's comfortable car and with the heater on and music to listen to, the journey passed easily. Daylight had almost crept upon us by the time we reached Rannoch Moor and we could look at the mountain bulk of the Buachaille, apparently isolated, across the cold emptiness. However, as we pulled into the lay-by nearest the foot of the mountain there was a hint of brightness between gaps in the clouds. "Perhaps we're in luck," I said.

"Mm. There seems plenty of snow in the gullies too." Rob didn't delay and after putting on a windproof we opened the back of the car and took out our gaiters and boots. With everything packed the night before it was only a few minutes before we were walking briskly down the path, across the river by the little footbridge, and were heading up towards our mountain.

The route we had chosen was the classic and long Crowberry Gully. I had not done this route before so it would be an interesting day for both of us. We slowed a little as we gained height and eventually stopped as the snow steepened. I stamped a level platform. "Seems a good place to sort out the kit."

"Right." Rob looked up the gully cut deep into the cliff. "Looks great."

I tilted my head backwards to look up. "Yes. We could do the normal route, which goes right at that fork, or we might even try the direct finish by the left fork."

Holding coils of rope, we moved together on good firm snow. The rock walls gradually closed in on either side and the climbing became more serious. We found a handy thread belay and Rob kicked a platform and tied on. In those days we still had only one ice axe each and with a string of gear round my neck I led on.

The climbing was easy but steep. Our tiny footprints could be seen a long way below and beyond them was the road, like a thread running down through the glen. We climbed easily, pitch after pitch, and the only problem was that spindrift snow would come slewing down the gully from time to time. It wasn't dangerous but came down like a little river and built up round our legs if we were standing still. On every little overhang we were careful to keep our hoods up and over our helmets or the fine powder snow would have poured down our necks.

A few hours had passed by the time we reached the fork in the gully. To the right was the traverse, which led, after a few moves, to the continuation of the open gully. It looked pleasant climbing. Straight above our heads a deep cut chimney, thick with ice, went almost vertically upwards to the top. This was the direct finish.

I studied the route for a minute. "Shall we try the harder finish?"

Rob shrugged. "Okay, if you're leading."

"Right, I'll have a look." I clipped the runners onto my harness and started bridging up. There was enough ice for my crampons to bite and I made good progress up to the chockstone that was jammed between the walls. This great boulder created an overhang and I moved my crampons to scratch into the ice on the edge of the walls. With my legs spread wide I was now in balance and the view between my feet was quite spectacular. After a few nervous moves I was able to reach over and drive the wooden shaft of my axe into the snow above the chockstone. The snow was sound and gave me confidence to grate upwards, spreading my weight evenly on feet and hands. With one ungainly thrust I was over and standing up above the crux.

"Peter," Rob's voice came up from below. "Only three metres of rope."

It took me a while to find a couple of doubtful belays so I used my axe as a foot brake for extra insurance. I called down the gully, "Rob, when you're ready."

"Climbing," he shouted, and as I took in the rope, I was free to look around.

Although the climb had not been particularly steep my position, perched above the overhang, felt awesome. The walls, black and glistening on either side, dropped down to a void that was now out of sight. I could only look out into space. The rope came in fairly well and then it stopped. After a minute or two Rob grunted and said, "Peter ... keep it tight."

I inched the rope as tight as I could and eventually Rob reached over the edge and did a belly crawl onto safe ground. He stood up. "Phew. Thanks."

The gully was not so steep above and Rob took the gear and led through. Better climbers than us might have moved together but we didn't want a slide that might have sent us over the chockstone and out into space. We climbed the last few pitches and stood together on level ground.

We could now look in all directions. Rannoch Moor ran away in the distance to our right; across the Glen was the long ridge of the Aonach Eagach and on our left were the complex summits of Stob Corrie and Bidean Nam Bian.

The wind was not too strong and although the sun was too shy to peer round the clouds it wasn't a bad afternoon. In a relaxed mood we went over the summit and round to the top of the great gully. A small cornice had broken away at the lip and I cautiously cut a couple of steps downwards. However, the snow was in perfect condition and we made a relaxed and easy progress downwards with Rob going first and me protecting him on the rope.

Eventually, off steep ground we stopped to take off the rope and put kit in our rucksacks. We stood looking around. Behind us the great cliffs were cut by chimneys and cracks. I liked the wild nature of it all but Rob had a broader interest. He pointed out to me features of glaciation and mountain structures that I would never have noticed. Lower down he showed a knowledge of plants that I had never possessed. He seemed an intelligent and well-rounded chap.

It was clear to me that for a long time I had been climbing the mountains, going down rivers and sailing the oceans, but had been missing many interesting things. I felt quite ignorant beside Rob. I decided that I would try to learn more about nature. We reached the car and although it wasn't late in the afternoon, I realised we would probably miss dinner.

We drove the short distance to the Kings House Hotel and I telephoned Roger. He arranged to have two meals left for us, so while Rob drove us home to Benmore, we talked.

"So, Rob, have you any plans this year?"

"Yes, we're going to the Alps."

"Your wife as well?"

"Yes, all of us. Of course, things will be different with the baby but we think we've sorted something out. We're going with Dave from Plas Y Brenin. They have a little girl about the same age as ours."

"Oh, I see. Good idea. I've met Dave. Seems a nice guy."

"Yes, he is. Safe on the mountains too. Dave and I hope to do a few good routes. The girls don't want to climb and they are happy with the children. I've bought a papoose and we shall all do some walking together."

"Mm. Should work out okay. Where are you going?"

"Chamonix. Plenty there for the family, and the chairlift is there to make the routes quicker for us."

From what I knew about the two families it seemed an ideal solution. Both of the chaps seemed pleasant family men and good on the hills. They should have had a good time …. But none of us can see into the future.

Winter gradually passed and with it any more chance of snow and ice climbing. Spring approached and I started to prepare for the sailing season.

*

It was August and I had long forgotten the day of climbing on Crowberry gully when I heard the terrible news about Rob.

It seemed that Rob and Dave had left their family camp in Chamonix to do a climb on the south side of the Aiguille du Midi.

It should have taken two days but after three days they failed to return. The two young mothers went to the gendarmerie. The police told them they were holding two bodies for identification. Rob and Dave had been killed. They had been caught in a huge avalanche while still approaching their chosen climb. Gone: two conscientious instructors and two fine husbands and fathers.

I still find it difficult to imagine the terrible situation the young mothers found themselves in. Two little babies in small tents on a campsite full of carefree holiday campers, overlooked by magnificent but deadly mountains. They had to pack their kit with their husbands' few possessions and drive the long journey home to face the future alone.

It must have been a terrible summer for them.

CHAPTER 32: CATH VISITS

That same summer was wonderful for me. I received a letter each day in the mail. The envelopes were always blue and the address was written in the same rounded style. I suppose it was only a matter of time before the rest of the staff started to ask questions about the letter that arrived from Yorkshire every single day.

It was still winter and we were all having coffee when Morag came into the staffroom holding a letter. "Now, Peter. Another letter for you." She laughed and held it up to the light in a pretence to see inside. "Another blue envelope with the very same handwriting."

I held out my hand but she snatched the letter back. "Och nooo. I think we need to know who writes to you every single day."

I laughed. "It's probably from home. It will be from my mother."

Morag peered closely at the postmark. "Yorkshire." She grinned knowingly. "It's always from Yorkshire. Och noo, your folks stay in London." She grinned. "I think we need to know who writes to you every single day."

Bill drummed the table with his hands. "Come on Pete, spill the beans."

Roger took the envelope and sniffed it. "I can smell scent."

Vic grinned and put an arm round my shoulder. "Now, Peter, we're all friends here."

Everyone was laughing and making comments. "Get it off your chest. Tell us who writes to you every single day?"

"Aye." Sheena from the office, usually quiet and serious, joined in. "And I've noticed he replies every single day too."

"A friend," I smiled. "Just a friend."

"Och noo," Morag laughed. "We'll noo accept that. You can do better than that."

I sat back and shrugged my shoulders. "It's a girl I met at college."

"Ah. That's better……... Well? Go on then!"

"Well…. She's from Yorkshire. We've been writing quite a while."

Roger laughed in exasperation. "We know that," he said, and passed me the letter.

"She's a teacher. In a primary school." I told them about Cath.

"Well," said Morag. "Are we going to see this Catherine?"

"Yes, probably. She would like to come up and visit for a while." I turned to Vic. "Would that be okay Vic, for her to stay for a week or so?"

"Sure. Just tell me when she wants to come."

It might seem strange that I kept Cath a secret, but there was a reason. When I had been applying for work as an instructor it seemed that most centres were keen to have single people so that they could live in the centre and be on duty during evenings and nights. When I applied for the Benmore job I did not 'advertise' my steady girlfriend. So, now they knew I had a serious girlfriend and were happy to meet her.

As a teacher, Cath had good holidays and I thought she would like to join me for a few days on one of our courses. I looked through the programme to see what course would be most suitable for her. In May I had a sailing course for teachers that lasted six days. Cath would also have a holiday from school at that time so that course would be perfect for us. She would see what my work involved and hopefully think this area was a good place to live.

Cath had left the school in Leicester and gone home to live with her mum and dad, and now taught in a local primary school in West Yorkshire. Cath still owned the grey mini van that she had at college. We arranged that she would drive up early on a Friday.

So, on that special Friday I joined Hamish on his shopping run into Dunoon and walked down to the pier so that I could meet her from the ferry. I had an hour to spare and as I looked around at 'my' ocean and behind to 'my' hills I felt that I was very much a local in this beautiful part of Scotland.

The ferry was approaching and I checked my appearance in the window of the waiting room. As the large ferry rolled gently just a few metres from the pier I saw Cath waving. I took a deep breath and waved back. Two seamen heaved up the heavy gangplank, which was kept lying on the dock, and tied the end securely before the patient line of passengers walked down. And with them came Cath looking excited and wonderful wearing jeans and a high neck jacket against the strong sea breeze. I gave her a great hug and kiss and we stood together talking about her journey while waiting for her mini van.

The ferries across the Clyde were not the modern 'roll on – roll off' type like the ones that plough across the English Channel. Cars had to be lifted off using the ship's crane. However, the seamen were efficient and we stood holding hands and watching her little van being lifted high into the air and gently lowered to the dock. She was a better driver than me but passed me the key. "You drive, Pete."

This gave me a chance to point out things as we went along. I showed her everything. The new swimming pool, the library, the primary school and the place where I had knocked the drunk man down in Vic's car. Then we were out of the town, by the fields and approaching the village of Sandbank. Peering out through the little windows I told her about the American submarine base, the expensive gleaming yachts and the boat builders on either side of the road. I even turned off onto the grass to show her our little sailing base.

I didn't want her to miss anything. But I could see she was tired after the long drive and we went quietly along the tree lined back road and across the cattle grid passing by the Golden Gates Lodge. "What a funny little house," she said.

"Yes, quaint isn't it? Rusty lives there with his wife, Pat and their baby girl."

"Rusty? Oh yes. He's one of the instructors you wrote about? And you say Pat was a teacher too?"

"Yes, and from Yorkshire." As I drove slowly along the crunching drive she was looking out to the gardens and the huge Rhododendron bushes. Then she saw the adventure centre across an immaculate lawn. She said nothing but I could tell she thought it looked wonderful and I was so very pleased that the sun was shining. To make a good impression I stopped on the wide terrace, right by the front door.

Nobody was around and I carried her case as she followed me up the wide main staircase to the guest room. "Is your room nearby?" she said.

"Yes, just along the landing." We went along and I showed her my room and we went out onto the covered balcony. She looked across the lawn to the cows grazing in the afternoon sunshine.

"Pete, you're lucky to live in such a lovely place," she said.

I didn't reply but I was hoping that she would also like to live in this lovely place. After a quick wash she joined me and we went down to the staff room where everyone had gathered as usual for afternoon tea.

I once had a crew haircut, and when my mother saw it, she said, "Peter, it's awful. With your long nose you look just like a horse."

Certainly, I was never what anyone would call handsome, so I think the men at the centre were amazed when they met Cath at afternoon tea. I might have had a smug grin as we stood together and I said, "Now, everyone. This is Cath."

I thought she was beautiful but it was obvious from the reaction of the men that they could not believe how someone who looked like me could attract a girl like Cath. Her trim figure suited the jeans, striped blouse and Scholl sandals that she was wearing. As she stood beside me with her blonde hair and blue eyes, I felt quietly proud.

210

I introduced her all round and poured tea for us. It seemed that she immediately became part of our working 'family' and soon got talking to Morag. "So, Cath, have you any plans this week?"

Cath took a sip of tea. "Well I hope to see the area a bit but Peter has said I can join his sailing course for a few days."

"Oh, that's grand. It's lovely here at this time of the year."

Cath certainly did think it lovely as we walked round the botanic gardens after dinner. The giant rhododendrons were covered with purple flowers. I showed her the formal garden area and the charming ponds. She stood on the little bridge for quite a while looking at the huge Japanese goldfish and then said, "What a beautiful place to live."

I just squeezed her hand. I think we both were thinking of the future. We walked along the main drive with the towering Western Red Cedars on either side and eventually strolled down the gravel pathway to the Golden Gates Lodge. Rusty and Pat had invited us down for evening drinks. Rusty's German shepherd barked a greeting and her whole body squirmed with the delight of meeting friends.

Before we could reach the door, Pat opened it. "Ah," she said. "So, you're Cath. Welcome to Benmore." Pat had a friendly open manner and as they shook hands, I knew they would get on well together. In fact, they got on so well they never stopped talking. They were both from Yorkshire and both teachers so they had plenty in common. By the time we left it was dark and we held hands on the walk back through the trees. I was so happy I didn't know what to say and we crunched along in silence.

*

The strength of the wind is crucial for a successful sailing course and we were certainly lucky that week. The first couple of days the wind was fairly light and then built up more strongly as the week progressed. The students were all teachers from Edinburgh and it was easy for them to progress in these perfect conditions.

By the first afternoon they were sailing by themselves with the instructors just keeping an eye on things. Cath joined the clients in one of the sailing dinghies and everyone seemed to enjoy the day of green ocean and blue sky. Perhaps it was too good for I noticed, at dinner, that the entire group had caught the sun after the day afloat. Cath also had quite a red face.

We joined the staff for afternoon tea in the staff room and Cath was keen to talk about her perfect day of sailing. Then it was a shower and change before the evening meal with everyone.

After dinner I took her on a drive along the shore of Loch Eck. I drove quietly north until we passed the end of the fresh water loch and met the sea again at Loch Fyne. Thick yellow broom bushes lined the road and we strolled a little way along the shore looking across the loch to the green hills beyond.

I talked on and on, pointing out everything, the names of birds we could see, the trees and flora and all I knew of the small farms in the area. Then I drove slowly back until we reached our local pub set back from the side of Loch Eck.

Ewan, the barman, raised his eyebrows when he saw us walk in. "Helloo Peter."

He smiled at Cath. "We don't often see Peter doon here."

I grinned. "Bill makes up for me, I'm sure." "Aye." He laughed. "Yes, most nights we see Bill."

"So, Ewan," I said. "This is Cath, a friend of mine."

"Aye, I know. Bill told me." He reached across the bar and they shook hands. "Welcome to Scotland."

"Now, Peter. What will it be? A pint of heavy?"

"Yes please … and an orange juice and lemonade for Cath."

We chatted with Ewan for a while about things like the lambing that year, work in the forests and fishing. When he started to get busy, we carried our drinks outside and walked across the road to tables that had been set up.

The beer garden was on a small terrace of grass that dipped down to Loch Eck. We sat down and Cath looked at the dark water of the loch and across the short distance to the wooded slope of Benmore mountain rising up the other side. "What a lovely spot. It seems a beautiful area."

"Yes," I looked around. "It certainly is beautiful when the weather is good like this."

She looked back at the pub that now had a few outside lights on. "I'm surprised there are so few tourists around."

"Mm. The tourists don't seem to find this area, down on the peninsula."

The sun had gone down and the air was soon cold so we went into the bar and sat near the log fire. Bert, the laird's shepherd, was there with our local farmer, Fergus. They showed a real interest in Cath and her teaching work. Fergus was keen to point out where she might work if she came up to this area. I was a little embarrassed but quietly delighted that they seemed to be assuming she would come up to live nearby.

It had been a long day for Cath and we left early and drove in darkness the short distance to the Centre. It had been a perfect first day.

The second day of sailing was very easy to instruct. The sailing conditions for learning were excellent and by lunchtime the boats had covered most of the basics. Onshore it was sunny and warm so I made a large pot of tea for everyone and we took our packed lunches and sat on the grass outside the sailing base.

The US factory ship seemed busy in the middle of the loch with four American submarines against its hull. They were low in the water as if sulking and landing craft were continuously chugging from the ship to their base along the shore. I talked to Cath about the impact all this activity had on the community.

"Mm." She was thoughtful for a minute and then said, "Are the sailors' families living here as well?"

"Yes. I believe some of the 'top brass' have their families here."

She nodded thoughtfully. "So, there will be a few American children in the local primary schools?"

"Yes. I believe they go to Strone." I pointed across the loch to where we could just see the cluster of houses edging the wooded headland. "Over there."

She smiled to herself as if answering her own question but said no more.

That afternoon I set the group a triangular course that I marked with three buoys. With each circuit they seemed to improve until they began to try and overtake the boat in front. It had developed into a race. Cath had done some sailing with me before and I was quietly pleased when I noticed that she was doing particularly well.

Cath already seemed to be part of our extended family at Benmore and she talked excitedly to Vic about sailing that day. Over coffee in the staff room, she spent some time talking to Roger and his wife Jenny about the local village schools their children attended. I was eventually able to take her off so that I could show her other localities.

I drove her little van past the Golden Gates Lodge and up the beautiful Glen Mason to where the forests finished and the open hillsides started. At this point the small river shoulders its way through a mini gorge. It has created deep pools and smooth arches cut through the clean rock. I parked on the empty road and we walked along the riverbank and scrambled over the rocks. "There are often trout in these pools," I told her. "The locals tell me they can catch them with their bare hands when the water is low."

For some time, we laid down on a flat rock overhanging the river. There was just one trout that we saw laying quite still under a grassy overhang.

She stood up and looked around the valley. She didn't say anything but I could tell she liked what she saw. I was so pleased.

213

"I'll show you another valley," I said as we strolled back to the van. After driving down to the coastal plain, I turned right and went up the winding road through a forest of dark conifers to reach the upper part of Glen Lean. Along this windswept glen were a few farms that reared cattle. The only trees were patches of alder in the wet areas by the river and a few silver birches and scattered rowans on the open hillside.

I drove on a few miles and descended to the bank of Loch Striven and parked. Cath stood looking up and down the narrow road. "The roads are so empty."

"Yes, I suppose they are. It's always like this." There was no noise from humans at all and as we walked along the seashore the only activity seemed to be the birds. There were plenty of small birds in the open oak woodlands and out over the water were terns and a couple of white gannets. We stood and watched the gannets as they swooped downwards, closing their wings just before plunging into the water. It had been a perfect day for me.

After a few days of racing and training in the Holy Loch the group were ready for a change. So, we packed the wayfarer dinghies with our lunches and spare clothes and set off in a little flotilla out past the great square bulk of the US floating dock and out of the Holy Loch. In the open water of the Clyde, I checked on the wind direction. It was south east and I looked around to see where we could go on a 'reach'. With the wind on the side, we would be able to sail fast and easily, out and back again. The other boats came close and I shouted across to the crews. "Helensburgh," I pointed across the Clyde. "We'll make for Helensburgh pier."

It was an easy, fast reach across the Clyde and in less than two hours we went alongside the pier. By carefully organizing the mooring ropes we tied the boats up so they were held clear of obstructions and out of the way of the big ferries that docked on the end of the high timber pier. When we had gathered on dry land, I looked at my watch. "Okay everyone, back here please at one thirty."

They split into groups to look round town and have their picnic lunch. Cath and I sauntered along and found a grassy terrace for a picnic. We wandered around the rocks to look for crabs and shoreline blennies. It was much warmer on land and I carried our waterproofs until it was time to return to the boats.

The journey back was uneventful and the group enjoyed the change of scene and a chance to cruise in open water.

After dinner Cath and I spent the whole evening strolling round the gardens and along our river. My interest in the wildlife had opened my eyes to all sorts of things and I was keen to show my 'finds' to Cath. Just outside the huge front door was a bird's nest built amongst the ivy and glorious flowering clematis. It was a flycatcher's nest and the birds spent the whole day flitting out from the wall to snatch flies. A small bright goldcrest was always by the bay window but I never did manage to find its nest.

We walked down the drive and onto the bridge that crossed the river. I had seen a pair of dippers here and sure enough they were still there. Their chunky black bodies with a clean white bib, bobbing up and down on rocks just above the rushing water. We went down to the bank and watched them for a long time. They were very busy flying out and back to the bridge where we could see two nests.

As we walked along the riverbank a Kingfisher kept flying a short distance in front to land on a suitable branch above the water. It was easy to see with its brilliant blue glinting in the evening sunshine. I thought it looked annoyed with us for disturbing its hunt and as we got to the rushing weir it swept back up the river again.

On the walk back across the fields a pair of buzzards circled the sky mewing to each other in ecstasy. I pointed out a red squirrel dray and a place where a badger went under a fence every night. As we got back towards the centre, we walked off the path for me to show Cath the nest of a coal tit. I had been amazed to find its entrance right at the base of a tall scots pine. It was a lovely evening.

On the last day of the course, I had chartered a keelboat from a sailing friend. It was on a mooring beyond Sandbank so we had to row out, three at a time in his little tender. The students were quite excited to be on a big yacht and walked around and below deck exploring everything.

Eventually we were all on board and I tied the tender to the stern. I showed them how to raise the mainsail and a couple pulled on the halyards with another easing the slides in place. The sail flopped gently from one side to the other. When everything seemed okay two volunteers raised the big genoa and I fed the sheets aft. I released the mooring line from the bow cleat and with the rope in my hand I slowly walked it back to the cockpit. As the wind gently filled the genoa the bow of the yacht swung slowly offshore and as both sails filled, I released the rope and took hold of the tiller. We were away and sailing.

A weather 'front' had gone through during the night and it was still rather grey but the forecast said it would soon improve. One of the group took the helm and we made our way to the open water of the Clyde. We beat down towards the Kyles of Bute with the sails tight and the water rushing close to the gunwale.

Wearing full waterproof suits, we all sat high on the windward gunwale to give a little weight to that side. We had to go a fairly long way, straight into the wind, but the hull was beautiful and with a long deep keel we made good progress. However, I believe the novelty of tacking back and forth had worn off by eleven o'clock. We were pleased when we could sail off the wind a little, ease the sails out and make for the Isle of Bute and its harbour at Rothesay.

There was just a gentle wind blowing in the harbour and it was peaceful but for me this was always a time for concentration. I took over the helm and looked for an empty mooring buoy that was not too far from the pier. I saw a rusty red one with a plastic bottle attached to it by a length of rope.

This was perfect and I carefully briefed everyone about the procedures. When they all knew their duties, I headed slowly up into wind and a tall chap on the bow scooped up the plastic buoy with the boat hook and tied it to a cleat. Two of the crew lowered the genoa sail and then more leisurely the mainsail was dropped. "Right, everyone," I shouted. "Prepare for shore leave."

They rowed each other across the short distance to a handy pontoon lying alongside the pier. Eventually it was our turn and I rowed us across and tied the tender to a bollard. The clients had walked off in various directions and Cath and I spent a pleasant hour looking round the little town.

I pointed out the swimming pool that we had used in the winter and we sat on a seat along the promenade and had our packed lunch and a coffee. We talked about all the things we could see: yachts, the harbour and the hills in the distance until it was time to return to the pier.

Everyone seemed happy to be setting sail and we gathered on the pontoon to ferry out to the yacht. The wind was blowing gently offshore so we hoisted the mainsail and then the genoa. I looked around carefully for any problems that might occur and then asked one of the ladies to release the bowline and bring it back towards the cockpit. The genoa sail filled with wind and the bow gently swung away and very soon we were clear of the harbour and out into open water.

One of the ladies took the helm and now I had time to look around. The Clyde looked wonderful and even the sun was shining. Cumulus clouds formed lumpy lines in the sky and their edges showed brilliant white against the darker greys. The sea was lively with steep little waves sparkling in the sunshine. The coast was interesting too, with small towns, each with a pier, fronting the green hills behind. A good sea breeze was setting in and the wind went quickly from force three to four. Within half an hour it went up to force five and white horses splashed into the bow as we surged along. We were making good time and the Cumbrae Islands, now a long way behind, were quickly losing definition.

With the increase in wind, people started to put on their waterproof jackets and a woollen hat to stay warm but the clients were still happy to sit about and enjoy the scenery. Some were on deck and a couple sat in the cockpit with me.

Cath, who sat opposite me, was looking out to the distant hills. "What a great day," she said.

"Yes." I raised my eyebrows. "We've been lucky this week. It's a good place to work and with a grin to Cath ......and to live." We sailed easily past our little town of Dunoon and I took over the helm as we sailed into the Holy Loch. I briefed the students about picking up the mooring buoy and with a tall chap at the bow I turned the yacht into wind and slowed to approach our yellow buoy. Using a boat hook the buoy was brought up and two students immediately dropped the genoa. More relaxed, the mainsail was lowered and everything stowed away neatly.

The crew started to row each other ashore and after checking around the boat Cath and I were rowed ashore. The clients were fairly quiet as I drove the mini buss down the wooded lane and into the beautiful Botanic gardens.

I was not on duty that evening so Cath and I went along to the Coylet pub and while looking over the beautiful Loch Eck I said, "Would you be happy living here?"

Cath didn't look at me but just smiled and nodded her head.

We had never really spoken of marriage; didn't think it necessary. I had never felt I had to go on 'bended knee'. We seemed to have grown together and knew we both felt that our future was going to be together. Now I had the type of work I wanted and Cath was very happy to join me in this glorious part of the world.

I was happy and relaxed so that evening we started to talk about a wedding in August. By the time Cath left Benmore in her little grey van a few days later, we had planned it all.

Our wedding would be in Yorkshire and we would honeymoon in Austria. The guest list was complete with relations from all sides and many of our student friends from college days. It all seemed sorted and the only thing we had not discussed was where were we going to live.

*

I spent many worried days trying to find a house without success. Then just two weeks before the wedding a friend from the sailing club told me about a place owned by the Forestry Commission. I phoned their office and they

217

agreed to let me look over a vacant cottage that was just three miles from the Benmore Centre and up in Glen Lean.

It was an old semi-detached bungalow off the glen road and just above the forest. It was rather spartan and cold but I could make it cosy.

I was pleased and paid the first month rent of £5 and then had just five days to sort things out to make it our first home. Morag helped me clean the place and Vic lent me some old furniture, bedding, kitchen utensils and crockery from the centre.

The Benmore staff insisted that I had a stag night in the Coylet pub and I was still feeling a little ill the next morning when Roger gave me a lift to Dunoon.

With a heavy rucksack and a suitcase of wedding clothes I walked up the timber gangplank onto the Clyde ferry to begin my journey to Yorkshire. As we pulled away from the pier, I went on deck to look in all directions and felt very content

I knew that when I next crossed on this ferry, I would be a married man with a wonderful wife.

You will find the next instalment of Peter's life story in his sequel ***Conway to Conwy***.

GLOSSARY

MOUNTAIN FEATURES
Cwm or **corrie**. A huge semi-circular bowl cut out of a valley side by a glacier. In Britain the ice has gone but it often leaves a lake with a river running down to the lower valley.

Valleys or **Glens** in Scotland in mountain areas are often cut by an ancient glacier and are U-shaped in section, often with steep cliffs on either side of the valley.

A **crib** in Wales is a rocky ridge, like the ridge of a house.

Buttresses are steep ridges running up the sides of the mountains. Like a buttress on the sides of a church.

A **gully** is a very wide crack running up a steep hill or cliff. In winter it is often filled with snow and ice.

Scree is a steep slope of broken stones.

Pass is a low point between two mountains. In Welsh it is a Bwlch. In French it is a Col.

CLIMBING
A **belay** is a fastening on a cliff face -sometimes natural like a tree or a spike of rock. A belay can be used to fix the climber onto a ledge.

A **Runner** is a fixture where the climbing rope runs through a karabiner/snap-link to safeguard the leader while climbing.

A **sling** is a loop of rope or tape used to provide a belay.

A **piton** is a spike of metal knocked into a crack or screwed into ice to provide a belay.

A **nut** is a general name for a variety of metal fixings that can be jammed into a crack to act as a belay.

SAILING
Bow and **stern** are names for the front and back of a boat.

Port and **starboard** are the names for the left and right side of a boat.

Gunwale is the top edge of the hull of a boat.

Sheets are the ropes that control the sails to be more loose or tighter.

Sails: The **Main** is the large sail fixed to the mast. **Jib** or **Genoa** are small or larger sails at the front of a yacht.

Mooring is a fixture to park a boat. Usually marked by a buoy.

CANOEING/KAYAKING

An **eddy** is where a river or sea current turns back on itself along a shore.

A **cockpit** is the seat enclosure in a Kayak.

A **sweeper** is a tree that has fallen into the river, usually on the outside of a river bend creating a trap with its branches.

CAVE FEATURES

A **pot** is a shaft or entrance of a limestone cave.

A **sump** is a dip in a passage that is completely filed with water.

Stalactites and **stalagmites** are the calcite formations that have been formed by dripping water that hang from the roof or grow up from the floor of a cave.

Resurgence: Water running out from a cave

Printed in Great Britain
by Amazon

86525290R00130